Legal Culture and the Legal Profession

Legal Culture and the Legal Profession

EDITED BY
Lawrence M. Friedman and Harry N. Scheiber

Routledge
Taylor & Francis Group
NEW YORK AND LONDON

First published in 1996 by Westview Press

Published in 2021 by Routledge
605 Third Avenue, New York, NY 10017
2 Park Square, Milton Park, Abingdon, Oxon OX14 4RN

Routledge is an imprint of the Taylor & Francis Group, an informa business

Copyright © 1996 by Taylor & Francis

All rights reserved. No part of this book may be reprinted or reproduced or utilised in any form or by any electronic, mechanical, or other means, now known or hereafter invented, including photocopying and recording, or in any information storage or retrieval system, without permission in writing from the publishers.

Notice:
Product or corporate names may be trademarks or registered trademarks, and are used only for identification and explanation without intent to infringe.

A CIP catalog record for this book is available from the Library of Congress.
ISBN 0-8133-8935-6 (HC)

ISBN 13: 978-0-3670-1756-9 (hbk)
ISBN 13: 978-0-3671-6743-1 (pbk)

Printed in the United Kingdom
by Henry Ling Limited

Contents

	Acknowledgments	vii
1	Legal Cultures and the Legal Profession: Introduction *Lawrence M. Friedman and Harry N. Scheiber*	1
2	American Lawyers, Legal Cultures, and Adversarial Legalism *Robert A. Kagan*	7
3	Are We a Litigious People? *Lawrence M. Friedman*	53
4	The Assault on Civil Justice: The Anti-Lawyer Dimension *Marc Galanter*	79
5	The "Globalization" of Judicial Review *Martin Shapiro*	119
6	Americanization of Law: Reception or Convergence? *Wolfgang Wiegand*	137
7	Courts and the Construction of Racial and Ethnic Identity: Public Law Litigation in the Denver Schools *Rachel F. Moran*	153
	About the Contributors	181
	About the Book	184

Acknowledgments

The editors and authors wish to thank the American Academy of Arts and Sciences for principal support of the project for which these studies were prepared. A vital additional contribution was made by the University of California's Humanities Research Institute, which underwrote and hosted an extended planning session for the authors. The Stanford Law School, UC Boalt Hall School of Law, and the UC Berkeley Center for the Study of Law and Society all provided important supplemental funding or secretarial staff support. Dr. Gerald Bradford of the Academy, Profs. Murray Krieger and Mark Rose of the UC Humanities Research Institute, and Prof. Malcolm Feeley of the Center for the Study of Law and Society all extended themselves personally and were generous in arranging for institutional support. Professor Robert Gordon is also owed warm thanks for his scholarly counsel and abiding interest in the project.

Dr. William Gallagher served as rapporteur for the project conferences and contributed to the preparation of materials for publication. The editors are grateful to him and also to Ms. Patricia Ramirez and Ms. Kiara Jordan of UC Berkeley for devoted and expert attention to the editorial and production processes; and to the Westview Press editorial staff for their supportive role in bringing these papers to publication.

Lawrence M. Friedman
Harry N. Scheiber

1

Legal Cultures and the Legal Profession: Introduction

Lawrence M. Friedman and Harry N. Scheiber

The papers collected in this volume were originally presented in May, 1993, at a conference held at the Center for the Study of Law and Society, University of California, Berkeley, under the principal sponsorship of the Western Center of the American Academy of Arts and Sciences. This conference brought together an international group of scholars in law, humanities, and the social sciences. The general topic of the conference was the relationship between legal systems and the cultures in which they are imbedded, with particular emphasis on the legal profession. The seven papers in this volume are lineal descendants of the seven principal papers presented at the conference.

A word should be said at the outset about the concept of "legal culture." Scholars have used the term in a number of senses. Sometimes the phrase describes legal consciousness—attitudes, values, beliefs, and expectations about law and the legal system. At other times, scholars employ the term in a broader but somewhat vaguer meaning—to capture what is distinctive about patterns of thought and behavior in, say, American law. Some sweep even more into the category: legal institutions and the distinctive ways they function. In any case, the term refers to *living* law, to law as a dynamic process; if the dry texts of statutes and cases, and the organizational charts that describe legal institutions are the bones and skeleton of a legal system, then legal culture is what makes the system move and breathe. The authors of the essays, however they make use of the term, never stray too far from the core meaning of legal consciousness: the law as image and incentive, in the minds of members of some public.

Lawyers and the Culture of Legalism

Three of the papers presented at the conference, and reprinted in this volume, focus on lawyers, litigation, and the use of the law. Their common theme is the much-discussed culture of legalism in American society. Robert Kagan's essay, "Do Lawyers Cause Adversarial Legalism?" takes as its starting point what he believes to be America's uniquely legalistic culture. Kagan calls the American style of governance and policy implementation "adversarial legalism." It is a style which is more legalistic, decentralized, and prone to litigation than the legal styles of other Western societies.

Where does this aspect of American legal culture come from? Why does there seem to be so much litigation, dissension, legal maneuvering? The average person tends to pin the blame on lawyers. Because of their training and their habits, their selfishness and greed, lawyers foment litigation, and encourage legalistic forms of governance and dispute resolution. The result is a plague of lawsuits, a plague of lawyering—a legal system choked by excess. Kagan sifts the evidence, and comes to the conclusion that there is some truth to the charge. Legal education and scholarship put a premium on traits which can only exacerbate adversarial legalism. Lawyers learn to look at law in instrumental terms. They learn to respect and honor an activist role for judges. They value rights and entitlement; and legal enforceability (in court) for just about every expression of policy.

Lawyers are engaged in whipping up legal business. Advertising—once strictly forbidden—serves to increase access to lawyers; but it also encourages the aggressive use of litigation to pursue even marginal legal claims. Many lawyers are battlers, whose litigation tactics make settlement and negotiation difficult or impossible. Other lawyers act as entrepreneurs and litigation brokers; they dream up or encourage high-stakes lawsuits (some of them of dubious merit), and end up lining their own pockets more than those of the clients they are supposed to be serving. Some lawyers use litigation as a tactic to fight policies they or their clients oppose: they may, for example, use environmental law as a tool to block projects that they find offensive. Finally, lawyers collectively lobby courts and legislatures to shape public policy on issues—tort reform would be one example—that have an impact on them and their clients. Even the system of ethics for lawyers plays a role in building the house of adversarial legalism. The code of ethics encourages aggressive advocacy; it emphasizes absolute loyalty to the client rather than the duty of the lawyer as an officer of the court, or any responsibility to the larger society.

Still, it would be hard to make the case that *all* of America's distinctive legal culture can be laid at the door of the lawyers themselves. Is it possible that lawyers and their activities are a consequence of adversarial legalism rather than the cause of it? There may be salient features of American society—the weak system of hierarchical political control; the common law vision of law as uncertain, malleable, instrumental; the radical decentralization of finance, business, and labor systems—which serve to create a demand for adversarial legalism. That is, they

Legal Cultures and the Legal Profession: Introduction

favor a style of governance and dispute resolution that relies heavily on individual use of law, litigation, and the legal profession. In other words, lawyers have a role in perpetuating adversarial legalism; but they act mainly at the urging, and the command, of client and interest groups, and with regard to the strategic needs of these groups. Kagan's conclusion, then, neither demonizes nor absolves the lawyers. Rather, he offers a more nuanced explanation; he identifies lawyers as a significant but ultimately secondary cause of an adversarial legalism which is deeply rooted in American culture.

His general approach aligns Kagan with one distinctive camp in the social study of law—the camp which tends to put heavier weight on general *social* forces, than on forces internal to the (formal) legal system, as variables to explain what is happening to the legal system, and why. The essay by Lawrence M. Friedman is very much in the same camp. Friedman admits, as he must, that some features of adversarial legalism do seem more pronounced in the United States, compared with European countries or with Japan—the vast army of lawyers, the claims-consciousness of the population. Like Kagan, he looks for cultural and structural factors outside the legal system for an explanation.

Part of the essay consists of a historical exploration of what makes America different—the abundance of land, the social mobility, the decay of traditional churches and authorities. But while history can be read as a story that explains what is different about America, the same story suggests that American uniqueness may be temporary. Europe, and even Japan, are moving in the same direction. The individual nations are becoming more heterogeneous. There is vast immigration—if not from outside, then from the countryside to the city. All of the modern, developed countries are welfare-regulatory states of a somewhat similar type. The forces that attenuated communitarian influences in the United States, and heightened individualism—the forces on which adversarial legal culture thrives—are present, more and more, in these other countries as well.

There is an obvious convergence in popular culture, all over the world. Business too is rapidly globalizing—and this too frays the local fabric that discourages the use of formal law. Legal cultures show their own patterns of convergence. American legal culture may be less a permanent mark of difference, than an omen of what is coming in other places as well.

In his essay, Marc Galanter puts lawyer-bashing under the microscope; and identifies it as one aspect of a counter-movement against adversarial legalism. Of course, criticism of lawyers is an old theme in American popular culture. People tell dozens of (anti)lawyer jokes; while there is really no equivalent for doctors, accountants, plumbers or other occupations and professions.

The current wave of lawyer-bashing differs, however, from the older waves. In the past, critiques stressed, among other things, the failure of lawyers to live up to professional ideals, and to provide access to justice. Behind the more recent attacks looms the image of the lawyer as economic predator. In fact, some people (including politicians) accuse lawyers of causing economic stagnation and decline in this country. The picture painted shows an army of lawyers, stirring up frivolous lawsuits, and in the process driving up insurance costs, health care costs, and the costs of just about all manufactured goods. Lawyers, in short, cost us billions in lost economic productivity. Other societies (Japan is always cast as the star of this drama) have far fewer lawyers and are therefore much more productive.

Galanter argues that this is in many ways a dubious thesis. The empirical evidence is murky; it certainly does not prove that America has too many lawyers, or that lawyers have any demonstrable effect on economic productivity. Where does the image of the lawyer as economic predator come from, then? It is, Galanter argues, primarily a creation of economic elites; and it is at least in part a reaction to the fact that the legal system is far more open than it used to be. Groups of litigants now have access who were formerly excluded; and they use litigation to address a range of social problems. But this, of course, stirs up resentment from those on the other side.

In the end, Galanter tends to reach a conclusion somewhat similar to Friedman's. American legal culture may not be quite so exceptional as it seems at first glance. As other societies, increasingly, address social demands, and face social problems, similar to those of the United States, they may well use lawyers more—and construct their own versions of anti-lawyerism (and, indeed, their own versions of adversarial legalism). American legal culture, we can conclude, is in part at least a response to issues and situations which are global—or at least widespread among modern, developed countries.

Legal Culture: An American Export?

One prominent aspect of American legal culture, by common consent, is the extraordinary role played by the courts—a role which is, in the broadest sense, deeply political. The most salient aspect of this "activist" role is judicial review. A good deal of the academic debate over the role of America's courts has focussed on the power of courts to strike down legislation as unconstitutional. Legal scholars, and political scientists, have generated a normative, descriptive, and explanatory literature on the subject that could fill dozens of rooms.

Martin Shapiro, however, in his essay, tries to bring into sharper focus one aspect of judicial review that tends to be somewhat neglected: the review of decisions by administrative agencies. If there is "too much" judicial policy-making, Shapiro feels, it is likely to be located at that level.

Shapiro's essay carefully sets out some of the factors that lead courts to make policy in the course of reviewing decisions of administrative agencies. There is, in the first place, the plain fact that legislatures have delegated a great deal of lawmaking authority to these agencies. Cultural distrust of technocracy, pressures from outside groups for more access to agency decision-making, and greater participation in the process of regulation—these lead to increased scrutiny of the work of bureaucracies. There are also expectations that "scientific perfectionism"

Legal Cultures and the Legal Profession: Introduction

should underlie technical decision-making, even when these expections really cannot be fulfilled, either because the data are not there, or because the expertise is simply lacking.

As Shapiro notes, these conditions and concerns are common to many industrialized nations, mostly in the West. They may be more striking in the United States, but they are not unique to that country. The "globalization" of judicial review, which seems to be under way, might be the sign of a further globalization: that is, the adversarial legal culture so pronounced in the United States, and particularly expressed in the American habit of judicial review, may have become an export product. Up to this point, Shapiro's conclusions fit those of the other contributors who describe or predict a process of convergence, among the world's legal cultures.

Shapiro shows, however, that concerns about these trends have led people to think about an alternative model of governance, which he calls "deliberation." His paper explains what is meant by this subtle and elusive concept; and he suggests the possibility of a style of judicial review, and of control of the discretion of administrative agencies, that might foster a truly deliberative style of decision-making, and thus provide an alternative to adversarial legalism.

Wolfgang Wiegand, in his paper, takes up the issue of convergence once again—in the form of the "Americanization" of European law. This process, he argues, is a contemporary event as important in legal evolution as the reception of Roman law in the eleventh century. Since the middle of the 20th century, there has been, according to Wiegand, a genuine "reception" of American law. Deep changes in European law and culture reflect this profound process of Americanization. Wiegand's essay identifies some of the ways in which American legal culture has seeped into and shaped European legal institutions, practices, and doctrines—and has even penetrated into the marrow of European legal culture.

For example, many European universities have adapted American styles of law teaching. The American corporate law firm is the model for the recent, very rapid rise of large law firms in Europe. Entire areas of European substantive and procedural law have been reshaped, in parallel with developments in American law. Most important, there have been shifts in legal concepts—in underlying principles. He notes an increased inclination to extend tort liability into novel areas (novel, at least, as far as European jurists are concerned), including lender liability suits and class action shareholder suits against corporate officers. This is only one example among many.

Wiegand does not think the process is one of "convergence" in the passive, automatic sense of that word. Rather, he argues, Europeans have consciously (and quite naturally) patterned legal culture on the American model. Wiegand's distinction between two forms of convergence is, of course, significant; but in essence, it is striking to what degree Wiegand's conclusions mesh with at least *some* of the assumptions and predictions that underlie the papers of Friedman and Shapiro, and perhaps of Kagan and Galanter as well.

Public Law Litigation: A Case-Study

Rachel Moran's essay on school desegregation litigation in Denver is a searching and intense case-study of what may be (thus far) a peculiarly American legal phenomenon: public law litigation. Lawsuits of this type aim to do much, much more than resolve some particular dispute between two parties. Their focus, rather, is multi-polar—they involve multiple parties, in complex relationships; and they engage the trial judge in an active and ongoing role in shaping a legal remedy—a remedy that addresses not only or even primarily private rights, but public policy considerations as well.

The lawsuit in Denver which she describes has been in court for a period of over 20 years. Moran analyzes the effect of the litigation on the parties—and discusses as well the threats to judicial legitimacy that may flow from lawsuits of this nature. Still, she concludes that such lawsuits can function as significant "safety valves," drawing off political pressure from other institutions (legislative or administrative) which find it impossible, for one reason or another, to provide effective responses to those pressures.

The authors of the essays reprinted here differ, of course, in style and subject matter. They would, however, agree that the elusive and difficult concept of "legal culture," whatever its conceptual failings, does reflect something real in the living law of the various legal systems of the world. Moreover, they would probably agree that *legal* culture is a more important aspect of the life of modern citizens, than was true perhaps in the past—that it has an impact on the hopes and thoughts and behaviors of everyone from multinational corporate executives to the parents of black and Hispanic children in Denver. They would probably agree that at least the dim outlines of a world legal culture are visible. They would certainly agree, and emphatically, that the subject sketched out in this volumes is deserving of major attention and research from legal scholars and social scientists.

2

American Lawyers, Legal Culture, and Adversarial Legalism

Robert A. Kagan

[1] Contemporary constitutional democracies all seem to value the rule of law, an independent judiciary, and a common core of basic legal principles. The rapid mobility of capital and ideas generates powerful pressures toward convergence among separate national bodies of substantive law. Nevertheless, convergence is far from complete. National legal styles and institutions stubbornly resist homogenization.

Some observers would attribute variability in domestic legal systems to differences in legal traditions or "legal culture." In this perspective, legal systems, at least in democratic regimes, are relatively autonomous. Bolstered by constitutional traditions and by the aura of professionalism, lawyers, judges, and legal academics dominate the formulation and evolution of legal ideas, norms, and reforms. Hence distinctive features of a nation's legal style would reflect distinctive currents (or unchallenged traditions) in that nation's "elite legal culture."

Other analysts, however, would look for an explanation in the realm of politics. In this second perspective, legal norms, institutions, and reforms are shaped primarily by broader political forces. The extreme version of this position is held by Marxists (and some of their intellectual descendants), for whom legal autonomy and professionalism are only myths, a smokescreen of words and rituals that mask the repressive violence of law and its subservience to the power and interests of capital. But many non-Marxist social scientists, too, believe that judges and lawmakers, especially in democratic societies, are responsive to political attitudes and demands (whose development legal officials do not control). In this view, a nation's distinctive legal norms, institutions, and practices may be polished and re-wrapped at the retail level by legal professionals, but the basic production process is dominated by political forces.

This essay examines the relative importance of "inside" and "outside" factors in explaining why the "legal style" of the United States continues to diverge from that of other constitutional democracies. Detailed cross-national case studies repeatedly reveal that compared to other economically advanced democracies, American methods of public policy implementation and dispute resolution are more adversarial and legalistic, shaped by exceptionally costly court action or the prospect of it. After briefly documenting that finding, the question to be addressed is "Why?"

I will contend that adversarial legalism stems *primarily* from enduring features of American political culture and governmental structure. Nevertheless, as I hope to demonstrate, American legal elites do play a significant *secondary* causal role—by independently promoting and perpetuating adversarial legal contestation as a method of governance.

I. The Dependent Variable: Adversarial Legalism

Everywhere in the modern world, it seems, law is intruding more deeply into social and economic life.[1] As European Community regulations, large law firms, and inch-thick commercial contracts proliferate, some observers speak of the "Americanization" of continental legal practice.[2] In fields such as workers' rights and land use controls, some European countries have "more law" and more legal contestation than the United States.

But the United States has a "legal style" that remains unique. Any talk of "convergence" is quite premature. The evidence lies in an accumulating body of detailed case studies, listed in Table 2.1, that compare how the United States and other democratic governments have responded to particular social problems—such as compensating injured people, regulating pollution, equalizing educational opportunity, and deterring malpractice by policemen, physicians, and product manufacturers. In every case, the relevant American legal process tends to be characterized by (1) more complex bodies of legal rules; (2) more formal, adversarial procedures for resolving political and scientific disputes; (3) more costly, litigant-dominated forms of legal contestation; (4) more punitive legal sanctions; (5) more frequent judicial intervention into administrative decision-making; (6) more political controversy about legal rules and institutions; and (7) more legal uncertainty, malleability, and unpredictability.[3] This cluster of legal propensities is what I attempt to capture in the summary concept "*adversarial legalism*."[4]

Adversarial legalism differs first of all from *informal* methods of resolving disputes or making policy decisions—such as mediation, reliance on expert professional judgment, or bargaining among political authorities. Secondly, in adversarial legalism, litigants and their lawyers play active roles in the policy implementation and decision-making process; hence, it differs from styles of governance that are legally formal but are more *hierarchical* or bureaucratic. Thus in Western European courts, bureaucratically-organized judges dominate fact-gathering and selection of expert witnesses.[5] In American adversarial legalism, attorneys for the parties dominate those processes. Similarly, the American tort law system for compensating victims of highway, medical, and product-related accidents is more adversarial, more driven by litigant activism, than European methods, which operate primarily through hierarchically-organized benefit-payment bureaucracies.

Even when compared to the British "adversarial system" from which it descended, American methods of adjudication are far more party-influenced, less hierarchically-controlled. American judges are more diverse, more political, more autonomous than British judges, and their decisions are less uniform.[6] Law in the United States is more malleable, open to novel legal and policy arguments put forth by parties and their lawyers. In the United States, lay jurors still play a large and normatively important role in civil cases, which in turn magnifies the importance of skillful legal advocacy by the parties and reduces legal certainty.[7]

Similarly, compared to European democracies, *regulatory* decision-making in the U.S. entails many more legal formalities—public notice and comment, open hearings, restrictions on *ex parte* and other informal contacts, legalistically-specified evidentiary and scientific standards, mandatory official "findings" and responses to interest group arguments. These legal devices facilitate interest group participation and judicial review of administrative decisions. Consequently, hierarchical authority in American agencies is weak, at least when compared to European regulatory bodies, where lawyers rarely participate and appeals to the courts are even rarer.[8]

Adversarial legalism, of course, does not pervade the American legal order uniformly or completely. In some policy arenas, litigation and even the threat of it is infrequent. Many individuals, communities, subcultures, and industries disparage and avoid legal contestation.[9] Most losses are dealt with by recourse to private or public insurance, not to litigation.[10] The point is that in comparative, cross-national perspective, adversarial legalism is far more common in the United States than elsewhere, and more fully characterizes American legal structures and processes.

The importance of adversarial legalism in the United States cannot be measured by litigation rates alone, any more than the significance of nuclear weapons rests on the frequency of nuclear war. Even in social arenas in which the processes of adversarial legalism often are invoked, full-scale legal contestation usually does not occur; the extraordinary costs and delays associated with formal adversarial litigation impel *most* disputants to negotiate an informal plea bargain or settlement, even if it means abandoning valid claims or defenses.[11] Moreover, even if only a small minority of aggrieved persons actually file lawsuits, the mere threat of costly litigation can deter malpractice by physicians, polluters, and bureaucrats. By empowering citizens to publicly challenge official decisions in

10   *Robert A. Kagan*

court, adversarial legalism, even if only sporadically invoked, can make the
insurance adjuster, the prosecutor, the welfare office, and the zoning board attend

TABLE 2.1   Cross-National Studies That Document American Adversarial Legalism

Study	Policy Area	Countries Compared with U.S.
Badarraco (1985)	Exposure to polyvinyl chloride	France, Germany, Japan, U.K.
Bayley (1976)	Police behavior	Japan
Bok (1971)	Selecting labor representatives	Several W. European
Braithwaite (1985)	Coal mine safety	Australia, France, Germany, Japan
Brickman et al. (1985)	Hazardous chemicals	Several W. European
Day & Klein (1987)	Nursing homes	Great Britain
Glendon (1987)	Regulating abortion providing child support	Several W. European
Jasanoff (1986)	Regulating carcinogens	Several W. European
Kelman (1981)	Workplace safety	Sweden
Kirp (1982)	Special education	Great Britain
Kirp (1979)	Racial discrimination in schools	Great Britain
Langbein (1985)	Civil litigation methods	Germany
Litt et al. (1990)	Banking regulation	Japan
Lohof (1991)	Hazardous waste cleanup	Various European
Lundqvist (1980)	Regulating air pollution	Sweden
Lynch (1987)	Criminal incarceration	Canada, Germany, UK
Quam et al. (1987)	Medical malpractice	U.K.
Schwartz (1991)	Products liability	Various European
Tanase (1990)	Compensation for motor vehicle accidents	Japan
Teff (1985)	Pharmaceutical products	U.K.
Vogel (1986)	Environmental regulation	U.K.

See text note 3 for study source information.

more carefully to the evidence and the equities of individual cases. Thus, it is
helpful to regard the concept of adversarial legalism as encompassing both

1. a set of legal structures, institutions, and rules that facilitate adversarial,
    party-dominated legal contestation as a mode of policy implementation
    and dispute resolution

American Lawyers, Legal Culture, and Adversarial Legalism

2. the day-to-day practice of adversarial legal contestation

Public discussion of American adversarial legalism has focussed primarily on whether it is good or bad. Critics argue that it diverts talent and money into dispiriting legal battles; that it induces excessive legal defensiveness; that it adds to governmental gridlock; and that by reason of its slow and expensive procedures it compels litigants or potential litigants to abandon just legal claims and defenses. Justice delayed and too complex, they claim, is justice denied. Defenders of adversarial legalism point out that it injects vitality and responsiveness into the legal and political order; that it gives voice to the political and social underdog, and that it offsets the biases, rigidities and inequities associated with more hierarchical governmental systems. There is merit, I believe, in both sets of arguments. The purpose of this essay, however, is not to assess or weigh the incommensurable costs and benefits of adversarial legalism. Its task is to explain *why* it is more common and important in the American legal order than elsewhere.

II. Political Structure, Political Culture and Adversarial Legalism

Professions, sociologists tell us, seek to create and preserve influence and economic advantages for their members.[12] American lawyers are well situated to do so. The American legal profession is extraordinarily large and lucrative; its collective income in 1992 was $100 billion (Sander, 1992:665), which undoubtedly accounted for a far larger share of gross national product than legal services in any other country. The American legal profession includes a very large number of especially intelligent, articulate, ambitious, wealthy, and well-connected people. Lawyers and legally-trained politicians outnumber representatives of all other occupations and professions at the commanding heights of American government. More than half of all U.S. Presidents have been lawyers. In the 1980s, more than half of all state governors were lawyers; so were slightly more than 60 percent of U.S. Senators and 44 percent of members of the House of Representatives. A majority of the heads of departments in President Clinton's cabinet are lawyers. In recent decades, more than two-thirds of presidential appointees to head the EPA and to serve on the EEOC, FCC, FTC, NLRB, and SEC have been lawyers.[13] And lawyers, of course, dominate the judiciary, legislative staffs, and law reform commissions.

Since American lawyers do the lobbying, draft the laws, promulgate the regulations, and decide the court cases, is it not plausible to regard lawyers as the "cause" of adversarial legalism? One would expect them, after all, to perpetuate those methods of governance which they learned to value in law school and in practice—and which also enhance the status, influence and incomes of lawyers. Those methods of governance promote adversarial legalism—*legal* remedies for social problems; legal rules (such as those concerning attorneys' fees) that reduce economic barriers to litigation; guaranteed rights to legal representation and formal adversarial procedures in administrative settings as well as in courts; preservation of trial by jury; and a strong policy-making and oversight role for the judiciary.

On the other hand, any implication that legal elites are the *primary* cause of adversarial legalism goes too far. It rests on the implausible assumption that in a democratic polity, other sources of power meekly acquiesce in whatever forms of law the legally-educated elites choose to impose on them. In reality, lawyers work for clients, and generally do what clients want. Lawyers in public office are accountable to powerful political constituencies. To explain the behavior of legislators, political scientists generally refer to variables such as political party, constituency characteristics, committee specialization, and the like; they do not seem to regard legislators' legal training or experience, or lack of it, as important.[14] There is little empirical evidence that law-trained politicians, legislative staff members or top administrative officials—whose very numbers suggest internal political diversity—differ systematically from non-lawyer colleagues.[15] Similarly, judges and private lawyers have diverse interests and political attitudes; some have been leading proponents of reforms that seek to *reduce* adversarial legalism.[16] For the most part, researchers observe, lawyers for powerful economic interests function as "conduits"—as agents, not as principals.[17] They do their clients' bidding, share their clients' political attitudes, and exercise relatively little independent influence on corporate clients' goals.[18] These studies suggest, therefore, that American lawyers do not play a major *independent* role in shaping public policy, in which their own views as lawyers (rather than their clients' and constituents' views) are what count.

Most importantly, if one views the American legal system in broad historical and comparative perspective, it seems clear that adversarial legalism stems from forces that lie well beyond the control of legal elites. It stems from the confluence of two conflicting features of the American political system:

1. a *political culture* that in recent decades has demanded increasingly comprehensive governmental protections from harm, injustice, and environmental dangers—and hence a more powerful, activist central government; and,
2. *governmental structures* based on *mistrust* of concentrated power—and hence that fragment power and check its exercise by means of privately-initiated lawsuits, appeals, and judicial review.

From this perspective, the salience of lawyers and lawyering in the United States is a consequence rather than a cause of adversarial legalism. Let me elaborate this lawyers-as-consequence thesis.

Political and Economic Structure

Liberalism, the dominant political culture in the United States,[19] emphasizes the primacy of individual rights vis-à-vis governmental control. Governmental power, in the liberal vision, must be limited and restrained by law, invoked and applied by citizens. The U.S. Constitution, accordingly, splintered governmental authority among separate "branches," limited the national government's powers, and added a judicially-enforceable Bill of Rights. Constitutionally limited and decentralized, 19th Century American government, as Stephen Skowronek put it, was "a state of [political] parties and courts."[20] Legislatures met for limited terms and were slow to act, which encouraged judges to become active policy-makers.[21] And where courts are politically potent, lawyers thrive.

By European standards, America's national administrative bureaucracy was slow to develop, retarded by a constitution that limited the central government's authority. Well into the 20th Century, economic life was dominated by private, market-based relationships, policed primarily by judicially-made rules, enforceable by litigation; this, too, exalted the role and prevalence of lawyers in legal development and the management of disputes.

America's general mistrust of concentrated power was replicated in the internal mechanisms of its legal system. These "legal structures of adversarial legalism" included trial by jury (which limited judicial power); a politically-selected judiciary (which maximized political responsiveness rather than centralized legal control); methods of adjudication that relied primarily on lawyers, rather than judges, to develop and manage the presentation of evidence and arguments; and legal doctrines that encouraged citizen access to courts. Among the latter are doctrines that authorize judicial review and reversal of governmental decisions on both statutory and constitutional grounds, that permit plaintiffs' lawyers to take cases on contingency fees, and that do not require unsuccessful litigants to pay the winners' legal fees.

A New Political Culture: "Total Justice"

The historical legacy discussed thus far—political liberalism, power-fragmenting political and economic structures, institutions conducive to litigation—suggests that the United States always would have had more "adversarial legalism in practice" than economically advanced European countries. Nevertheless, the adversarial legalism that has pervaded the United States in the last few decades seems different, both in intensity and scope, from that of the late 19th and the first half of the 20th Century. As recently as the early 1960s, the decisions of American administrative agencies, school boards, police officers, and zoning boards rarely were challenged in court. Litigation was not an omnipresent consideration in electoral redistricting, the practice of medicine, corporate acquisitions, and the formulation of regulatory rules. Both criminal and civil trials were far shorter. Litigation between business enterprises was less common. Consider these indicators of change:

- Between 1960 and 1987, expenditures on lawyers grew sixfold, from $9 billion annually to $54 billion (in constant 1983 dollars), almost tripling the share of GNP consumed by legal services.[22]

- Civil rights cases against government in federal courts increased from 280 filings in 1960 to about 27,000 in 1980.[23]
- In 1980, federal courts of appeal decided an estimated 2000 cases involving seriously-contested constitutional issues, compared to about 300 in 1960.[24]
- The volume and rate of state appellate and federal court cases involving public schools, roughly stable from 1920 through 1960, doubled in the 1967-1981 period.[25]
- In the early 1980s, more than 80 percent of the Environmental Protection Agency's new regulations were suspended by court challenges,[26] as was virtually every U.S. Forest Service management plan,[27] National Highway Traffic Safety Administration regulation,[28] and Department of Interior lease for offshore petroleum exploration.[29]
- Employment discrimination suits filed in federal district courts, at a minimal level in the 1960s, grew to about 2000 cases per year in 1973 and then quadrupled to over 9000 per year in the 1980s.[30]
- Medical malpractice suits were uncommon until the late 1960s. Then, according to the largest medical insurance company, claims rose from 4.3 per 100 insured physicians in 1970 to 18.3 in 1986.[31]
- Legal complaints against unfair labor practices filed in the National Labor Relations Board (the administrative "court" for such charges) grew from about 13,000 annually in 1960 to about 45,000 in 1980, even as the events that might occasion such complaints (representation elections, collective bargaining negotiations, work stoppages) remained at a steady level.[32]
- Several studies suggest a dramatic increase in intra-business litigation. In federal courts, contract cases filed under diversity jurisdiction grew eightfold, from about 4000 in 1960 to 32,000 in 1986.[33]

These increases in adversarial legalism reflected an extraordinary explosion of new legal rules and institutions—the Warren Court's "due process revolution"; sweeping changes in tort law; the founding of public defender offices, federally-funded legal services offices, and public interest law firms; the "judicialization" of administrative rulemaking; the judicially-reviewable environmental impact statement; and a barrage of ambitious regulatory statutes, designed to control pollution, protect consumers, and attack discrimination based on race, gender, age, and disability. The new regulatory statutes, unlike those enacted during the Progressive Era and the New Deal, invited adversarial legalism: they contained detailed legal provisions that made it easier for citizens to haul implementing agencies into court, as well as technology-forcing obligations and harsh penalties that triggered legal resistance by regulated enterprises.[34]

But why was there such an outpouring of new law? Most obviously, it stemmed from the dramatic political movements and ideas that swept through the

American polity in the 1960s. Beginning in mid-1960s, the United States experienced what political scientist Samuel Huntington calls a period of "creedal passion." During such periods, he argues the citizenry becomes intolerant of the gaps between the soaring ideals of the American creed and the sordid reality of institutional practices. They leap the channels of "normal politics," turning to demonstration and protest.[35] Thus in the 1960s and early 1970s, the political techniques and moral urgency of the civil rights movement spread into the anti-Vietnam War movement, and then to the environmental, consumer protection, and feminist movements. Congress, the courts, and state governments responded, promulgating a stack of new legal rights and obligations.

To some observers, however, the legal changes of recent decades reflect not merely a periodic burst of idealism but a more enduring change in American political culture. After all, legal change and adversarial legalism have persisted even as the United States, encountering an era of financial limits, turned politically conservative. To Aaron Wildavsky, the crucial development has been the growing strength of the egalitarian strain in American political culture—critical of inequalities of wealth and power, eager for governmental action to contain the technological risks and economic vulnerabilities associated with capitalism.[36] Lawrence Friedman, surveying American culture in recent decades, points to rising expectations of "total justice"[37]—the notion that technologically and organization-ally sophisticated modern societies can (and hence should) compensate victims of unfair treatment, personal injury, unexpected economic loss and health care costs, and also provide *ex ante* regulatory protections against sources of harm.

Total Justice Meets Fragmented Government

Growing popular expectations of "total justice," however, are not unique to the United States. In the post-World War II period, rich European democracies, too, have expanded governmental protections against misfortune, environmental degradation, and unfair treatment. But they have done so without creating American levels of adversarial legalism. The difference stems primarily from the European democracies' more hierarchical or corporatist political structures and traditions. There, national governmental bureaucracies and corporatist bodies implement new regulations and welfare-state entitlement programs without much interference from courts and lawyers.

In the United States, on the other hand, popular demands for "total justice" and regulatory protections are filtered through a political culture that mistrusts "big government"[38] and through a political structure that fragments power. Hence the satisfaction of demands for "total justice" has been left in large measure to state and local governmental agencies, even for the implementation of federally-enacted programs and policies. But how could reformers ensure that local police officers, environmental inspectors, school districts, and businesses would faithfully elaborate and implement those new legal rules and policies? The answer was to grant ordinary citizens and advocacy groups the right to haul errant officials and corporations into court. In the United States, lawyers and adversarial legalism thus substitute for the hierarchical bureaucratic and political mechanisms of accountability that European reformers could rely upon.

Even as political demands for total justice extended the responsibilities and powers of the federal government, the American electorate grew *more* mistrustful of government, and political leaders grew more mistrustful of each other. This tension was resolved by *further fragmenting authority* within the government, presumably to increase its responsiveness. The electorate repeatedly chose a President and Congress of different parties. A subcommittee-dominated Congress decentralized legislative power. Within the political parties, power was further dispersed.[39] Democratic Congresses, mistrustful of Republican presidents, began to enact more detailed statutes, so that courts could be called into play to monitor the executive branch. Interest groups that mistrusted government pushed for laws that enabled their constituents to challenge unsympathetic administrators and recalcitrant businesses in court.[40] Weak political party control over individual legislators and committee chairs led to cumbersome, legally complex statutes that were burdened with concessions to interest groups, substantively incoherent compromises, and ill-drafted last minute amendments[41]—all of which, of course, encourage litigation.

Pressured to respond to popular demands for more ambitious, socially transformative policies, the American judiciary, too, became more politically divided. Since the 1960s, high courts have been riven by higher dissent rates.[42] Political struggles over the composition of the judiciary have intensified. Changes in judicial personnel led to rapid doctrinal shifts. As court decisions became more changeable and unpredictable, disputants had more incentive to hire lawyers in order to reshape the law to their own ends.

In the private sector, too, increases in adversarial legalism reflect the interaction of a fragmented power structure and new demands for justice. American business and corporate finance are much more decentralized and competitive than their European counterparts,[43] as is American labor.[44] American pension, insurance, and health care systems are left more fully to the private sector, and are more fragmented and competitive. Hence as American businesses have been buffeted by greatly intensified competitive forces, there have been no strong industry associations, labor federations, bank holding companies, or governmental ministries which (like those in Germany and Japan) can help contain the resulting financial difficulties and power struggles.[45] In the more fragmented U.S. economy, short term market relationships and the risk of opportunism have become more pervasive.[46] Lengthy contracts, legalistic government regulation, and litigation help fill the need for governance. Adversarial legalism and demand for lawyers grow.

III. Lawyers and Adversarial Legalism

Even if government structures, economic fragmentation, and political attitudes are the *primary* causes of adversarial legalism, that does not mean that the large, aggressive, and politically active American legal profession plays *no* causal role. Lawyers may not be the locomotive of adversarial legalism, I will argue, but they do have their hands on the throttle. They can (and do) make it go faster and block attempts to slow it down.

A. Lawyers as a Secondary Cause

Consider, for example, the relationship between federalism and adversarial legalism. In the United States, top officials in Washington, D.C. do not have direct supervisory powers over local governmental officials who violate national policies; they can neither fire them nor offer them promotions for future good behavior. That is one reason why federal statutes give private citizens and advocacy groups the right to sue state and local officials who are responsible for implementing federal environmental laws. That is why Supreme Court rulings designed to control local police behavior empowered criminal defense lawyers to bring motions to exclude evidence obtained in violation of federally-elaborated Constitutional norms.

The causal arrow, in this analysis, runs from *governmental structure* (federalism, which weakens centralized bureaucratic control) to accountability by means of *adversarial legalism*. But federalism does not *automatically* give rise to legal rights to challenge local officials in court. To ensure that local officials follow national rules, federal policymakers could instead insist on detailed reporting by local officials. They could send in federal auditors, or suspend federal funding for noncompliant local entities. They could bypass local government entirely by funding new federal administrative offices to implement federal laws. Reliance on the techniques of adversarial legalism, therefore, needs some additional explanation.

The landmark federal Education for All Handicapped Children Act (P.L. 94-142), enacted in 1973, required local public schools to provide all children, regardless of handicap, an "appropriate public education." How was compliance to be assured in thousands of school districts, controlled by locally elected boards, which had incentives to hold down the costs of "special education"? Congress's solution—in contrast to the method adopted in Great Britain[47]—was to grant parents of handicapped children a series of legal rights: to participate in a prescribed meeting with educational officials, to negotiate a contractual educational plan for their child, and to appeal, first administratively, then to court, from educational plans with which they disagreed. Predictably, thousands of educational decisions have resulted in adversarial, legalistic hearings,[48] and federal courts became the principal forums for defining "appropriate public education."[49]

Congress's decision to rely on lawyer-assisted private legal challenge, rather than top-down bureaucratic review, *seems* to flow directly from the limitations imposed by American political structure, in this case a politically decentralized educational system. But that decision was not inevitable. Early versions of PL 94-142 called for oversight of school-level compliance by federal or state *administra-*

tive entities. However, two public interest law firms—the Children's Defense Fund and the California Rural Legal Assistance Foundation—"played a key role . . . as advisors to the congressional conferees. . . . Their experience [in civil rights and poverty litigation] produced a belief in the efficacy of rights, courts and court-like procedures, and profound mistrust of bureaucratic accountability."[50]

In this case, it appears that a *legal culture* dedicated to due process procedures and judicially enforceable rights operated as an "intervening variable." And the influence of lawyer lobbyists in shaping the implementation method was palpable. Whether legal culture and lawyers' influence were *decisive* in the special education case or in others is hard to "prove." Nevertheless, it does seem justifiable to hypothesize that the culture and actions of American lawyers often act as secondary causes of legal measures that expand adversarial legalism. Lawyers' causal impact is channelled, I will attempt to demonstrate in the pages that follow, through three streams of activity:

1. Promoting legal ideas that *legitimate* adversarial legalism and *extend* the realm of issues subject to that mode of governance.
2. Aggressive case by case advocacy, in which some lawyers choose to magnify (rather than temper) adversarial legal contestation.
3. Mounting organized resistance to reforms that would reduce adversarial legalism.

Lawyers or Clients. When lawyers lobby for statutes and judicial rulings that extend adversarial legalism, or engage in aggressive case-by-case advocacy, they typically do so on behalf of clients. How, then, can we properly view the lawyers rather than the clients as the "cause" of adversarial legalism? Often we can't. However, in a number of settings, situations, and roles, lawyers plausibly can be thought of as acting wholly or partly "on their own account."

First, members of the legal profession do not formally represent particular clients, organizations or interest groups when they serve as judges, law professors, bar association officers and committee members, members of law reform commissions, legislators, legislative staffers, and administrative policy-makers. Those roles obligate them to serve a wider public interest as they discern it. Thus when lawyers in those roles promote legal measures that expand rather than retard adversarial legalism, they can be regarded as independently responsible.

Second, some lawyers enjoy a great deal of discretion in deciding which clients or interests to represent, and how to do so. For example, public prosecutors, lawyers in public interest law firms, and lawyers who serve as leaders of advocacy groups typically have considerable authority to decide "on their own" whether and how to litigate and what kind of legal or policy arguments to make.[51]

Third, lawyers who are financially dependent on a particular kind of litigation have their own economic stake, independent of the interests of particular clients, in initiating certain kinds of litigation and in fighting for legal rules and institutions that foster adversarial legalism in their area of practice.

Fourth, some lawyers have reputational interests, philosophies, or personalities that may lead them to engage in adversarial legalism, and they may influence clients to accept the *lawyer's* preferred course of action.

Lawyers as "Dampeners" of Adversarial Legalism. In a society pervaded by the threat of legal action, many lawyers *prevent* litigation simply by advising their clients about potential liabilities.[52] Corporate lawyers prevent litigation by drafting detailed contractual terms for resolving potential future conflicts.[53] Many attorneys decline on moral grounds to advance claims or defenses that seem to them unjustified.[54] Other lawyers, emphasizing the costliness of the adversarial process, push clients intent on moral and legal vindication to accept financial compromise.[55] Bar associations dominated by elite lawyers often have fought to reduce "ambulance chasing" and certain types of litigation in hopes of enhancing the profession's image.[56] Some corporate counsel have insisted on using private mediation firms, rather than litigation, to resolve disputes; the leading mediation firms are run and staffed by lawyers and ex-judges.[57] Some law professors have been at the forefront in recommending no-fault insurance schemes to replace costly tort litigation.[58] During the administrations of Presidents Reagan and Bush, government lawyers persuaded conservative judges to restrict appeals to federal courts from state criminal convictions.

In sum, even if some members of the American legal profession consciously and on their own account work to amplify adversarial legalism, there are many, possibly more, members of the profession who work to dampen it. Perhaps, then, the *net* contribution of lawyers is to *reduce* adversarial legalism.

Perhaps, but probably not. The relative number of lawyers in each camp does not resolve the question. The burglary rate can go up even if most people try to deter burglary. Relatively small numbers of determined people can have a big impact. The fact remains that adversarial legalism, by most measures, has increased in the last quarter century. The issue is whether the actions of American lawyers—not all lawyers, but lawyers—have contributed to that net increase, even though many of their professional brothers and sisters may have prevented the increase from being greater. Or perhaps the profession has changed in ways that have increased the relative power and impact of amplifiers as compared to dampeners. The question to be examined, therefore, is not only *how* lawyers help generate adversarial legalism, but whether there has been any discernible *change* in American lawyers' ideas, practices, and professional roles.

B. Lawyers and the Culture of Adversarial Legalism

Law as Politics by Other Means. In March, 1993, an Alabama trial court judge held that the state's entire public school system violated the state constitution's mandate to "maintain a liberal system of education throughout the state." The system was unconstitutional, Judge Eugene Reese said, because the academic performance of many students fell short of basic standards. Many school buildings were woefully ill-supplied and badly maintained. Judge Reese's opinion specified that the schools, inter alia, must provide students with an opportunity to attain sufficient skills to compete with other students throughout the world and "sufficient understanding of the arts to enable each student to appreciate his or her cultural heritage and the cultural heritages of others."[59]

This decision, remarkable both for its interpretive creativity and for its ambition, nevertheless exemplifies an approach to adjudication that is common, if not predominant, in American legal culture. The law, in this view, is not simply a set of authoritative norms, set down in statute books and judicial precedents. Law is a set of evolving tools that judges must use to help achieve broader ends, such as individualized justice and social welfare. That instrumentalist, social engineering view of law contrasts sharply with the legal culture of the civil law countries of Western Europe and even of Great Britain, America's common law ancestor. In other democracies, law is generally regarded as a set of relatively stable, binding rules or principles. Changing law to attain social ideals is viewed as a job not for judges but for democratically elected legislatures.[60]

Judge Reese's instrumental approach to the judicial role is by no means uncontested in the United States. Its prominence ebbs and flows with political eras, issues, and movements, and it varies across courts in the same era. But it has long been a major stream in American legal culture, and has flowed with unusual energy in recent decades. High court judges now seek control over their dockets, they candidly acknowledge, in order to maximize their courts' capacity to decide major policy issues.[61] Chief Justice Earl Warren of the U.S. Supreme Court and Judge Roger Traynor of the California Supreme Court, creative, precedent-discarding instrumentalists, are both praised as shining examples of the American judicial tradition.[62] To the extent that the American legal profession—the social grouping in which beliefs about law are most consciously and continuously articulated, debated, shaped, and reshaped—endorses and promotes an instrumentalist vision of law and of adjudication, then it seems fair to infer that lawyers themselves, as advocates and as judges, help extend adversarial legalism.

Law Professors and Adversarial Legalism. After Judge Reese declared the Alabama school system unconstitutionally inadequate, Professor Eric Neisser of Rutgers University Law School, interviewed by a news reporter, said "I think [courts] would like to get out of the business [of defining standards schools must uphold], but unless someone takes control of the problem, the courts feel that they have to respond to the constitutional mandate."[63] Neisser, moreover, apparently endorsed that view—if the other branches of government are not doing the job adequately, the courts, however reluctantly, are *obliged* to see that basic justice is done.

Is that what American law professors teach future advocates, judges, legislative staffers, and politicians? Many American law professors do not. Some teach that whether the other branches of government are failing to "do the job" or to "take control of the problem" depends on a complex set of educational, economic and political judgments that the courts are not well suited to evaluate. Some professors would argue that the courts are not likely to be able to solve social problems, or that the courts have no warrant to try without clear legal justification in the text of existing constitutions, laws and precedents.

Nevertheless, Professor Neisser is not alone. "Someone," writes Yale Law School Professor Owen Fiss, "has to confront the betrayal of our deepest ideals and be prepared to turn the world upside down to bring those ideals to fruition."[64] And that someone, Fiss argues, should be the courageous judge. I know of no survey that directly measures support for this instrumentalist philosophy among the law school professoriat. But some surveys suggest that a majority of elite law school professors endorse a critical, social problem-solving approach to law.[65] When I ask American law professors what they think their colleagues think, most say that a view much like Professor Neisser's, if not predominant, is quite prominent.

A cross-national perspective underscores the point. Atiyah and Summers observe that English legal academics defer to barristers and judges in shaping law and legal culture.[66] British law students are expected to learn the rules of law as laid down in rather dogmatic textbooks, and Continental European students are expected to master the theoretical underpinnings of their legal systems. American law students, however, are taught to question the merits of legal doctrines and judicial opinions in terms of the fairness, economic efficiency, or equality of their social consequences. They are prodded to formulate legal arguments that support their gut feelings about what the results *should* be. The law journals they edit bulge with articles calling for new legal rights and changes in old ones,[67] along with essays stressing the indeterminacy and political character of legal rules. Reviewing the last decade's debates among the leading schools of legal thought, one professor concluded, "Now all sides agree that in some ultimate sense law . . . is unavoidably political."[68]

American professors teach their students that judges are often incompetent and are as apt to be influenced by their political allegiances as by the letter of the law. The legal system thus is portrayed as a field of political struggle, shaped by creative lawyering and argumentation (at best) and by raw economic and political power (at worst). So the lawyers job is to pick her way through that uncertain minefield, striving for justice as best she can when she sees an opening, whether as lawyer or judge. Not surprisingly, that is the view of the system that American lawyers convey to their clients.[69]

Law Schools and Distrust of Governmental Power. If judicial authority, when viewed through the lens of American legal education, is not entirely rational, the rest of government is portrayed as even more arbitrary. In law schools, American political culture's skepticism about governmental competence is honed to a fine edge. "The best insurance against autocracy," says an introduction to the law, "is to diffuse power as much as possible throughout society. This is exactly what lawyers in America do!"[70] Little wonder, then, that lawyers-to-be are taught, first and foremost, to question the bureaucrat's or the police officer's word, to favor strict (or at least "heightened") judicial scrutiny of legislative enactments for signs of bias or "rent-seeking," and to view due process procedures and lawyer-assisted access to the courts as the best way to structure governmental processes.

For those who might be skeptical about the virtues of adversarial legalism, American legal culture offers no equally well-developed countervailing ideal. Skeptics can argue that further legalization would be costly, might overburden the courts, or (perhaps most effectively) would be "a full-employment program for lawyers." But those are crimped, negative arguments, devoid of the high-sounding values that permeate the arguments in favor of rights and adversarial legalism. A countervailing legal ideal would entail greater emphasis on cooperative attainment of collective goals as opposed to individual rights, on legal stability rather than legal responsiveness, and on the notion that professional administration usually will be better than litigation in protecting the public interest and equity. Those are ideals discussed in European legal scholarship. But that is not what one generally encounters in American legal scholarship and classroom talk.[71] In the legal culture developed in American law schools, therefore, the proponents of adversarial legalism tend to occupy the moral high ground.

Law Professors as Lobbyists. The generally pro-adversarial legalism views of the American law professoriat are channeled directly to the judiciary. Some legal scholars frequently write briefs in Supreme Court cases.[72] Student law review editors become clerks to high court judges, bringing the latest scholarship to the pages of judicial opinions. Law professors rush their articles into print in time to be quoted in briefs in controversial cases. Atiyah and Summers write:

> A striking and far from isolated illustration of the extraordinary impact which academic ideas have on the daily administration of law can be found in the way in which in the 1970s and 1980s American state courts across the country accepted the arguments of a junior law professor . . . for allowing punitive damages more generously in products liability cases.[73]

Law professors also serve as reporters and chief drafters of the American Law Institute's influential "model statutes" and "Restatements" of the common law—documents which often have advocated more expansive legal rights and more equal (hence easier) access to courts.[74]

The most important influence of the law schools, however, has been indirect. They shape a legal culture that is invoked, day in and day out, by practicing lawyers and legally-trained governmental officials (including judges) when they make arguments based on an instrumentalist vision of law and when they call for judicially-enforceable legal rights and penalties as a way of implementing public policy.[75]

C. *Extending Adversarial Legalism in Courts and Legislatures*

Connecticut attorney Robert Farr, when serving as a state legislator, tried unsuccessfully to push through legislation that would ban smoking in restaurants. After Congress passed the 1990 Americans with Disabilities Act, designed primarily to bar workplace discrimination against disabled people, Farr saw another opportunity. The American Lung Association put him in touch with three mothers of children with asthma. On their behalf, Farr brought suit against Wendy's, McDonald's, and Burger King, arguing that by failing to bar smoking entirely—their current practice was to restrict smoking to some sections—the restaurants discriminated against people with respiratory ailments, forcing them to eat elsewhere.[76]

Farr may or may not win his case. While his cause is arguably just, it is highly unlikely that Congress, in enacting the Disabilities Act, intended to bar smoking in all stores, restaurants, and workplaces. On the other hand, the Act's language is both sweeping and unclear, so Farr had at least a chance of winning.[77] Many ADA suits have been filed on behalf of injured workers in order to obtain larger damages than those provided by workers' compensation laws—although again, that probably was not Congress's intent.[78] Like Farr, many American lawyers feel no compunction about using litigation to persuade the courts to extend statutory rights in previously uncontemplated ways.[79] Their legal culture, which values legal creativity in the pursuit of justice, validates their behavior. In day-to-day advocacy, therefore, lawyers (not all, but some, and cumulatively many) pound away at the frontiers of law. They lose many cases, of course. But in the aggregate they extend the universe of litigatable claims a bit further, and thereby reinforce the culture of adversarial legalism.

Creative Judging. Innovative lawyering aimed at extending the boundaries of adversarial legalism would be fruitless, of course, if judges were not responsive. Consider again, therefore, the Alabama trial judge who declared the state school system inadequate and hence unconstitutional. If his decision is upheld, the threat of appeal to court will become a pervasive feature of decision-making concerning Alabama public schools. The judge's decision was "invited," one might say, by the basic structural factors discussed earlier—growing expectations of "total justice" (in this case the social injustice of substandard educational facilities and programs) and a fragmented political system seemingly incapable of establishing and administering nationwide educational standards. Still, the Alabama judge's decision was not "compelled" by law or by political pressure. It was the decision of a law-trained judge, secured in his position by the traditions of judicial independence, responding simultaneously to a serious social problem and to legal and policy arguments advanced by public interest lawyers.

Of course, many, perhaps most, American judges are judicially or politically conservative, inclined to reject arguments that would expand adversarial legalism. But new legal rights and remedies established by activist judges persist and spawn litigation despite the reluctance of others to further expand those rights and remedies. Thus in the last 30 years "net" judicial contributions to adversarial legalism have been enormous. American judges, acting without political or legal compulsion, abolished the defense of contributory negligence in tort cases. They elaborated new doctrines which encouraged litigation concerning medical malpractice, product liability, "toxic torts," and dismissal of employees without just cause. They created constitutional rights to suppress illegally obtained evidence, obtain free legal defense in criminal cases, demand decent treatment in prisons and mental institutions, and obtain due process hearings in welfare administration, schools and other settings. All of these rulings gave rise to new, institutionalized patterns of adversarial legalism.

The judges who issued these decisions often were responding to deep social concerns, widely expressed in the media or by prominent politicians. Lawyers and judges, therefore, did not act alone, without encouragement from the wider society. Nevertheless, the innovative judicial decisions were suggested and defended by a lawyer-dominated legal discourse that endorses social problem-solving via judicial action and advocates litigation as a mechanism for implementing the new legal norms.

Policy-oriented judges also have extended *statutes* in ways that invite private litigation. Judges created "implied" private rights to sue governmental officials for insufficiently aggressive enforcement of civil rights and regulatory statutes.[80] Civil rights lawyers and sympathetic judges reshaped the 1965 Voting Rights Act, which guaranteed equal rights to vote, into a vehicle for judicial invalidation of electoral rules under which minority candidates have difficulty winning elections;[81] in consequence, few electoral redistricting statutes now take effect without a lawsuit. Similarly, judges read the National Environmental Protection Act to give environmental groups the right to sue agencies for inadequate environmental impact statements,[82] which helped make adversarial legalism a recurrent feature of governmental efforts to build highways and license power plants, implement forestry plans, dredge harbors, construct waste disposal facilities, and issue offshore oil exploration leases. Not surprisingly, a cross-national comparison of styles of statutory interpretation classified the American judiciary as the most freewheeling.[83]

Organized Lawyering for Legal Change. Many innovative judicial rulings arise from systematic, lawyer-dominated campaigns of legal advocacy. No other nation has such a large number of, or such effective, "public interest" legal advocacy organizations—acting primarily on their own initiative, relatively free from pressure from particular clients. Most salient, perhaps, are the American Civil Liberties Union and the NAACP, whose dedicated lawyers lobbied the courts to expand the legal rights of criminal suspects, limit capital punishment, ban school prayer, attack racial segregation, and promote busing for racial balance in schools. ACLU and NAACP successes in court led to further reliance on adversarial legalism as a means for protecting those newly-won rights. In addition, the NAACP, the ACLU, and the National Lawyers Guild persuaded Congress to insert a provision in the 1964 Civil Rights Act authorizing judges to order governments or businesses who violated the Act to pay the plaintiffs' attorneys' fees.[84]

In the late 1970s, the Ford Foundation funded a number of public interest law firms, that specialized in litigation on behalf of ostensibly under-represented interests.[85] Congress provided for attorney fee recovery in other major pieces of legislation. Litigation became a mainstay funding source for "private attorneys general."[86] In the past twenty years, lawyer-dominated advocacy organizations filed innumerable lawsuits, appeals, and amicus briefs to extend the legal rights of welfare recipients, tenants, children, women, consumers, disabled and mentally handicapped persons, and prisoners. Many have been successful.[87] Politically conservative public interest law firms, too, were established, lobbying courts to protect property owners from regulatory restrictions and exactions.

It is not only "private attorneys general" who lobby the courts to extend the law into new realms. Ambitious public prosecutors—not a majority of them, but enough to make a difference—seek to enhance their reputations by "making law." In the 1960s and 1970s, according to Suzanne Weaver's study of the Antitrust Division of the Justice Department, lawyers competed to devise innovative legal theories that would extend the reach of antitrust law.[88] In the wake of Watergate, ambitious U.S. Attorneys crafted legal arguments that transformed the federal Mail Fraud Act, the Hobbs Act, the Travel Act, and the RICO (Racketeer Influenced and Corrupt Organizations) statute, none of whose "statutory language nor . . . legislative histories . . . authorize their application to local political corruption," into vehicles for prosecuting dishonest state and local officials.[89]

Lawyers in private practice for profit also systematically lobby the courts. Loose networks of plaintiffs lawyers regularly are formed to urge the courts to expand legal rights for victims of particular hazards, such as asbestos, cigarettes, or pharmaceutical products. The lawyers circulate newsletters, operate clearing houses, and hold conferences to discuss possible legal arguments.[90]

Persistent advocacy by claimants' lawyers gradually transformed California's workers' compensation program, originally designed to provide insured benefits to injured workers without costly legal conflict, into an intensely adversarial and legalistic system.[91] J. Anthony Kline, legal affairs secretary to Governor Jerry Brown between 1975 and 1980, says, "The lawyers began to take over. The more lawyer involvement you get, the more procedural rules you get. The labor union movement gradually became dependent on the lawyers."[92] In 1990, litigation costs amounted to two-thirds the average award in disputed cases.[93]

Congressional support for the "private attorney general" concept reflected a broader lobbying campaign by public interest law firms, designed to make adversarial legalism the primary mode of accountability in the expanding regulatory-welfare state. Analyzing the public interest movement of the 1960s and 1970s, Michael McCann found that the reformers advocated a "judicial model of democracy."[94] Public interest lawyers wanted to expand governmental regulatory power, but they also mistrusted politicians and administrators. Their solution was to fight for administrative processes that would mimic the formal adversarial procedures of courts—the governmental institution they felt they could trust most fully. Congress responded accordingly, enacting regulatory statues that (a) empowered advocacy groups (like trial lawyers) to cross-examine and counter the arguments of regulated entities; (b) instructed administrators (like judges) to provide written justifications for their decisions;[95] (c) expanded the rights of advocacy groups to challenge administrative decisions in court; and (d) enacted strict statutory deadlines for achieving regulatory objectives, thereby enabling public interest lawyers to sue agencies for moving too slowly.[96]

One cannot be sure, of course, that these legal changes were "caused" by reform-oriented lawyers. Circumstantial and anecdotal evidence, however, suggests that lawyers and their legal cultures mattered. According to a law school magazine, John Phillips, co-founder of the Center for Law in the Public Interest in Los Angeles, is "best known for his instrumental role in Congress in reviving and updating the False Claims Act in 1986."[97] The Act, aimed at preventing fraud and waste in military procurement, relied more on adversarial legalism than on better top-down auditing. It empowered citizens to force a government investigation by filing a lawsuit, rewarding them with a bounty of fifteen to thirty percent of any moneys recovered from contractors. By 1993, over 500 cases has been filed, resulting in $400 million in governmental recoveries, and as John Phillips gloated, "unprecedented opportunities for private lawyers."[98]

The 1980 Act creating Superfund is another example. Unlike European regulatory programs for cleaning up hazardous waste disposal sites,[99] the Superfund statute reads as if it were designed by a plaintiff's personal injury lawyer. It imposes absolute, joint and several, and retroactive liability for clean-up costs on any enterprise whose wastes found their way into the disposal site—regardless of the disposer's *share* of the wastes, regardless of whether it acted perfectly lawfully under the legal rules and containment practices prevailing at the time of disposal, regardless of any demonstrated current harm to human health. EPA enforcement officials bring lawsuits against a few large corporate waste disposers, who then sue other "potentially responsible parties" (PRPs). As Landy and Hague describe the result, "the shovels often remain in the tool shed while the EPA pursues PRPs along the slow and tortuous path of litigation."[100] Litigation and related transaction costs, governmental and private, add up to at least one third of the funds actually expended on clean up,[101] and "by mid-1990, . . . after 10 years of program operation, only sixty-three of the more than twelve hundred National Priorities List sites had been cleaned up."[102] Superfund was not *all* lawyers' doing. It was supported by EPA, the hazardous waste treatment industry, and Congress members who could take a symbolic stand in favor of clean up without having to appropriate general funds revenues.[103] But Superfund also reflects—indeed it virtually epitomizes—a legal culture that espouses adversarial legalism as a mode of governance, and (although direct evidence is lacking) it bears the imprint of legally-trained legislators and staff members.

D. Constructing Lawyers' Ethics

The American legal profession long has stressed the ethic of zealous advocacy, in contrast to the legal professions of England and Western European nations, where "the ethical rules of conduct set greater limits on the lawyer's duty to protect client loyalty and confidentiality in deference to larger societal and third party interests."[104] American lawyers have fought for rules of evidence that provide a broader, more absolute lawyer-client privilege than exists in most other countries.[105] The American bar recently rebuffed proposed changes in the code of ethics that would have tempered lawyers' obligations of loyalty and confidentiality to corporate clients which engage in illegal behavior or fraud.[106] In contrast to most other legal professions, the American bar supports contingency fees, on grounds that they facilitate litigation by the non-wealthy. American legal ethics endorse lawyers' pre-trial coaching of witnesses, a practice strongly discouraged by the legal profession in Germany and other countries.[107]

The American legal profession's emphasis on the lawyer's duty of zealous advocacy—as opposed to her duty to serve as "officer of the court"—encourages a more entrepreneurial form of legal practice than prevails in Europe. It also encourages lawyers to advance novel legal claims and arguments, asserting that it is the court's job, not the lawyer's, to separate the wheat from the chaff.[108] The profession's adversarial ethic also validates a super-aggressive style of lawyering that intensifies the incidence and costs of adversarial legalism—as elaborated more fully in the next section.

V. Case-by-Case Lawyering and Adversarial Legalism

Socio-legal studies indicate that most attorneys serve as stolid gatekeepers for the courts, advising clients *not* to litigate. Most day-to-day, non-law-reform litigation is stimulated not by lawyers but by clients. Suppose, however, that 10 percent or 15 percent of legal contestation is the *lawyer's* idea—lawsuits, petitions, or motions filed or threatened in order to advance *lawyers'* pecuniary or strategic interests. It is difficult to tell, in any quantitative sense, how much legal contestation *is* lawyer-induced. Nevertheless, a great deal of anecdotal evidence, and limited systematic evidence, suggests that there is a significant amount of what we might call superaggressive lawyering, adding to the volume, costs and delays of "adversarial legalism in practice." This section surveys several subspecies of superaggressive lawyering. None dominate the legal rainforest, but neither do they appear to be on the endangered list.

A. Ambulance Chasers

Big Yank Corporation's sales of work clothing fell from $110 million in 1991 to $65 million in 1992, and the company told the 225 workers in its Wewoka, Oklahoma factory that the money-losing plant would be closed. Soon thereafter, according to company officials, a representative of a workers' compensation law firm met with employees and told them how to file claims. Two days before the plant closing, 247 claims for work-related injuries were filed—compared to 6 for that factory in the previous year. Much litigation ensued, between Big Yank's insurer and workers whose claims it disputed, and between the insurer and Big Yank, which claimed the insurance company had been lax in challenging fraudulent claims.[109] Statewide studies suggest that as in Wewoka, sudden surges in workers compensation claims, many of them legally questionable, often occur when factories close.[110] It is difficult to escape the inference that some workers' compensation lawyers engage in this particular form of litigation-stimulating ambulance-chasing.

Some American lawyers, of course, almost literally chase ambulances. They send runners to hospitals and union halls to give the attorney's business cards to injured people. Aided by modern technologies and communications systems, and motivated by the far higher damage awards now attainable in serious injury cases, contemporary ambulance chasers almost certainly dwarf the efforts of their counterparts earlier in this century. Some lawyers dispatch representatives by airplane to the scene of publicized train wrecks, chemical spills, hotel fires, and explosions. Others seek out individuals who may have had some exposure to harmful substances. In 1986 two lawyers formed the National Tire Workers Litigation Project, equipped vans with x-ray machines, and traveled to tire plants, offering examinations of workers who had been exposed to asbestos; they filed suit on behalf of 6000 workers. A federal trial judge accused the attorneys of "indifference as to whether any of the 6000 claims met professional standards or not."[111]

Most injured persons never hire an attorney.[112] Some people in ambulances have valid cases. Ambulance chasers, therefore, sometimes advance the cause of justice. But they do actively turn injuries into legal claims, adding to the sum of adversarial legalism and fostering the wider culture's acceptance of litigation as an appropriate social response.[113] Some lawyers help generate "claims conscious" American subcultures:

- Claims rates pursuant to the Longshore and Harbor Workers Compensation Act are far higher in the Ports of Los Angeles and Long Beach than for essentially identical stevedoring operations in the Ports of Oakland and Seattle. Employers who operate in all three harbors contest many more Los Angeles claims as unfounded or inflated. The difference, they claim, arises from the entrepreneurial behavior of claimants' attorneys whose offices abut the port area on San Pedro Bay and who station representatives in union halls.[114]
- New York City's municipal liability payments for slip-and-fall accidents in 1991, calculated on a per capita basis, were double those in Detroit and more than 50 percent higher than Chicago's. The City's attorneys, according to a *New York Times* reporter, claim that lawyers whose clients are injured in car accidents or sidewalk stumbles scrutinize the pavement for defects that can drag the city into the case.[115]

- One might suspect that attorney behavior is involved when research reveals that in Southern California, employers' first notice of worker injury claims in 1991 came from the claimant's attorney in almost 55 percent of claims, while attorneys were initially engaged in only 29 percent of Northern California claims. Similarly, in 1991 the workers' comp litigation rate (an indicator of how often insurers contend that claims are unfounded or exaggerated) was 17.5 percent for Southern California claims, but only 8.2 percent for Northern California 1991 claims.[116]

Flamboyant advertising by lawyers, a practice only about 10 or 15 years old, might be considered a sub-species of ambulance chasing. A Boston lawyer advertises on the radio, telling tenants that lawsuits for damages can be filed against landlords for exposure to lead paint.[117] Annual TV advertising expenditures by lawyers, the Television Bureau of Advertising reports, grew from about $17 million in 1983 to over $100 million in 1991.[118] A televised ad shown in Florida portrayed a boy squirming in a barber's chair. "If you don't stop moving, Jonathan, I'll cut your ear off," said the barber. The boy spun his chair and replied, "Yeah, and if you do, I'll call attorney David Singer." Singer then appeared on screen to intone, "No client is too small to benefit from our legal protection." Another Florida TV ad featured a man who said that after his third arrest for drunk driving, "They wanted to put me in jail for a year and take away my driver's license for 10 years. That's when I called the lawyers at the Ticket Clinic. They got my case thrown out of court. No jail. No suspension. Nothing."[119] Of course, much lawyer advertising is *not* tasteless; some of it may convey useful information about access to justice. Nevertheless, lawyers who advertise do legitimate and spread a culture supportive of adversarial legalism.

B. Wholesale Ambulance Chasing: Entrepreneurial Class Actions

In 1990, a New York law firm filed a state court class action against seven major brokerage houses on behalf of all investors—a class of about 1 million—who held margin accounts between 1984 and 1990. The suit claimed that the brokerage houses illegally charged compound interest—on the credit they extended *and* on accumulated unpaid interest. According to a newspaper account:

> The brokers countered that the interest rate charges on margin accounts, which are applied in a similar manner to those of credit cards, are part of a long-standing policy well understood by their customers. In addition, they said it was completely lawful.

> Thousands of hours of legal work later, the lawyers for both sides agreed to settle the suit without any resolution of the legal issues involved. (In fact, the New York Legislature recently clarified state law to make it clear that compounding interest

on margin accounts is legal.) The defendants agreed to notify customers about the compound interest rates . . . and to pay legal fees to the plaintiffs' attorneys.

A spokesman for defendant Merrill Lynch & Co. said the company has long included a notice to margin customers about interest charges, but that it agreed to pay a portion of plaintiffs' legal fees, which totaled $1 million, in order to avoid further litigation expenses.[120]

After learning of a government investigation of alleged price fixing by major airlines, attorneys filed 21 cases on behalf of 12 million passengers. After three years, the consolidated cases were settled for $458 million in cash and discount coupons, and $14.4 million in fees for the plaintiffs' lawyers—even though, according to a *Wall Street Journal* account, the presiding judge said he "would assess the chances of the plaintiffs recovering as not good" and that "I think the case would have a hard time surviving a motion for summary judgment."[121] But it made sense for the defendants to settle once they hit on the idea of paying the actual plaintiffs in discount coupons (worth 10 percent off purchased tickets for off-peak travel). Again, the plaintiffs' attorneys got a big payoff while providing their "clients"—those who bother to go to the trouble of proving they fall within the affected class and collect the coupons—with minimal benefits.

In these cases opportunistic lawyers themselves initiated litigation and used the club of costly adversarial legalism to extract settlements that primarily benefitted the lawyers themselves. Are these isolated stories, or are they commonplace? Apparently the latter, as indicated by these studies:

- Janet Cooper Alexander found that in 1983, a handful of entrepreneurial California law firms routinely filed a class action suit against *every* computer company, nine in all, whose stock declined substantially in the half-year following its initial stock offering.[122] The plaintiffs' lawyers clearly filed suit merely on the basis of the stock decline, without any prior evidence of fraud or other securities laws violations, and then sought detailed pretrial discovery that probed for evidence that management had in some way exaggerated the company's product quality or sales prospects. Regardless of the apparent strength (or weakness) of the claim, defendants felt compelled to settle the case on the eve of trial for about 25 percent of the potential damages. They did so, Alexander concluded, because (1) the potential damages claimed were "astronomically high"; (2) "insurance and indemnification rules . . . make substantial sums of money . . . available for negotiated settlements but not for judgments after trial"; and (3) the rules for paying plaintiff lawyers counsel fees made it very advantageous for them—if not for the class of investors they putatively represent—to settle before trial (but after conducting a vigorous round of pre-trial discovery). The plaintiffs, lawyers ended up with fees of $2-$3 million (averaging 27 percent of the recovery), defendants' lawyers with even more, and most of the "damages" (averaging $9 million) did not go to small investors but served to "insure a relatively small number of institutional investors against market losses from a speculative investment. . . . " The resulting "non-merits-based settlement regime also encourages the filing of more and weaker suits."[123]

- Roberta Romano, in an equally brilliant study of a broader population (n=139) of shareholder suits, found that the settlement pattern is consistent with the proposition "that a significant proportion of shareholder suits are without merit"; that the litigation did not produce significant structural changes in board composition or other changes in corporate governance; and "that the principal beneficiaries of cash payouts in shareholder suits are attorneys."[124] Of the 83 resolved cases in Romano's sample, only half involved a monetary recovery for stockholders, while plaintiffs' attorneys were paid in 90 percent (75 cases), and in 7 cases the only relief was attorneys' fees. Of the 32 adjudicated cases, plaintiffs won only one (or perhaps two).[125]

- Similar patterns have been found in studies of class actions in other spheres of law.[126]

Undoubtedly some class actions are socially useful, punishing and hence deterring unlawful corporate behavior. But quite often, it seems, the lawyers who claim to serve as "private attorneys general" really only "pile on" after the government has imposed criminal sanctions.[127]

C. Ideological Ambulance Chasers

Many public interest law firms chase not ambulances but governmental and corporate misconduct. They are legal knights errant, looking for the dragon of authority to sue, whether or not they were called into action by any particular damsel in distress. Thus the American Civil Liberties Union monitors governmental processes for violations of free speech. Natural Resources Defense Council lawyers scour the compliance reports that permit holders must file with the EPA pursuant to the Clean Water Act; from these reports, they target self-reported violators whom they then sue for damages.[128]

Public interest lawyers add deterrent punch to public law. They defend individuals and values that otherwise would lack representation. In so doing, they enhance governmental accountability. Their technique, however, is lawyer-initiated litigation; hence they "independently" add to adversarial legalism in the United States.

D. Warrior Litigators

According to journalist James B. Stewart, George Kern, Jr., a senior partner in Sullivan & Cromwell, "wasn't entirely satisfied with his defensive legal efforts" to prevent a hostile takeover of his client, the giant Kennecott Copper corporation, by T. Roland Berner, a lawyer who was chairman of Curtiss-Wright Corporation. Kern "began a plan which would put Kennecott on the offensive—and silence Berner as a threat forever."[129] The plan included a lawsuit designed to block Curtiss-Wright's tender offer on far-fetched anti-trust grounds, as well as Kennecott's own hostile takeover of Curtiss-Wright. There followed a furious round of additional legal actions, requests for *ex parte* injunctions, countersuits, motions, and appeals, scattered through several jurisdictions. None of the legal claims or arguments focussed on whether a Curtiss-Wright takeover of Kennecott (or vice-versa) would be good or bad for Kennecott shareholders, or for the copper industry, or for the national economy. All the litigation was designed simply to slow down or derail the other corporation's tender offers. Finally, the two companies, exhausted by the legal struggle, agreed to settle without either taking over the other. Kennecott had expended $1.5 million in legal fees. "In the end," Stewart concludes, "little was accomplished."[130]

Strategic Lawyering. In the Kennecott struggle, top attorneys deployed groups of younger lawyers like *panzer* divisions. Their purpose was to create obstacles and impose costs, not to vindicate their clients' deeply-felt legal rights. To paraphrase Mae West, justice had nothing, to do with it. Stewart's account, based on interviews with lawyers, may downplay the role of the clients, but it is plausible to believe that in these legal maneuverings, the lawyers devised the strategies. They deliberately searched the law and its procedures for any available charge or defense, manipulating the techniques of adversarial legalism for ends not contemplated by the lawmakers.

How often do lawyers suggest or agree to engage in such manipulative use of the legal system—or what sometimes is called "strategic litigation"? It surely does not characterize *most* commercial and financial litigation. But it is not uncommon.[131] For example:

- Canan and Pring systematically studied SLAPP suits ("strategic lawsuits against public participation"), identifying 100 damage suits (mostly for defamation). Parents were sued by a board of education for complaining about allegedly unsafe school buses. Homeowners who sponsored a referendum petition to block a proposed project were sued by the real estate developer. Police officers sued those who complained of official misbehavior. From the fact that most of these suits seek large money damages, rather than injunctive relief, Canan and Pring conclude that the goal was primarily to impose high litigation costs and hence silence critics. Legal judgments favored the citizen-defendants in 80 percent of the SLAPP suits that reached a legal disposition.[132] This suggests that lawyers for the SLAPPers not only were ineffective gatekeepers for the courts but willingly participated in the use of legal processes for purposes of intimidation.
- Opponents of development, too, use lawsuits as obstructive tactics in a broader ideological war. Some advocacy groups and their lawyers are inclined to oppose highway construction, logging, waste incinerators, or offshore oil

development on principle. The lawsuits they bring, however, often are cast as technical challenges to environmental impact statements. The best legally-obtainable result, in many cases, would be not to stop the project but to compel a rewriting of the impact statement.[133] The purpose of the litigation is the hope, often not unfounded, that the lawsuit-induced delays and costs will compel the developers or public agencies to curtail or abandon the project altogether.[134]

- Attorneys opposed in principle to the death penalty routinely file multiple state and federal appeals and habeas corpus petitions, often on legal grounds that are highly unlikely to succeed. They hope that the extraordinary delays, the build-up of death row populations, or the publicity attending frantic last minute appeals will increase political pressures for clemency or for legal change. To many who oppose capital punishment, the defense lawyers' actions are morally justifiable and even commendable. And their efforts are clearly justified when there is any doubt of the defendant's guilt. But it is hard to deny that many death penalty appeals represent a manipulative form of adversarial legalism, devised and extended by lawyers.

Pre-Trial Discovery Abuse. According to Second Circuit Court of Appeals Judge Ralph K. Winter, a member of the federal courts' Advisory Committee on Civil Rules:

> [The Advisory Committee found] a no-stone-left-unturned . . . philosophy of discovery governs much litigation and imposes costs, usually without correspond-ing benefits. . . . Second, discovery is sometimes used as a club against the other party . . . solely to increase the adversary's expenses.[135]

Abusive discovery doesn't occur in the average case, where the monetary stakes are not very large.[136] But in high stakes cases, lawyers often use discovery demands and other pretrial maneuvers to grind down the opposition. Professor Robert Rabin, reporter to an ABA commission on the liability system, concluded:

> The . . . most troublesome aspect of the spiralling costs of the system is not excessive litigation *per se* but . . . strategic resort to delay and imposition of burdensome costs of trial preparation. The many forms of this abuse include spurious motions practice, excessive deposition taking, unnecessary continuances, frivolous claims, and multiple lawyering.[137]

Chicago lawyers who frequently are involved in large-stakes litigation admitted to a researcher that they often (that is, in 40 percent of their cases or more) had used discovery tools simply to impose work burdens or economic pressure on their adversaries.[138]

Trial practice is not much better. Trial attorneys—not all, but many—routinely endeavor to prevent the introduction of unfavorable facts, attack the credibility of adverse witnesses by exaggerating small inconsistencies, and engage in a variety of obstructionist tactics.[139] Similarly, some lawyers transform a system of pre-trial pleadings designed to foster non-technical, non-adversarial behavior into patterns of obfuscation and costly motion practice. Rule 9(b) of the Federal Rules is designed to avoid unnecessary contentiousness by requiring plaintiffs to state claims of fraud "with particularity." But according to Michael Kaufman, "One would be hard-pressed to envision a lawsuit with common law fraud, securities fraud or RICO claims that did not get bogged down in a Rule 9(b) dispute," because the plaintiff's lawyer, unwilling to help the defendant prepare, "typically resists the nonadversarial spirit of Rule 9(b) by alleging fraud in a general notice-pleading manner."[140] If the reader's response is "Of course!" that only shows the extent to which lawyers have propagated a legal culture that leads us to accept unnecessary adversarial legalism as normal.

Criminal Defense and Prosecution. Attorneys representing poor or near-poor criminal defendants, it is commonly observed, often *fail* to mount aggressive legal defenses. Sometimes, that reminds us, there is not enough adversarial legalism. But in some proceedings and in some kinds of cases, intensely adversarial and calculatedly obstructive litigation tactics are very common. Indeed, they are encouraged by the conventional lawyer-generated interpretation of the defense attorney's proper role. Criminal lawyers thus routinely tell suspects never, never to say anything to investigators. They treat the *right* to silence as an *obligation*, encouraging offenders to adopt an adversarial rather than a cooperative or repentant stance—at least until the attorney first uses that silence to try to extort a reduced sentence. Once the possibility of a criminal investigation arises, corporate defense lawyers routinely try to prevent corporate officers and employees from speaking with regulatory officials.[141] Some criminal defense lawyers as a matter of course bring unwinnable motions to suppress evidence. In a study of several criminal courts, Peter Nardulli found that only 17 percent of motions to suppress physical evidence were granted, and only 5 percent of motions to suppress confessions.

The ethic of zealous advocacy also seems to draw some public prosecutors into a posture in which "winning" becomes the primary goal; the result is more adversarial legalism:

- Many state and county prosecutors' offices retain some or all of the large fines that can be obtained through successful prosecution of environmental crimes or from civil suits seeking "natural resource damages." Thus one can find accounts of district attorneys striving to "build up" damage claims in the style of a plaintiff's personal injury attorney.[142]
- The federal Office of Thrift Supervision is responsible for recovering government-insured losses paid out on behalf of "thrifts" that have failed. "In those instances," Dennis Curtis observed, the OTS legal staff "resembles plaintiffs' lawyers in mass disaster cases. The objective is to identify any party with a pocket deep enough to repay the expense of pursuing it . . . [e.g., not only] the officers and directors of the failed association [but also] the

accountants, the lawyers, and anyone else who furnished professional services, and the insurers of all of the above."[143]

- Church and Nakamura observed that in some EPA regional offices, which are responsible for remediation of hazardous waste disposal sites under the Superfund statute, "The informal language of government lawyers is often tough and uncompromising . . . [Potentially responsible parties] become 'slam dunk' PRPs or 'deep pockets'. . . ."[144] The effect, however, is to close doors to cooperative cleanup. Church and Nakamura came to believe that "The adversary process, with its assumptions about self-seeking behavior, discourages unilateral candor and openness" on the part of the prosecutors. The result is legal resistance and slower environmental remediation.[145]

VI. Lobbying to Preserve Adversarial Legalism

Lawyer-dominated organizations, such as the Federal Judicial Council, the American Bar Association, and state bars, sometimes work for legal reforms that would curtail adversarial legalism.[146] On the other hand, highly-organized subgroups of lawyers have been prominent and not infrequently successful in *resisting* such reforms, especially those that would make a *large* dent in the scope and intensity of adversarial legalism.

The Civil Justice System Reform Movement

In April 1993, the Governor of New York, a lawyer himself, proposed legislation that would create a fund, supported by a fee on hospital births, to compensate families whose babies sustained costly-to-treat injuries in the course of birth; compensation would be paid without the need to bring a lawsuit and prove negligence on the part of the doctor or hospital.[147] "The bill," cautioned the *New York Times*, "faces steep opposition from trial lawyers" and "has an uncertain outlook in the Legislature."[148] The trial lawyers' opposition to this adversarial legalism-reducing reform is not unusual: they have persistently lobbied to preserve the jury system for civil cases and to maintain the primacy of tort law for compensating accident victims.

The American tort law system, with its unexplained jury verdicts, loosely-structured law of damages,[149] and cumbersome methods of decision-making,[150] is an extraordinarily costly and inconsistent way of compensating accident victims.[151] Tort claims have driven auto insurance rates so high that many drivers go uninsured.[152] American medical malpractice and product liability insurance costs apparently are 5 to 10 times as high as insurance rates abroad,[153] even though most victims of medical malpractice or product injuries recover nothing and many settlements apparently result in much less than full compensation.[154]

State workers' compensation laws provide one alternative model: employers must insure against and cover employees' medical expenses and most of their lost earnings in the event of work-related injuries, regardless of fault; disputes are diverted from slow and costly jury trials to administrative tribunals. In some European democracies, this "no fault/mandatory insurance" model has gradually been extended beyond the workplace, covering accidents at school, at home and on the highway, as well as injuries stemming from pharmaceutical products and medical care.[155] Specialized compensation and mandatory insurance programs are designed to eliminate costly disputes about fault and to provide victims modest but certain compensation for out-of-pocket losses.[156] In the U.S., however, the no fault/mandatory insurance model has not been extended, except for a few programs such as the 1986 Childhood Vaccine Injury Act and a federal law covering lung damage to coal miners. Workers, compensation is still restricted to on-the-job accidents. Indeed, injured workers have been authorized in a variety of circumstances to *circumvent* workers' compensation programs' exclusive remedy provision and to bring potentially more remunerative tort cases against employers, contractors, and manufacturers of products used in the workplace.

In the mid-1980s, insurance, medical, and business groups, with support from some legal academics and from municipal governments, mounted a political campaign to curtail or reform tort litigation. Some 800 civil justice reform bills were introduced in state legislatures in 1986, 1000 in 1987, and 1400 in 1988.[157] The bills sought to modify rules on joint and several liability (so that "deep pockets" only partly responsible for injuries would not be stuck with the whole bill); shorten statutes of limitations; put caps on "pain and suffering" and punitive damage awards; change the collateral source rule (under which tort victims can claim damages even for losses covered by their own insurance); penalize refusals to accept reasonable settlement offers; limit contingency fees; institute self-insured "no fault" plans for motor vehicle accidents; and require arbitration or mediation as a prerequisite to a jury trial.

ATLA v. Tort Law Reform. The reform proposals were fiercely opposed by the Association of Trial Lawyers of America (ATLA) and its state-level affiliates. ATLA did not always win. Scores of reform laws were enacted, and some of them did tend to reduce litigation and award levels.[158] But ATLA often did win, bottling up the bills in lawyer-dominated legislative committees,[159] or managing to weaken the proposed laws.[160] In at least 17 states, the plaintiffs' bar successfully pursued the battle in the courts, persuading judges to hold tort reform statutes, particularly those imposing caps on damages, violative of state constitutions.[161]

When a federal no-fault bill was introduced in the Senate in 1971, it was supported by labor and consumer groups as well as by large stock insurance companies.[162] ATLA, raised its dues, hired lobbyists, used its well-funded political action committee to reward Congressional foes of no-fault, and bombarded members with anti-no-fault telegrams. Throughout the 1970s, the Senate Commerce Committee voted almost annually to support the Bill, but ATLA lobbyists managed to prevent it from being brought to a vote, typically by getting it referred to the lawyer-dominated Judiciary Committee.[163]

Political reporters credit ATLA lobbying for the Senate's rejection of an international treaty limiting plaintiffs' damages in air crash cases—even though the American Bar Association *favored* ratification. "They [ATLA] have a lot more raw political power than the ABA," a former Senate staff member was quoted as saying.[164] ATLA's lobbying approach, another staffer said, "is characterized by pure political power as much as it is by policy arguments." ATLA and its 100 person Washington staff also helped block a federal product liability statute designed to standardize liability rules and limit damages. Alarmed by Vice-President Quayle's civil justice reform ideas—particularly a proposal for a modified "loser pays" rule for counsel fees—ATLA made massive contributions to the Clinton campaign,[165] and Clinton's election seems to have squelched any such federal proposal.

Asbestos. The American method of compensating victims of exposure to asbestos epitomizes adversarial legalism's approach to social problems. Imaginative plaintiffs' lawyers used litigation to expose the asbestos industry's shortcomings. Innovative judges empowered diseased workers to circumvent the workers, compensation system and file tort suits against asbestos manufacturers. The ensuing avalanche of lawsuits sent a powerful deterrence message to all industry. Even supporters of product liability litigation, however, acknowledge that "Asbestos litigation . . . has come close to crippling the entire litigation capabilities of the American judiciary."[166] The volume of cases is enormous. Employers and insurance companies are embroiled in endless litigation over who is responsible for occupational exposures that occurred decades earlier. The potential damages are far larger that the net worth of the asbestos industry. Close to 75 percent of insurance company expenditures in asbestos cases have gone to lawyers and experts for both sides rather than to asbestos victims and their families. It is hard to imagine a more costly and inequitable way of dealing with tragedy.[167]

As the dimensions of the asbestos problem became apparent, proposals were made to create a federally-administered fund to compensate victims, without the need for costly payment-delaying civil litigation. It never was enacted. ATLA opposed the idea—although it is not clear whether the failure to enact such a plan is more attributable to ATLA's opposition or to the inability of proponents to agree on plans for funding it.

Workers' Compensation. In most European worker compensation plans, disputes about degrees of permanent disability are resolved by panels of government physicians and other experts. In U.S., it is common for each side to hire their own doctors, selected for their propensity to favor either employer or employee respectively.[168] Dissatisfaction with workers' compensation is rife, not only among employers but among injured employees and claimants, attorneys. Yet claimants, attorneys' associations routinely have lobbied against reform proposals that would call upon government-appointed physicians (instead of "dueling doctors") to determine the extent of disability.

It is hard to find a more inefficient and costly system than the one that operates under the Federal Employers' Liability Act (FELA). Under FELA, injured railroad workers cannot turn to workers' compensation systems, but can sue their employers in tort for damages; disputes are tried by juries and the worker must prove that the injury was the employer's fault. Awards are very high for some victims, which leads to high total costs and high lawyer bills, but many injured workers get nothing. Year after year, attempts to replace* FELA with a workers' compensation remedy (absolute employer liability, but limited damages) have been killed in Congress, often by Senator Metzenbaum, a former FELA lawyer who was heavily lobbied by (and received large political contributions from) the FELA bar.[169]

VII. Conclusion

Lawyers and the legal culture they generate are not the *primary* sources of American adversarial legalism. The legal system is far from autonomous. What lawyers do is determined principally by the preferences of lawyers' clients. The governmental functions of legal institutions are shaped by nfluential political leaders and interest groups. At bottom, adversarial legalism is the product of a populist political culture, more inclined to trust courts than "big business" and "big government," and disinclined to endorse the expensive welfare state and social insurance programs that could displace much civil litigation. Adversarial legalism also reflects a Constitutional tradition that has limited central bureaucratic government and has encouraged litigation as a mode of checking governmental arbitrariness.

On the other hand, there is abundant evidence that American lawyers, acting on their own preferences, play a substantial contributory causal role. Lawyers, law professors, and judges generate a legal culture that supports adversarial legalism as a desirable or even an essential mode of governance. Organized groups of lawyers systematically lobby courts and legislatures to extend the realm of adversarial legalism and to block reforms that would reduce it. Lawyers have created and defended an ethic of zealous advocacy that in the hands of some practitioners—but not merely a few—legitimates superaggressive legal contestation.

Moreover, the American legal profession has changed in recent decades, magnifying its contribution to adversarial legalism. The legal profession has become much larger and richer. Law penetrates far more deeply into economic and social life. Hence there are more lawyers with both the capacity and the opportunity to engage in the aggressive lawyering examined earlier.

The growth of the legal profession, to be sure, was not brought about primarily by lawyers. To explain that, we must return to the lawyers-as-consequence thesis. It was the advent of a distinctively American style of activist government—one that relies on decentralized governmental and economic institutions, legalistic regulation, and adversarial legal challenge to help attain the ideals of "total justice"—that vastly increased the demand for lawyers. Nevertheless, once new lawyer-pervaded programs and institutions were put in place, lawyers did play a large role in a wider array of policy fields. Legal organizations of all kinds, public and private, became larger and better funded. There were more opportunities to engage in the high-stakes legal actions that warrant huge investments in aggressive and creative lawyering. And those lawyers who either believe in or profit from extending adversarial legalism thereby acquired far greater opportunities to pursue those ends. To put the same point metaphorically, broader political forces and governmental structures are the sorcerers that called forth adversarial legalism, and hence the need for more legally-trained apprentices. But the sorcerers' apprentices then could pursue their own agenda, extending legalism further and even thwarting the sorcerer's efforts to rein in it.

One might ask, however, does the sorcerer really want to rein it in? As we have seen, American lawyers create a legal culture that legitimates adversarial legalism. Legal ideas, generated by law professors and activist lawyers, influence politicians, who repeatedly enact laws that actively call for legal contestation as a method of policy implementation.

But here, too, the legal culture of adversarial legalism is at least as much consequence as cause. In the last two generations, elite (or lawyers') legal culture changed. It became more supportive of an instrumental, or even political, vision of law and the judicial role. It became more egalitarian, stressing expanded access to courts and an ever-growing panoply of individual and group rights. This shift did not occur because of the inexorable logic of the debate in law reviews. Lawyers' legal culture changed in response to the political upheavals in the 1960s and 1970s. Government, responding to political pressures, sought to transform society. Law professors and activist lawyers began to address the same agenda.[170] Lawyers' legal culture was reshaped by a turbulent, encompassing political culture that called upon the legal order to address its hopes for "total justice."

How important in the whole scheme of things, then, are the lawyers' own ideas and aggressive practices? Even if all the lawyers who consciously work to extend and preserve adversarial legalism were exported to Japan *en masse*, it is hard to believe that the resulting change in the legal order (in either country) would be truly massive. In Japan, political traditions stressing hierarchy, deference, and cohesion would continue to limit the lawyers' role. And in the United States, the social divisions, economic conflicts, political fragmentation, and popular beliefs that generate adversarial legalism surely would not disappear.

Imagine, however, that American lawyers and legal scholars chose to rework legal ethics and procedural rules in ways that would strongly discourage super-aggressive litigation. Suppose they lobbied for social insurance programs that would supplant tort law for compensating injured persons. What if they fought hard for creation of cheaper, less adversarial dispute-resolution forums, and fostered administrative law that limited judicial subversion of administrative authority? If the bulk of the legal profession did these things, it almost certainly

40   Robert A. Kagan

would have a considerable effect on the level of adversarial legalism. For what lawyers think and say, the legal culture they generate and the behaviors they exhibit, influence what clients, interest groups, legislators, journalists, and the general public think appropriate to demand of the legal order.

In sum, the influences between political culture and lawyers' legal culture flow in both directions, especially in the United States, where law schools and judiciaries are especially open to democratic influences and lawyers play such a large role in politics. Lawyers' legal culture reflects a surrounding political culture that also mistrusts authority, that also values the jury system and the right to challenge government in court, and that also prefers a politically-responsive to a pro-fessionalized, bureaucratic judiciary. Conversely, lawyers' distillations of those broader sentiments into a more focussed ideology of adversarial legalism have worked themselves into the warp and woof of legislative hearings, the drafting of laws, administrative and business procedures, the news media, and the dramas shown on television and in movie theaters. In late 20th Century United States, therefore, politicians, lawyers, and the public alike tend to equate adversarial legalism and the forms that promote it with law itself.

Notes

For especially valuable comments, the author is grateful to Peter Schuck, Richard Lempert, Steve Bundy, and participants at the Conference on Legal Cultures and the Legal Profession, Center for the Study of Law and Society, University of California, Berkeley, May 7-8, 1993. The College of Law and the Socio-Legal Center at Ohio State University provided generous research support. An earlier version of this chapter is "Do Lawyers Cause Adversarial Legalism?" *Law and Social Inquiry* 19:1 (1994).

1.   Marc Galanter, "Law Abounding: Legalization Around the North Atlantic," *Modern Law Review* 55:1 (1992); Martin Shapiro, "The Globalization of Law," *Indiana Journal of Global Legal Studies* 1:37 (1994).

2.   See, e.g., Wolfgang Wiegand, "The Reception of American Law in Europe," *American Journal of Comparative Law* 39:229 (1991); D. Trubek, Y. Dezelay, R. Buchanan, and J. David, "Global Restructuring and the Law: The Internationalization of Legal Fields," Working Paper, Global Studies Research Program, University of Wisconsin, Madison, August 1993.

3.   See Joseph Badaracco, *Loading the Dice: A Five Country Study of Vinyl Chloride Regulation* (Boston: Harvard Business School Press, 1985); David Bayley, *Forces of Order: Police Behavior in Japan and the United States* (Berkeley: University of California Press, 1976); John Braithwaite, *To Punish or Persuade: Enforcement of Coal Mine Safety* (Albany: SUNY Press, 1985); P. Day and R. Klein, "The Regulation of Nursing Homes: A Comparative Perspective," 65 *The Milbank Quarterly* 303 (1987); R. Brickman, S. Jasanoff and T. Ilgen, *Controlling Chemicals: The Politics of Regulation in Europe and the United States* (Ithaca: Cornell University Press, 1985); Sheila Jasanoff, *Risk Management and Political Culture* (New York: Russell Sage Foundation, 1986); Steven Kelman, *Regulating America, Regulating Sweden: A Comparative Study of Occupational Safety and Health Policy* (Cambridge: MIT Press, 1981); David Kirp, *Doing Good by Doing Little: Race and*

Schooling in Britain (Berkeley: University of California Press, 1979); David Kirp, "Professionalization as a Policy Choice: British Special Education in Comparative Perspective," *World Politics* 34:137 (1982); John Langbein, "The German Advantage in Civil Procedure," *University of Chicago Law Review* 52:823 (1985); Lennart J. Lundqvist, *The Hare and The Tortoise: Clean Air Policies in the United States and Sweden* (Ann Arbor: University of Michigan Press, 1980); Lois Quam et al., "Medical Malpractice in Perspective," *British Medical Journal* 294:1529, 1597 (1987); Gary Schwartz, "Product Liability and Medical Malpractice in Comparative Context," in P. Huber and R. Litan, eds., *The Liability Maze* (Washington, D.C.: Brookings institution, 1991); Takao Tanase, "The Management of Disputes: Automobile Accident Compensation in Japan," *Law and Society Review* 24:651 (1990); David Vogel, *National Styles of Regulation: Environmental Policy in Great Britain and the United States* (Ithaca: Cornell University Press, 1986); Derek Bok, "Reflections on the Distinctive Character of American Labor Laws," *Harvard Law Review* 84:1461 (1971); Robert J. Flanagan, *Labor Relations and The Litigation Explosion* (Washington, D.C.: The Brookings institution, 1987); Mary Ann Glendon, *Abortion and Divorce in Western Law* (Cambridge: Harvard University Press, 1987); Robert Reich, "Bailout: A Comparative Study in Law and Industrial Structure," *Yale Journal on Regulation* 2:163 (1985); Harvey Teff, "Drug Approval in England and the United States," *American Journal of Comparative Law* 33:567 (1985).

4.   See Robert A. Kagan, "Adversarial Legalism and American Government," *Journal of Policy Analysis and Management* 10:309 (1991).

5.   Langbein, "The German Advantage," 823.

6.   P.S. Atiyah and R. Summers, *Form and Substance in Anglo-American Law: A Comparative Study of Legal Reasoning, Legal Theory, and Legal Institutions* (Oxford: Clarendon Press, 1987).

7.   Surveys and experiments have shown that attorneys and insurance claims managers assign widely different settlement values to the same or similar civil cases. See Marc Galanter, "The Quality of Settlements," *Journal of Dispute Resolution* 1988:55; Gerald Williams, *Legal Negotiation and Settlement* 6:111-114 (St. Paul, Minn.: West Publishing, 1983); Douglas Rosenthal, *Lawyer and Client: Who's in Charge?* 202-207 (New York: Russell Sage Foundation, 1974); Michael Saks, "Do We Really Know Anything About the Behavior of the Tort Litigation System—And Why Not?" *University of Pennsylvania Law Review* 140:1215, 1223 (1992).

8.   Badaracco, *Loading The Dice*; Brickman et al., *Controlling Chemicals*; Vogel, *National Styles of Regulation*; Teff, "Drug Approval in England and the United States."

9.   Carol Greenhouse, *Praying for Justice: Faith, Order and Community in an American Town* (Ithaca: Cornell University Press, 1986); Robert C. Ellickson, "Of Coase and Cattle: Dispute Resolution Among Neighbors in Shasta County," *Stanford Law Review* 38:623 (1986); Stewart Macaulay, "Non-Contractual Relations in Business: A Preliminary Study," *American Sociological Review* 28:55 (1963); David Engel, "The Oven Bird's Song: Insiders, Outsiders, and Personal Injuries in an American Community," *Law and Society Review* 18:551 (1984).

10.   See Robert A. Kagan, "The Routinization of Debt Collection," *Law and Society Review* 18:323 (1984).

11.   Malcolm M. Feeley, *The Process is The Punishment: Handling Cases in a Lower Criminal Court* (New York: Russell Sage Foundation, 1979); Stewart Macaulay, "Lawyers and Consumer Protection Laws," *Law and Society Review* 14:115 (1979).

12. Richard L. Abel, *American Lawyers* (New York: Oxford University Press, 1989); Andrew Abbott, *The System of Professions: An Essay on the Division of Expert Labor* (Chicago: University of Chicago Press, 1988); Ronen Shamir, "Professionalism and Monopoly of Expertise: Lawyers and Administrative Law, 1933-1937," *Law and Society Review* 27:361 (1993).

13. Mark C. Miller, "Lawyers and American Politics: An Interdisciplinary Perspective." Paper presented at Annual Meeting, Law and Society Association, Philadelphia, May 1992.

14. Justin Green et al., "Lawyers in Congress: A New Look at Some Old Assumptions," *Western Political Quarterly* 26:440 (1973); Larry Bert et al., "Judicial Regime Stability and the Voting Behavior of Lawyer Legislators," *Notre Dame Law* 49:1012 (1974); David Derge, "The Lawyer as Decision-Maker in the American State Legislature," *Journal of Politics* 21:408 (1959).

15. John Plumles, "Lawyers as Bureaucrats: The Impact of Legal Training in the Higher Civil Service," *Public Administration Review* March/April 1981:220-228. One noteworthy exception is Jerry Mashaw and Daniel Harfst's study of the National Highway Safety Administration (NHTSA). There, top legal officials regularly clashed with engineers concerning regulatory strategy. Lawyers tended to emphasize recalls rather than mandatory design standards. Lawyers, moreover, clashed with engineers as to whether recalls were warranted in particular cases. To the lawyers, a primary consideration was whether they could "win in court." Jerry Mashaw and David Harfst, *The Struggle for Auto Safety* 183 (Cambridge: Harvard University Press, 1990). See also Robert A. Katzmann, *Regulatory Bureaucracy: The Federal Trade Commission and Antitrust Policy* (Cambridge: MIT Press, 1980).

16. Laura Nader, "The ADR Explosion—The Implications of Rhetoric in Legal Reform," *Windsor Yearbook of Access to Justice* 8:269 (1988).

17. R. Kagan and R. Rosen, "The Social Significance of Large Firm Law Practice," *Stanford Law Review* 37:399 (1985).

18. John Heinz, "The Power of Lawyers," *Georgia Law Review* 17:891 (1983); Robert Nelson, *Partners With Power* (Berkeley: University of California Press, 1988); R. Nelson and J. Heinz, "Lawyers and the Structure of Influence in Washington," *Law and Society Review* 22:237 (1988).

19. Louis Hartz, *The Liberal Tradition in America: An Interpretation of American Political Thought Since the Revolution* (New York: Harcourt, Brace & World, 1955). Of course, profoundly illiberal political ideas, such as nativism, sexism, and racism, have contended with liberalism in American political culture and law. See, e.g., Rogers Smith, "Beyond Tocqueville, Myrdal, and Hartz: The Multiple Traditions in America," *American Political Science Review* 87:549 (1993). Still, viewed comparatively, liberalism is what best distinguishes the American political culture from that of most other economically advanced democracies.

20. Stephen Skowronek, *Building a New American State: The Expansion of National Administrative Capacities, 1877-1920* (Cambridge University Press, 1982).

21. Morton Horwitz, *The Transformation of American Law, 1780-1860* (Cambridge: Harvard University Press, 1977).

22. R. Sander and E. D. Williams, "Why Are There So Many Lawyers? Perspectives on a Turbulent Market," *Law and Social Inquiry* 14:431, 434-35 (1989).

American Lawyers, Legal Culture, and Adversarial Legalism 43

23. Peter Schuck, *Suing Government: Citizen Remedies for Official Wrongs*, 199-202 (New Haven: Yale University Press, 1983).

24. Robert A. Kagan, "Constitutional Litigation in the United States," in R. Rogowski and T. Gawron, eds., *Constitutional Courts in Comparison* (Gummersbach, Germany: Theodor Heuss Academie, 1987).

25. David Tyack and Aaron Benavot, "Courts and Public Schools: Education Litigation in Historical Perspective," *Law and Society Review* 19:339, 348 (1985).

26. Laurence Suskind and Gerland McMahon, "The Theory and Practice of Negotiated Rulemaking," *Yale Journal on Regulation* 3:133, 134 (1985).

27. "The Forest Service: Time for a Little Perestroika," *The Economist*, March 10, 1990, p. 28.

28. Mashaw and Harfst, *The Struggle for Auto Safety*.

29. Charles Lester, "The Search for Dialogue in The Administrative State: The Politics, Policy, and Law of Offshore Oil Development." Ph.D. Dissertation, University of California, Berkeley, 1991.

30. John Donohue and Peter Siegelman, "The Changing Nature of Employment Discrimination Litigation," *Stanford Law Review* 43:983 (1991).

31. Lois Quam et al., "Medical Malpractice in Perspective." See also Donald Dewees et al. "The Medical Malpractice Crisis: A Comparative Empirical Perspective," *Law and Contemporary Problems* 54:217 (1991).

32. Robert Flanagan, *Labor Relations and the Litigation Explosion* (Washington: Brookings Institution, 1987), p. 33.

33. Marc Galanter, "The Life and Times of the Big Six; or, The Federal Courts Since the Good Old Days," *Wisconsin Law Review* 1988:921, 943. See also William Nelson, "Contract Litigation and the Elite Bar in New York City, 1960-1980," *Emory Law Review* 39:413 (1990); T. Dungworth, M. Galanter and J. Rogers, "Corporations in Court: Recent Trends in American Business Litigation." Paper delivered at Annual Meeting of Law and Society Association, Berkeley, California, 1990.

34. B. Ackerman and W. Hassler, *Clean Coal/Dirty Air* (New Haven: Yale University Press, 1981); E. Bardach and R. Kagan, *Going By The Book: The Problem of Regulatory Unreasonableness* (A Twentieth Century Fund Report; Philadelphia: Temple University Press, 1982).

35. Samuel Huntington, *American Politics: The Promise of Disharmony* (Cambridge: Belknap Press, 1981).

36. Aaron Wildavsky, "A World of Difference—The Public Philosophies and Political Behaviors of Rival American Cultures," in Anthony King, ed., *The New American Political System*, second version (Washington, DC: AEI Press, 1990); D. Polisar and A. Wildavsky, "From Individual Blame to System Blame: A Cultural Analysis of Historical Change in the Law of Torts," *Journal of Policy History* 1:122 (1989).

37. Lawrence M. Friedman, *Total Justice* (New York: Russell Sage Foundation, 1985).

38. Seymour Martin Lipset, "A Weak Concept of the Common Good," *The Responsive Community* 1:81 (Fall, 1991) and Lipset, *Continental Divide: The Values and Institutions of the United States and Canada* (New York: Routledge, 1990).

39. Nelson Polsby, *The Consequences of Political Party Reform* (New York: Oxford University Press, 1983); Stephen Griffin, "Bringing the State into Constitutional Theory:

44   *Robert A. Kagan*

Public Authority and the Constitution," *Law and Social Inquiry* 16:659, 701-709 (1991), provides a review and compelling synthesis of the literature on declining popular confidence in government and on structural impediments to governmental action.

40. Terry Moe, "The Politics of the Bureaucratic State," in J. Chubb and P. Peterson, eds., *Can the Government Govern?* (Washington, DC: Brookings institution, 1989).

41. Atiyah and Summers, *Form and Substance*; Peter Schuck, "Legal Complexity: Some Causes, Consequences, and Cures," *Duke Law Journal* 42:1, 27-30 (1992); Martin Shapiro, *Who Guards the Guardians?* Athens, GA: University of Georgia Press, 1988), p. 172.

42. L. Friedman, R. Kagan, B. Cartwright and S. Wheeler, "State Supreme Courts: A Century of Style and Citation," *Stanford Law Review* 33:773 (1981).

43. Mark Roe, "A Political Theory of American Corporate Finance," *Columbia Law Review* 91:10 (1991); Lester Thurow, "Communitarian vs. Individualistic Capitalism," *Responsive Community* 2:24 (Fall, 1992); but see John C. Coffee, Jr., "Liquidity Versus Control: The Institutional Investor as Corporate Monitor," *Columbia Law Review* 91:1277 (1991).

44. Joel Rogers, "Divide and Conquer: Further Reflections on the Distinctive Character of American Labor Laws," 1990 *Wisconsin Law Review* 1990:1; Robert A. Kagan, "How Much Does Law Matter? Labor Law, Competition, and Waterfront Labor Relations in Rotterdam and U.S. Ports," *Law and Society Review* 24:35 (1990).

45. For an interesting comparative case study, see Robert Reich, "Bailout: A Comparative Study in Law and Industrial Structure," *Yale Journal of Regulation* 2:162, (1985).

46. Ronald Gilson, "How Many Lawyers Does It Take to Change an Economy?" *Law and Social Inquiry* 17:637, 638 (1992).

47. Kirp, "Professionalization as a Policy Choice."

48. D. Neal and D. Kirp, "The Allure of Legalization Reconsidered: The Case of Special Education," in Kirp and D. Jensen, eds., *School Days, Rule Days: The Legalization and Regulation of Education* (New York: Falmer Press, 1986), p. 355.

49. R. Shep Melnick, *Between the Lines: Interpreting Welfare Rights* (Brookings Institution, 1993).

50. Neal and Kirp, "The Allure of Legalization."

51. For example, staff attorneys in national environmental groups told a researcher that decisions to litigate are for the most part made in a decentralized way by the lawyers, and usually "by the individual advocates who are working on the particular matter." Cary Coglianese, "Environmental Litigation as a Political Strategy," paper presented at Annual Meeting of the Law and Society Association, Chicago, May 27-30, 1993.

52. See Kagan and Rosen, "The Social Significance" (corporate lawyers as "conduits"), and William K. Muir, Jr., *Law and Attitude Change* (Chicago: University of Chicago Press, 1967; p. 112) (school board lawyer who successfully promoted compliance with Supreme Court decision barring prayer in public schools).

53. Ronald Gilson, "Value Creation by Business Lawyers: Legal Skills and Asset Pricing," *Yale Law Journal* 94:239 (1984); Kagan and Rosen, "The Social Significance."

54. Reporting on his interviews of Wisconsin attorneys in connection with their handling of consumer claims, Macaulay ("Lawyers and Consumer Protection Laws") says: "A number of attorneys suggested that a lawyer has an obligation to judge the true merits of a client's case and to use only reasonable means to solve problems. . . . For example, several attorneys were very critical of other members of the bar who had used the Wisconsin

American Lawyers, Legal Culture, and Adversarial Legalism   *45*

Consumer Protection Act so that a lender who had violated what they saw as a 'technical' requirement of the statute would not be paid for a car which the consumer would keep. While this might be the letter of the law, apparently a responsible lawyer would negotiate a settlement whereby the consumer would pay for the car but would pay less as a result of the lender's error."

55. Macaulay, "Lawyers and Consumer Protection Laws," 153-155; A. Sarat and W. Felstiner, "Law and Strategy in the Divorce Lawyer's Office," *Law and Society Review* 20:93 (1986).

56. Shamir, "Professionalism and Monopoly," 361, 374.

57. Ellen Joan Pollock, "Mediation Firms Alter the Legal Landscape," *Wall Street Journal*, March 22, 1993; pp. B1, 6.

58. R. Keeton and J. O'Connell, *Basic Protection for the Traffic Victim: A Blueprint for Reforming Automobile Insurance* (Boston: Little, Brown, 1965); Stephen D. Sugarman, *Doing Away With Personal Injury Law: New Compensation Mechanisms for Victims, Consumers, and Business* (New York: Quorum Books, 1989).

59. *Alabama Coalition for Equity v. Hunt* (1993), Circuit Court for Montgomery, Ala., Civil Action No. CV-90-883-R (excerpted in Edward Felsenthal, "School System in Alabama Gets 'F' From Court," *Wall Street Journal*, April 6, 1993, p. B1). See also P. Applebome, "Its Schools Ruled Inadequate, Alabama Looks for Answers," *New York Times*, June 9, 1993, pp. A1, A13.

60. Atiyah and Summers, *Form and Substance*; R. Kagan, "What Makes Uncle Sammy Sue?" *Law and Society Review* 21:717, 728-30 (1988).

61. R. Kagan, L. Friedman, B. Cartwright, and S. Wheeler, "The Evolution of State Supreme Courts," *Michigan Law Review* 76:961, 980-84 (1978).

62. G. Edward White, *The American Judicial Tradition* (New York: Oxford University Press, 1976).

63. Felsenthal, "School System in Alabama."

64. See Owen Fiss, "Against Settlement," *Yale Law Journal* 93:1073, 1086-87 (1984).

65. Charles Kelso, *The AALS Study of Part-Time Legal Education* (Washington: Association of American Law Schools, 1972) found that teachers at larger "high resource schools" (primarily university law schools) thought that law schools should teach a more theoretical (and presumably more critical) approach to law, while those at "low resource" (usually proprietary) schools tended to think they should teach in a more positivist, law-applying manner. A Carnegie Commission on Higher Education survey (in 1969 and 1974) found that at least two-thirds of professors in the twenty top-ranked law schools agreed with the proposition that their institutions "should be actively involved in solving social problems." More than half of American law professors, and higher proportions in the top twenty law schools, identified themselves as politically "left or liberal," and only small percentages as "moderately or strongly conservative," which put them far to the left of most other academic and professional faculties. Carl Auerbach, "The Silent Opposition of Professors and Graduate Students to Preferential Affirmative Action Programs: 1969 and 1975," *Minnesota Law Review* 72:1233 (1988).

66. Atiyah and Summers, *Form and Substance*.

67. Michael Saks systematically compared American law reviews published in 1960 with those published in 1980. He found that in 1960, "the ratio of articles criticizing [the legal status quo] to articles defending was 0.84—for every article defending there was less than one article criticizing. For 1985 articles, the ratio had risen to 2.59—more than two and a half articles criticizing doctrine for every article defending it". Saks, "Law Journals: Their

46   *Robert A. Kagan*

Shapes and Contents, 1960 and 1985," pp. 5-6. Paper presented at Annual Meeting, Association of American Law Schools, New Orleans, January 6, 1989.

68. Michael Wells, "Behind the Parity Debate: The Decline of the Legal Process Tradition in the Law of the Federal Courts." *Boston University Law Review* 71:609 (1991) (quoting Richard Posner, "The Decline of Law as an Autonomous Discipline: 1962-1987," *Harvard Law Review* 100:761 (1987)).

69. Sarat and Felstiner, "Law and Strategy."

70. Richard Moll, *The Lure of the Law* (New York: Viking Press, 1990), p. 10.

71. Mary Ann Glendon, *Rights Talk: The Impoverishment of Political Discourse* (New York: Free Press, 1991).

72. Emily Couric, "Profiles in Power," *National Law Journal*, April 15, Special Report, p.19 (1985).

73. Citing David Owen, "Punitive Damages in Products Liability Litigation," *Michigan Law Review* 74:1257 (1956), "an article said to have been cited within a few years in at least 20 jurisdictions." Atiyah and Summers, *Form and Substance*.

74. ALI Committees, of course, do not always endorse rule changes that encourage adversarial legalism. For a fascinating case study, see Edward Rubin, "Thinking Like a Lawyer, Acting Like a Lobbyist: Some Notes on the Process of Revising UCC Articles 3 and 4," *Loyola of Los Angeles Law Review* 26:743 (1993). Rubin's account does indicate, however, that both ALI as an institution and individual law professors not infrequently lobby legislatures for the changes they prefer.

75. It is not only in the United States of course, that legal scholars are influential. See, e.g., Martin Weston, *An English Reader's Guide to the French Legal System* (New York: Berg, 1991), p. 117; John Henry Merryman, *The Civil Law Tradition*, 2nd ed. (Palo Alto: Stanford University Press, 1985), p. 56. What matters for our purposes is whether the approach to law recommended by the scholars fosters adversarial legalism. And far more than their French or German counterparts, that is what the American professoriat tends to do.

76. Edward Felsenthal, "Disabilities Act Is Being Invoked in Diverse Cases," *Wall Street Journal*, March 31, 1993, p. B1.

77. The court dismissed Ferr's suit, but he appealed. Other similar cases, however, were not dismissed. Frances McMorris, "Disability Case Widens Fight Over Smoking," *Wall Street Journal*, January 30, 1995, p. 31.

78. Felsenthal, "Disabilities Act."

79. Atiyah and Summers, *Form and Substance*.

80. Peter Schuck, *Suing Government*.

81. Abigail Thernstrom, *Whose Votes Count? Affirmative Action and Minority Voting Rights* (Cambridge: Harvard University Press, 1987).

82. Serge Taylor, *Making Bureaucracies Think: The Environmental Impact Statement Strategy of Administrative Reform* (Palo Alto: Stanford University Press, 1984).

83. R. Summers and M. Taruffo, "Interpretation and Comparative Analysis," in D. N. MacCormick and R. Summers, eds., *Interpreting Statutes: A Comparative Study* (Aldershot: Dartmouth Publishing, 1991).

84. K. O'Connor and L. Epstein, "Bridging the Gap Between Congress and the Supreme Court: Interest Groups and the Erosion of the American Rule Governing Awards of Attorneys' Fees," *Western Political Quarterly* 28:238, 239-40 (1985).

85. Robert L. Rabin, "Lawyers for Social Change: Perspectives on Public Interest Law," *Stanford Law Review* 28:207 (1976).

86. O'Connor and Epstein, "Bridging the Gap," 241-45; Michael Greve, "Environmentalism and Bounty Hunting," *The Public Interest* 97:15 (1989). According to the Council on Competitiveness established by the Bush Administration, by 1990 Congress had enacted more than 150 one-way fee-shifting statutes, under which plaintiffs who prevail can recover lawyers' fees from losing defendants. Victorious defendants get no such recovery.

87. For selected accounts of activist public-interest lawyering that extended adversarial legalism into new areas of welfare, educational, regulatory, mental health, and penal policy, W. Robert Curtis, "The Deinstitutionalization Story," *The Public Interest* 34 (Fall, 1986); Robert Mnookin, ed., *In the Interests of Children: Advocacy, Law Reform and Public Policy* (New York: W.H. Freeman, 1985); Jeremy Rabkin, *Judicial Compulsions: How Public Law Distorts Public Policy* (New York: Basic Books, 1989); John J. DiIulio, Jr., ed., *Courts, Corrections and the Constitution* (New York: Oxford University Press, 1990).

88. Suzanne Weaver, "Anti-Trust Division of the Department of Justice," in James Q. Wilson, ed., *The Politics of Regulation* (New York: Basic Books, 1980).

89. Arthur Maass, "Public Policy by Prosecution," *The Public Interest* 107, 114 (Fall,1987).

90. See Robert Rabin, "Institutional and Historical Perspectives on Tobacco Tort Liability," 110, 128 (n.27) in R. Rabin and S. Sugarman, eds., *Smoking Policy: Law, Politics, and Culture* (New York: Oxford University Press, 1993) (discussing Tobacco Products Liability Project); David Stipp, "Dogma in Doubt: Extent of Lead's Risk to Kids, Need to Remove Paint," *Wall Street Journal*, September 16, 1993, p.A1, 12 (newsletter concerning lead litigation); Bill Richards, "Elusive Threat: Electric Utilities Brace for Cancer Lawsuits Though Risk is Unclear," *Wall Street Journal*, February 5, 1992, p.A1 (computerized data bank by coalition of law firms named Electromagnetic Radiation Case Evaluation Team).

91. Philippe Nonet, *Administrative Justice* (New York: Russell Sage Foundation, 1969).

92. Dan Walters, "Workers' Compensation: A New Approach to an Old System," *California Lawyer* 40, 41 (February, 1983).

93. "Twitching Millionaires," *Economist* 29 (Oct. 3, 1992); "Research Notes," California Workers Compensation Institute (1991).

94. Michael McCann, *Taking Reform Seriously: Perspectives on Public Interest Liberalism* (Ithaca: Cornell University Press, 1986), p. 114.

95. McCann, *Taking Reform Seriously*, 112-113; Martin Shapiro, *Who Guards the Guardians? Judicial Control of Administration* (Athens: University of Georgia Press, 1988).

96. R. Shep Melnick, "Pollution Deadlines and the Coalition for Failure," in M. Greve and F. Smith, eds., *Environmental Politics: Public Costs, Private Rewards* (New York: Greenwood, 1992).

97. *Boalt Hall Transcript*, Fall 1993, p. 72, 85.

98. Ibid.

99. Andrew Lohof, *The Cleanup of Inactive Hazardous Waste Sites in Selected Industrialized Countries* (Washington: American Petroleum Institute, 1991); R. Kopp, P. Portney and D. DeWitt, "International Comparisons of Environmental Regulation" (Washington: Resources for the Future, 1990) (Discussion Paper QE90-22-REV).

100. M. Landy and M. Hague, "The Coalition for Waste: Private Interests and the Superfund," in Greve and Smith, eds., *Environmental Politics* (1992).

101. Timothy Noah, "Clinton, Facing Conflicting Advice on Superfund, May Attempt to Ease the Burden of Business," *Wall Street Journal*, December 2, 1993, p. A16; Peter Menell, "The Limitations of Legal Institutions for Addressing Environmental Risks," *Journal of Economic Perspectives* 6:93 (1991).

102. T. Church and R. Nakamura, *Cleaning Up the Mess: Implementation Strategies in Superfund* (Washington, Brookings institution, 1993).

103. Landy and Hague, "The Coalition for Waste" (1993).

104. Mark J. Osiel, "Lawyers as Monopolists and Entrepreneurs: Review of *Lawyers in Society*, edited by Richard L. Abel and Philip P.C. Lewis (1988)," *Harvard Law Review* 103:2009, 2019 (1990).

105. Osiel, "Lawyers as Monopolists," 2018.

106. See Ted Schneyer, "Professionalism and Bar Politics: The Making of the Model Rules of Professional Conduct," *Law and Social Inquiry* 14:677 (1989).

107. Langbein, "The German Advantage," 823, 833-834.

108. Osiel, "Lawyers as Monopolists," 2009, 2060.

109. Peter Kerr, "The High Cost of Job Injury Claims," *New York Times*, Feb. 22, 1993, pp. C1, C7.

110. Ibid.

111. M. Geyelin and M. McCarthy, "Judges Chides Lawyers Facing Suit for Thousands of Asbestos Claims, *Wall Street Journal*, June 7, 1990, p. B8. For other examples, see M. Geyelin, "Texas Lawyers Seek Bill to Curb Their Soliciting," *Wall Street Journal*, May 25, 1993, p. B1. Conversely, it should be noted, insurance companies long have dispatched representatives to disaster scenes in order to make quick payments to victims, asking for releases in return.

112. Deborah Hensler et al., *Accidents and Injuries in the U.S.: Costs, Compensation, and Claiming Behavior* (Santa Monica: Rand Institute for Civil Justice, 1991); R. Miller and A. Sarat, "Grievances, Claims and Disputes: Assessing the Adversary Culture," *Law and Society Review* 15:525 (1980-81).

113. For an analysis of survey evidence indicating that Americans are more likely to blame others for accidents than the English, and more likely to make legal claims for compensation—even when the injured person thinks he or she is partly at fault, see Herbert Kritzer, "Propensity to Sue in England and the United States of America: Blaming and Claiming in Tort Cases," *Journal of Law and Society* 18:400 (1991).

114. Interviews by author with shipping line and stevedoring company officials.

115. Allen Myerson, "Soaring Liability Payments Burden New York's Budget," *New York Times*, June 29, 1992, p. A15.

116. CWCI, *Workers Compensation Litigation Costs*.

117. David Stipp, "Dogma in Doubt: Some Question Extent of Lead's Risk to Kids, Need to Remove Paint," *Wall Street Journal*, September 16, 1993, pp. A1, 12.

118. Milo Geyelin, "Debate Intensifies Over State Regulations That Restrict TV Advertising by Lawyers," *Wall Street Journal*, Aug. 31, 1992, p. B1.

119. Ibid.

120. Jonathan M. Moses, "Accord Enriching Only Lawyers Assailed," *Wall Street Journal*, January 23, 1992, p. B8.

121. "Crass Action," *Wall Street Journal*, April 1, 1993, p. A14. For a similar example, see "Coupon Clipping for Lawyers," *Wall Street Journal*, November 17, 1993, p. A18.

122. Janet Cooper Alexander, "Do the Merits Really Matter? A Study of Settlements in Securities Class Actions," *Stanford Law Review* 43:497, 513 (1991). For a profile of an attorney specializing in these suits, see L. Fisher, "William S. Lerach: The Pit Bull of Silicon Valley," *New York Times*, Sept. 19, 1993, Sec. F, p. 4; Andrew Serwer, "What to Do about Legal Blackmail," *Fortune*, Nov. 15, 1993, pp. 136-140.

123. Alexander, "Do the Merits Really Matter?", 501, 575.

124. Roberta Romano, "The Shareholder Suit: Litigation Without Foundation?", *Journal of Law, Economics and Organization* 7:55, 65 (study of all shareholders' suits against a random sample of publicly traded corporations, late 1960s through 1987).

125. Romano, "The Shareholder Suit," 61.

126. Bryant Garth, "Power and Legal Artifice: The Federal Class Action," *Law and Society Review* 26:237, 257 (1992) ("the facts do not add up to a strong picture of litigation that makes lasting improvements in the lives of class members"); M. Peterson and M. Selvin, "Mass Justice: The Limited and Unlimited Power of Courts," *Law and Contemporary Probs.* 54:227, 231, 241; Peter H. Schuck, *Agent Orange on Trial: Mass Toxic Disasters in the Courts* (Cambridge: Belknap Press, 1986); Peter Huber, "Environmental Hazards and Liability Law," in R. Litan and C. Winston, eds., *Liability: Perspectives and Policy* (Washington: Brookings institution, 1988).

127. Thomas Hetherington, "When the Sleeper Wakes: Reflections on Corporate Governance and Shareholder Rights," *Hofstra Law Review* 8:183 (1979); John C. Coffee, Jr., "No Soul to Damn, No Body to Kick: An Unscandalized Inquiry into the Problem of Corporate Punishment," 79 *Michigan Law Review* 79:386, 435 (1981) (antitrust class actions).

128. Michael Greve, "Environmentalism and Bounty Hunting," *The Public Interest* 97:15, 18 (1989).

129. James B. Stewart, *The Partners: Inside America's Most Powerful Law Firms* (New York: Simon & Schuster 1983), 146.

130. Stewart, *The Partners*, 282.

131. Ronald Gilson, "How Many Lawyers Does It Take to Change an Economy?", *Law and Social Inquiry* 17:635, 639 (1992). See also Ross Cheit, "Corporate Ambulance Chasers: The Charmed Life of Business Litigation," *Studies in Law, Politics and Society* 11:119 (1991).

132. Penelope Canan and George Pring, "Studying Strategic Lawsuits Against Public Participation," *Law and Society Review* 22:385 (1988).

133. See Taylor, *Making Bureaucracies Think*.

134. M. O'Hare, L. Bacow and D. Sanderson, *Facility Siting and Public Opposition* (New York: Van Nostrand, 1983); Lester, "The Search for Dialogue."

135. Ralph K. Winter, "Foreword: In Defense of Discovery Reform," *Brooklyn Law Review* 58:263, 264 (1992).

136. Trubek et al., "The Costs of Ordinary Litigation."

137. Robert L. Rabin, "Some Reflections on the Process of Tort Reform," *San Diego Law Review* 25:13, 42 (1988).

138. Wayne Brazil, "Views From the Front Lines: Observations by Chicago Lawyers About the System of Civil Discovery," *American Bar Foundation Research Journal* 1980:219.

139. Michael J. Kaufman, "The Role of Lawyers in Civil Litigation: Obstructors Rather Than Facilitators of Justice," *Illinois Bar Journal* 202, 203 (Dec. 1988).

140. Ibid.

141. Bernard Penner, "The Prosecutor and *Ex Parte* Communications," *National Environmental Enforcement Journal* 3 (May, 1992); Kenneth Mann, *Defending White Collar Crime* (New Haven: Yale University Press, 1985).

142. John Privatera, "Using CERCLA's Natural Resource Damage Provision to Focus and Organize a State Environmental Penalty Case: A Personalized Case Study," *National Environmental Enforcement Journal* 3 (March 1992).

143. Dennis Curtis, "Old Knights and New Champions: Kaye Scholer, the Office of Thrift Supervision and the Pursuit of the Dollar," *Southern California Law Review* 66:985, 1003 (1993).

144. T. Church and R. Nakamura, *Cleaning Up the Mess*, 27.

145. Ibid.

146. Shamir, "Professionalism and Monopoly"; Terrence Halliday, *Beyond Monopoly: Lawyers, State Crises, and Professional Empowerment* (Chicago: University of Chicago Press, 1987).

147. Under the tort law system, New York governmental officials said, few birth injury suits on behalf of infants are successful; those who win in court often have to wait a decade or more to see any money. Under the proposed system, they argued, "instead of a small number of individuals getting very large awards," a much larger number of families would receive moderate compensation. Determinations about eligibility and benefits would be made by a panel consisting of two doctors, a lawyer, a parent of an injured infant, and an expert in developmental disabilities. Sarah Lyall, "A Bill Would Pay for Birth Injuries," *New York Times*, April, 21, 1993, p. B12.

148. Ibid.

149. J. Blumstein, R. Bovberg and F. Sloan, "Beyond Tort Reform: Developing Better Tools for Assessing Damages for Personal Injury," *Yale Journal on Regulation* 8:171 (1990).

150. Langbein, "The German Advantage," 823.

151. See Stephen Sugarman, Doing Away With Personal Injury Law; R. Bovberg, F. Sloan and J. Blumstein, "Valuing Life and Limb in Tort: Scheduling Pain and Suffering," *Northwestern Law Review* 83:980 (1989); C. Hammett and Relles, "Tort Standards and Jury Decisions," *Journal of Legal Studies* 14:751 (1985); Jeffrey O'Connell, *The Lawsuit Lottery: Only the Laywers Win* (New York, Free Press, 1979); Peter Huber, "Junk Science and the Jury," *University of Chicago Legal Forum* 1990:273.

152. See Stephen Sugarman, "The California Vehicle Injury Plan (VIP): Better Compensation, Fairer Funding, and Greater Safety." Working Paper, Earl Warren Legal Institute, University of California, Berkeley, 1993.

153. F. Nutter and K. Bateman, *The U.S. Tort System in the Era of the Global Economy* (Schaumberg, IL: Alliance of American Insurers, 1989), 20; Peggy Berkowitz, "In Canada, Different Legal and Popular Views Prevail," *Wall Street Journal*, April 4, 1986, p. 21; D. Dewees et al., "The Medical Malpractice Crisis: A Comparative Empirical Perspective," *Law and Contemporary Problems* 54:217 (1991).

154. Saks, "Do We Really Know Anything," 1147.

155. In Germany, for example, mandatory worker compensation (industrial accident) insurance coverage was extended to cover students and travel to and from work and school, and thus covers at least one-third, possibly half, of all traffic accident injuries (Nutter and Bateman, *The U.S. Tort System*, 46.) Switzerland extended workers' compensation insurance coverage to injuries at home and at play (T. Duffy and R. Landis, "Workers' Compensation

in Switzerland)," *NCCI Digest* 3:31 (March, 1988).

156.   In 1961, Germany enacted an "enterprise liability" law for compensating persons harmed by vaccines, and added a similar law in 1978 for injuries caused by all pharmaceuticals (Nutter and Bateman, *The U.S. Tort System*, 44). Sweden, in addition to making social insurance and medical care the primary recourse for tort victims, established special no-fault insurance regimes for motor vehicle injuries, injuries to patients caused by medical procedures, and pharmaceuticals. Carl Oldherz, "Security Insurance, Patient Insurance, Pharmaceutical Insurance in Sweden," *American Journal of Comparative Law* 34:637 (1986); Jan Hellner, "Compensation for Personal Injury: The Swedish Alternative," *American Journal of Comparative Law* 34:613 (1986).

157.   Nutter and Bateman, *The U.S. Tort System*, 16.

158.   Patricia Danzon, "The Frequency and Severity of Medical Malpractice Claims: New Evidence," *Law and Contemporary Problems* 49:57 (1986).

159.   See Vic Pollard, "Sacramento Scene," *California Lawyer* 55 (December, 1984).

160.   U.S. Department of Transportation, *Compensating Auto Accident Victims: A Follow-Up Report on No-Fault Auto Insurance Experiences* (Washington: U.S. Department of Transportation, 1985); David Foppert, "Does No-Fault Stack Up?" in *Best's Review: Property-Casualty Insurance Edition* (Oldwick, NJ: 1992).

161.   Nutter and Bateman, *The U.S. Tort System*, 16-18.

162.   P. Heymann and L. Liebman, "No Fault, No Fee: The Legal Profession and Federal No-Fault Insurance Legislation," 309, in Heymann and Liebman, eds., *The Social Responsibilities of Lawyers* (Westbury, NY: Foundation Press, 1988).

163.   Heymann and Liebman, "No Fault, No Fee," 325-330.

164.   Steve Nelson, "Trial Lawyers Blaze Aggressive Trail," *Legal Times*, March 14, 1983, p.1.

165.   L. Gordon Crovitz, "Lawyers Seek Senators as Advocates Against Quayle Reforms," *Wall Street Journal*, Sept 18, 1991, p. A15. In the 1992 elections, ATLA's political action committee was the nation's fourth largest in total contributions, ranking ahead of the National Education Association and falling just short of the National Association of Realtors, the American Medical Association, and the Teamsters. "Who Gave the Most," *New York Times*, June 11, 1993, p. A12.

166.   J. Henderson and A. Twerski, "Stargazing: The Future of American Products Liability Law," *New York University Law Review* 66:1332, 1336 (1991).

167.   Peter Schuck, "The Worst Should Go First: Deferral Registries in Asbestos Litigation," *Harvard Journal of Law and Public Policy* 15:541, 553-568 (1992); Lester Brickman, "The Asbestos Litigation Crisis: Is There a Need for an Administrative Alternative?", *Cardozo Law Review* 13:1819 (1992); James S. Kakalik et al., *Costs of Asbestos Litigation* (Santa Monica, CA: Institute for Civil Justice, 1983).

168.   One study of permanent disability claims indicated that in Maryland, New Jersey and some categories of cases in Wisconsin, "dueling adversary experts" were employed in 63 percent, 79 percent, and 63 percent of cases, respectively, and "friction costs" added up to 38 percent, 46 percent, and 42 percent of the total disability payments awarded (WCRI, *Reducing Litigation: Evidence from Wisconsin* (Cambridge: Workers' Compensation Research Institute, 1988).

169.   See J. Birnbaum, "Political Contributions of Narrow-Focus Groups Seen by Some as Growing Campaign Funds Issue," *Wall Street Journal*, December 22, 1989, p. A8.

170.   See Bruce Ackerman, *Reconstructing American Law* (Cambridge, MA: Harvard University Press, 1984).

3

Are We A Litigious People?

Lawrence M. Friedman

The Problem Stated

In many countries, the problem of litigiousness has been much discussed. The debate has been particularly strong in the United States. Any number of commentators have noticed, or thought they noticed, that Americans claim a lot, demand a lot, sue a lot. Exactly how much suing there is, and what it all means, has been hotly disputed; but it is an uphill struggle to argue that there is nothing to the notion that Americans are addicted to law suits. The issue is interesting in and of itself, and for the legal profession; but I also think the question of a litigious society opens the door to more general questions—questions worth exploring for other countries as well as for the United States.

Much of the debate in the United States, about the "litigious society," has been on a fairly low level, intellectually speaking. There has been a lot of invective, a great deal of political posturing, and not much careful and rigorous study. Horror stories and anecdotes abound—stories about strange cases, huge damages, and juries that award astronomical amounts of damages.[1] There are, however, a number of honorable exceptions, that is, serious scholarly study or discussion of litigation.[2] Robert Kagan, among others, has contributed very thoughtful work on the subject. In this work, Kagan has introduced the concept of *adversarial legalism*.[3] Adversarial legalism is a particular style of policymaking and dispute resolution. It is formal, rather than informal (hence "legalism"), but it is also dominated by the parties involved, rather than being "hierarchical" (hence "adversarial"). In other words, a society can be described as having more or less "adversarial legalism." It ranks high on this scale when its citizens tend to resort to formal legal mechanisms, rather than mediating, or pursuing customary methods of dispute-resolution or, perhaps, simply swallowing their anger and hurt. In such a society, too, the choices (to sue or not to sue; to use legal mechanism or not) are made by ordinary citizens themselves, and do not get imposed from the top down.

This definition tries to get at a situation which many people in the United States would describe in more vivid and feverish terms: a quarrelsome, rights-conscious, legalistic, litigious population; everybody suing everybody else at the drop of a hat; businesses folding under the crushing blows of litigation; sharpsters collecting fees for trouble-making; noble doctors driven out of their offices or the operating room by shysters eager to make dishonest money; and so on. The debate is, of course, far from academic. The notion is that "adversarial legalism" is extremely harmful. It is destroying the fabric of society.

Too Many Lawyers

Is the United States guilty, as a society, of "adversarial legalism" or something like it? There are certainly facts pointing in that general direction. Exhibit A, according to many people, is the legal profession itself: too many lawyers. There were almost three-quarters of a million American lawyers as of 1988,[4] and by now probably over 800,000—an astonishing (and growing) horde of women and men—arguably the most bloated legal profession in the world; and one that continues to grow, almost without visible limits. This army of advocates is performing quite a few functions; and much of what they do is beyond criticism. They defend people against accusations of crime; they help to enforce the rights of the downtrodden (at times); and they make it possible for people to pursue their claims in court. Lawyers also do many things that have little or nothing to do with courts, and which can be best described as "facilitating." The public image of the lawyer is the image of a battler, a struggler, a tough advocate. But in fact, many lawyers are almost the opposite: they try to avoid battles; they mediate controversies, they negotiate, they help businesses and individuals reach the structural goals they want to; they patiently clear away obstacles from the path. They develop "innovations," creative new strategies which can be used by clients in their business life.[5] Lawyers also help clients "manage uncertainty;"[6] in some industries, they act as middle-men between investors and entrepreneurs—making life simpler for both of these.[7]

Many lawyers, too, work in jobs where they act as representatives or lobbyists.[8] They are information brokers; they learn and absorb messages from the government, and digest it in a form that their clients can use.[9] They provide information for individuals, groups and institutions, about "law," or about the activities of government; they monitor those activities; and they step in to make sure that government, at all levels, listens to the voice of their clients. "Lobbyists" are not popular figures; they have a bad image; but in many ways their work is vitally important, and it does not fit the picture of adversarial legalism.

Still, honesty requires us to admit that not all lawyers by a long shot spend their time mediating, calming, bridging, or representing; a lot of them are indeed battlers who get paid for being tough and fighting as hard as they can for their clients. And the number of lawyers who are *involved* in litigation has apparently skyrocketed in the last generation.

"Toughness," of course, is not a concept which can be easily defined or measured. It is not easy to say more than that there is a lot of tough, hard litigation (and negotiation) in the United States, and that lawyers are involved in these affairs. Lawyers almost surely also cause or foment *some* of this fighting and gouging; in the popular mind, they foment a lot of it, or even most of it. Lawyers, as we have seen, have been accused of hurting the economy—retarding growth, choking enterprise. But the evidence seems on the whole to be against this point;[10] and lawyers would have to be the very devil incarnate to *cause* all of the litigation, battling, and adversarial activity in American society. Many people, to be sure, apparently do think the worst of the profession; "lawyer-bashing" is a growing American sport.[11] But if there is in fact a great deal of adversarial litigation in the United States, there must be some general tendency in society that accounts for it; it cannot be pinned entirely on the lawyers. If one had to choose, it would seem more plausible to guess that adversarial legalism is the *cause* of the huge size of the legal profession, rather than the effect of it.

I am referring here to general tendencies. It seems pretty likely that lawyers contribute *something* to the sheer bulk of litigation. Kagan himself, in a recent article, reviewed the evidence carefully. He concluded, on the one hand, that lawyers are "not the only or even the primary source of American adversarial legalism." But, on the other hand, he did find "abundant evidence" that some segments of the legal profession make a contribution to the problem.[12] In any event, the sheer size of the profession calls for some explanation. One factor seems certain: the amount of money America spends on law and lawyering has risen dramatically in recent decades.[13] One estimate is that the United States spends about 100 billion dollars a year on legal services; in 1970, it spent less than a third as much (in constant dollars).[14]

Too Many Lawsuits?

The second "fact" adduced to support the charge of adversarial litigation is the flood of lawsuits. We hear a good deal about a "litigation explosion" in the United States—and in other countries as well.[15] A "litigation explosion" must refer to some sort of rise in overall rates of litigation, per thousand population. Can we demonstrate such an increase? There is, in fact, a great deal of dispute about how much litigation actually occurs in American society; and whether this amount, whatever it is, represents some sort of explosive increase over time. Many scholars have expressed grave doubts about the reality of the "litigation explosion."[16] To begin with, there is the evidence of longitudinal court studies; these do not, on the whole, support the idea that modern litigation rates are dramatically higher than they have been in the past. Indeed, there are even theoretical reasons to expect the opposite to occur—that is, a *falling* litigation rate—in developed societies. In 1974, José Juan Toharia published a pioneering study of Spanish litigation in the 20th century;[17] in this study, Toharia suggested that rapid economic development would lead to a *decline* in litigation rates, at least in the formal courts. This is because courts are slow, formal, and in general a drag on business activity. Modern business, then, should tend to shun the courts. In any event, it also turns out that a "litigation rate" is not at all easy to measure; not every "case" in a "court" really counts as "litigation," if by litigation we mean actual disputes in court, where the judge does something more than act administratively.[18]   How heavy is the use of courts in the United States? For the year 1991, over 93,000,000 cases were filed in trial courts, in the country as a whole. This seems like an alarming number; but over 60,000,000 of these "cases" were "traffic and other ordinance violations." The total number of *civil* cases filed, other than these, was just under 19,000,000. These civil filings had increased some 33 percent since 1984, although population had gone up only 7 percent.[19]

But even this awesome figure of 19,000,000 has to be further broken down. Most of these "cases" were filed in courts of "limited jurisdiction," typically handling small claims and relatively petty matters. A full third of the cases in the courts of general jurisdiction consisted of "domestic relations." The overwhelming majority of these were uncontested divorces. Whether this is "litigation" under anybody's definition is very questionable. Another 7 percent were "estate" matters—probating wills, handling the affairs of deceased persons.[20] These are normally uncontested, and again are hardly "litigation;" whatever name we give to these matters, they are not what all the fuss and controversy is about. The fact is that the actual amount of "litigation," meaning *contested* cases, is all but unknown.

What we are left with are some bland generalizations. There is a lot of activity in court, though we are unsure of its exact nature and scope. Court activity is *perhaps* rising, although no one who actually studies the situation can be 100 percent sure of what is going on. The huge size of the legal profession does call for some sort of explanation. We also have to be able to account for the *impression* of a litigation explosion, even if the actual evidence is ambiguous.

It is undeniable that certain *kinds* of litigation are more common in the United States than they were in earlier times.[21] There is unquestionably an enormous expansion in liability for tort. Medical malpractice—suing a doctor for negligence—was theoretically possible in the 19th century; but it did not happen very often. The same is true of products liability. Civil rights cases hardly existed before the 1950's; now there are thousands and thousands of complaints filed every year with government agencies; there are also a substantial number of lawsuits—on race and sex discrimination, discrimination against certain nationalities, or against members of minority religions; not to mention age discrimination, and, recently, discrimination against the handicapped, a new and growing category.

It is worth pausing for a moment to look more closely at this type of litigation. Women, for example, bring a considerable number of cases into court every year, on the grounds of sex discrimination.[22] How do we account for all this activity? To begin with, of course, there has to be a cultural or psychological element: that is, a sense of right, joined with a willingness to bring the claim. But this element is not enough. People will not, as a rule, throw their money and time away on a lawsuit, if they feel they have no chance to win. There has to be a *legal* element, an opening, a favorable doctrine and structure. And, to be sure, the law now favors or at least encourages such claims. The American Congress, after all, passed a major civil rights law in 1964, which made all this claiming possible. The courts, too, have been basically receptive to civil rights cases; enough decisions and rulings have been favorable to plaintiffs to encourage new litigants with decent claims.

In other words, both structure and culture come together to permit this kind of lawsuit. Presumably, claims-consciousness is a personality or culture trait; but it cannot exist without channels to flow in and institutions receptive to claims. Did the Civil Rights Acts *create* a culture of claiming—or did they merely untie a knot, releasing energies that were there before, only in a dormant or frustrated sense? Of course, this is an impossible question to answer. But the Civil Rights laws themselves did not fall from heaven; they too were creations of structure and culture, and they flowed out of a specific history and context.

The same kind of question can be asked about other kinds of "new" litigation—protests against administrative action, very notably. How much can be explained by legal innovation, how much by cultural change? The question, as I said, cannot be answered; both facets are necessary, and they are hopelessly intertwined. It is equally important to explore the cultural and the structural roots of forms of litigation. In any event, the importance of law and lawsuits in the modern American state is dramatic. New York City or Los Angeles or the state of Nevada could not possibly decide to build a new airport, or a major highway network, without running into the threat of one, two, or many lawsuits. Every organized group (and some disorganized ones) know this trick. So, for example, people who are eager to save the environment have made strategic use of litigation, fighting projects in National Parks, trying to save old forests, rescue endangered species, keep the air and water clean, and so on. The whole field of environmental law is new; nobody heard of it before the 1950's, essentially. But, again, these forms of action presuppose a particular legal culture *and* structures that make the lawsuits possible; not to mention procedures that smooth the way for claimants and for groups of claimants.

The best evidence, then, suggests that there are changes in legal structure and in legal culture which underlie the widespread *perception* of adversarial legalism. The evidence, too, is about qualitative changes in litigation, rather than quantitative ones. The idea of a culture of claims cannot rest, in other words, on sheer numbers of cases. The law itself—the way it has developed—does suggest a certain social ferment. It is the *kind* of litigation, not the amount that makes the whole issue controversial. People are not uneasy because courts are crowded, because there are backlogs and delays; but rather because they are disturbed by what they read and hear about—the specific abuses and outrages lovingly dished up in the media or elsewhere. Medical malpractice is a good example. Malpractice cases or the threat of malpractice cases makes doctors extremely uneasy; even angry. Insurance companies pontificate about these cases, which cost them money or drive up their rates. Pharmaceutical companies are alarmed about products liability cases. Big employers worry over sex discrimination cases. Mayors and city officials detest litigation that threatens to saddle their towns with huge liability. After all, why should anybody care about litigation in the abstract, or the litigation *rate* as a number? Basically, nobody *does* care. It is always some specific kind of litigation that raises people's hackles. And when newspapers report huge recoveries for ingrown toenails or psychic damage, people are ready to believe that greedy claimants and shyster lawyers are killing the country.

The case for adversarial legalism is not as strong as some critics of American law make out. But we cannot dismiss it, either. Lawsuits that are "adversarial," and create a certain amount of social turbulence, may in fact be growing in number—it is hard to tell. A certain amount of adversarial legalism does seem to be a structural and cultural feature of American society. It would be hard to imagine much litigation among people who truly believe that it is wrong to make a fuss, or who value harmony and compromise above most other values.[23] The structural aspects, as we have said, are equally important. Indeed, the two *must* be connected; any important cultural trait is bound to have a structural aspect. Obviously, the nature of the judicial system is one of the key structural factors. Doctrines and rules can choke off litigation, if that is their job. If courts are too expensive, too formalistic, the climate will be wrong for certain kinds of lawsuit. Indeed, this was the point of Toharia's study of Spanish courts.[24] Modernization and litigation (in the regular formal courts) moved in opposite directions.

Of course, litigation *is* expensive; and courts are (or seem to be) formalistic. Doctrine can also act as an important structural barrier. Doctrinal barriers of certain types have greatly lessened over the years, in the United States. The law has moved, on the whole, in such a way as to eliminate immunities, or zones of immunity, that is, areas where law is not allowed to penetrate, where no lawsuits are permitted, where power enjoys unbridled sway. Generally speaking, large institutions (schools, prisons, businesses) enjoyed vast power and authority, in the 19th century, over the lives of their workers, clients, and inmates. In the free-market climate of the 19th century, this was only to be expected, certainly as far as employers were concerned.

These zones of immunity are now only a shadow of what they used to be. The law has "invaded" many areas of life and law that once were immune. "Labor law" is basically a series of laws, institutions, and doctrines that cut down on the absolute power of bosses. The 19th century knew nothing of "prisoners rights," or "students rights;"[25] today, these developments have chipped away at the prerogatives of authorities that once ruled their little domains with almost absolute power.[26]

The United States and the World

The thesis of adversarial legalism has another aspect to it, however; and that is the notion of American exceptionalism. The point is not only that Americans fight and sue and fight some more; but that they do this more than most other people or even that they are world champions at legalism and litigation.[27] The

Are We A Litigious People? 59

comparative literature on the subject is not very large; but it does suggest that Americans are more claims-conscious than, say, the English, or Australians;[28] and that Germans (for example) are more individualistic and rights-conscious than, say, Kurds or Lebanese.[29] If Americans are the bad boys of litigation, then the good boys are the Japanese, who (so the story goes) mediate and compromise and apologize and make nice, to the everlasting benefit of their economy and polity. Japan, it is said, is a kind of (almost) lawyerless wonderland; and the same can be said of many other countries of the Far East—Korea, for example—which supposedly share in Eastern culture, with its emphasis on compromise and moderation.[30] The argument, in short, is that litigiousness and claims conscious-ness are part of American culture. Furthermore—so the argument goes—the country pays a high price for that culture, in social and economic terms.

In fact, the evidence of American uniqueness is rather thinner than most people think it is. It would be foolish to deny differences between American culture and Japanese culture. But (in the first place) there are serious doubts how far these cultural differences go to explain differences in lawyering and litigation. Structural aspects of law, and differing incentive systems, may explain more than "culture."[31] And, even if we concede the cultural point, perhaps it is Japan (or the far East in general) that constitutes the exception, rather than the United States. If we compare the United States with European countries, the differences seem not quite so stark as they do in the case of Japan. Many European countries have very sizeable numbers of lawyers.[32] Complaints about a "flood of litigation" are heard in Europe as well as in the United States, as we have mentioned.[33] The evidence is, at best, ambiguous.[34] Even in the far East, in countries like Korea, which (like Japan) have relatively few members of the bar, the *numbers* of lawyers are increasing.[35] In Japan, it is extremely difficult to pass the bar examination—about 2 percent of those who take it actually do—and this is one major reason why there are so few Japanese lawyers. The rest of the law-trained people, who fail the bar, have to content themselves with some other title—they cannot call themselves lawyers. In Taiwan, too, the state severely restricts the number of lawyers; between 1950 and 1991, less than 5 percent of the candidates who took the bar examination actually passed the test.[36]

American-style law practice, however, appears to be spreading to other countries—the grouping of lawyers into very large partnerships or firms, for example. In England, firms of solicitors were limited to 20 partners until 1967; no firm had even ten partners before World War II; today, there are "megafirms" with hundreds of solicitors,[37] and the sheer *number* of solicitors doubled between 1969 and 1985.[38]

Once again, our conclusions have to be somewhat tentative and modulated. If we could construct a scale to measure adversarial legalism, the United States *might* score rather high—perhaps near the top, though that is not so easy to prove. And there are interesting examples of countries that appear to rank lower on the scale. Japan, for all our doubts, would have to be the prize exhibit in this category. This is a country that relies heavily on informal networks and administrative

Adversarial Legalism: The Sources

This leads us to ask about the source of adversarial legalism. What are its social roots? How long has this condition existed in the United States, and what brought it about? This is not simply an exercise in history. The answer to the question might shed some light on the essential nature of adversarial legalism. If we understood what it is and where it came from we would have a better chance of knowing how to cope with it, assuming we want to. But whether to cure this disease, and what kind of cure to offer, depends on the cause of the ailment.

Kagan himself emphasizes the role of structural elements. Adversarial legalism, he says, "has been stimulated by a fundamental mismatch between a changing legal culture and an inherited political culture."[39] As he sees the problem, "the socially transformative policies of an activist, regulatory welfare state" get squeezed into the meshes of a "reactive, decentralized, nonhierarchical governmental system."

Kagan's "adversarial legalism," rests, as we have seen, on two pillars. One is formality; the other is the absence (or weakness) of hierarchy. The society, in other words, is egalitarian, individualistic; it is not a communitarian society, not a love-thy-neighbor kind of place. The result is formalism, legalism, a multiplicity of laws, lots of suing, much rigidity of structure. Both the formalism and the weak authority system are elements of the culture of the United States; and they both express or reflect the decay of customary norms. Both also have become part of the marrow of American governmental structure—federalism, for example, is an expression of a more general looseness of authority, a weakness of the national government, an absence of firm controls from the center. America is a society of little enclaves—townships that thumb their noses at the cities they feed on; independent "authorities" that manage ports, bridges, harbors; everywhere within government, and between government and its citizens, we find checks and balances running riot.

Perhaps it is unwise to emphasize these *formal* elements of structure. I would not want to argue, for example, that there is more adversarial legalism in Germany and Switzerland, which are federal states, than in France, which is highly centralized. If we say hierarchy and centrality are weak, we may not be referring to the formal structure of government at all. Medieval life was highly decentralized. In some parts of Europe, each village had its own dialect, its own local customs. There were no real "nations" in the modern sense, nothing like France or Italy today. What glued society together was not a powerful centralized state, but pre-modern ways of thinking, acting, and obeying. Each community was a tightly-ordered hierarchy. American government is to be sure extremely

Are We A Litigious People? 61

fragmented: This might reinforce "legalism," in some instances—it certainly provides many points at which "government" is vulnerable to attack from private citizens. I am less certain that it is a necessary condition for the kind of legalism that Kagan is describing.

"Law" in the sense of formal rules and formal institutions is, no doubt, a reflex of the weakness or absence of *informal* rules and institutions. Where "custom" is king, there is no need for "law."[40] "Law" emerges historically where the norms leave off; in disputes between members of different customary groups, or in areas where custom for one reason or another fails, perhaps because there is no body of shared norms to fall back on. A tiny society—say, a society of hunters and gatherers—might have nothing that most people would describe as law, that is, no police, judges, courts, lawyers, or specialized law-trained staff. In modern life, those realms that are most strongly governed by informal norms—family life, for example—are the least thoroughly "legalized."

This point should not be overemphasized. The "law" that replaces custom is not *independent* of custom; it is a sign of the weakness of consensus, but it does not mean that there are no norms, no consensus at all. Without some minimum basis of agreement, "law" is impossible. Hence, Karst is not wrong when he says that law, within a "community of shared values dampens aggression and promotes cooperation."[41] Law serves "communitarian purposes" by "standing as a totem, a symbol that community exists." Law is, however, a symbol of the *limits* of community, as well as a symbol *of* community; it is a "totem" of the place where community trails off and a no-man's land begins.

Law is also a sign of the fragmentation of community; where there are dozens of little power-centers, there have to be formal rules about the way these little kingdoms relate to each other. This point reminds us of structure again—of American federalism, for example. But we do not have to understand "power-center" literally, that is, as an actual government. Any society which is strongly pluralistic, which has people of many different identities living inside its borders—races, ethnic groups, culture groups, interest groups—will tend toward multiplicity of "law," toward a kind of legal pluralism that matches the pluralism of its population.

These remarks would seem to fit many countries, and not just the United States. Hence, we approach with some skepticism the strong claim that America is incurably, ineluctably "different." The hypothesis of difference does invite us to poke about in American history to find some explanations for American "difference." Why is it that this country *seems* more egalitarian, more individualistic than European societies, or the societies of Latin America and the far East: less communitarian and traditional? It is, in fact, not too hard to make out a case, scratched together out of historical experience. Paradoxically, the case, I believe, strengthens the argument *against* American exceptionalism, at the very moment that it tends to prove it.

Historical Roots

American national history begins with a revolution against royal authority; but royal authority had probably rotted away even before the outbreak of hostilities in the late 18th century.[42] This was, after all, an immigrant society, and had been an immigrant society from the beginning of its history.[43] It became even more of an immigrant society in the 19th century. Millions of newcomers streamed into the country, mainly from Europe. Many immigrants, of course, traveled in family groups; occasionally whole villages pulled themselves up and left the old country for America. Nonetheless, immigration to the United States almost always involved a certain element of rootlessness, change, people wrenched out of their moorings.

Within the United States, there was tremendous mobility in the 19th century—geographic and social mobility; people shifting about from place to place, and sliding up and down the social ladder as well. There was also a tremendous amount of social *isolation*; young people (almost always male), who lived deracinated lives, in boarding and lodging-houses, or who drifted from place to place. The young man "out to seek his fortune" was one side of the coin; the tramp or drifter was the other side of the coin, and the drifter was always the object of scorn and distrust.[44] In general, of course, a mobile society, a society in which people come and go and rise and fall, is more individualistic than one in which social roles are fixed and unchanging. It is also a society less cushioned and protected from conflict, litigation, dispute, compared to a society which is stable, patriarchal, family-bound, strongly communal.[45]

The United States is also very *pluralistic*, or at any rate heterogenous. This is a country of many races, many national groups, many different religions. Of course, this is certainly not an unusual situation in the modern world. There are, in fact, many countries that are, if anything, *more* heterogeneous than the United States—Nigeria, or Russia, or India—countries with many "nations" harbored or trapped inside their boundaries. In some ways, the United States does not suffer from the problems that afflict countries seriously split along one or more ethnic fault lines—Belgium or Canada, for example; unlike Spain with its Basques and Catalans, it does not have compact, sharply defined sub-nations.[46] The country sucked in immigrants by the millions, but the dominant ethos was always the ethos of the melting pot, that is, the goal was to absorb, and assimilate the immigrants—to turn them into "real" Americans—with some egregious exceptions, to be sure.[47]

American heterogeneity is somewhat different from the heterogeneity of many other countries. In Europe, the mixture of peoples and races is typically the product of a long historical development, or borders drawn arbitrarily as a result of wars and conquests, or the debris of old empires. In the United States, heterogenity is, in essence, the product of immigration; and of mobility, which has weakened the ties of primary groups. The revolution in transport and communication, in the 20th century, has increased mobility still further, and more emphatically

Are We A Litigious People? 63

weakened the older traditions of authority. I do not mean to suggest, of course, that the United States is unique in these particular regards. There are many other nations of immigrants (Australia, Argentina); and the transport and communication revolution is global. I will return to this point.

The United States was not always a rainbow of races and nationalities (and religions). There were black slaves from the 17th century on; and a handful of Jews. For most of American history, it is fair to say that white Protestants from northern Europe were politically, economically, and culturally dominant. Millions of Irish Catholics streamed across the ocean in the first half of the 19th century. The Civil War in the 1860's freed slaves; but the black population remained oppressed and subordinated. Blacks lived mostly as landless farm workers in the South, desperately poor, segregated, and denied the right to vote. Chinese immigrants were concentrated on the West Coast, where they met with extreme hostility and persecution. The Chinese were, in fact, shut out of citizenship in the late 19th century, and barred from entering the country.[48] Vast numbers of foreign immigrants from southern and eastern Europe entered the country in the late 19th and early 20th centuries; but they were much less welcome than the earlier waves of immigrants from Protestant Europe. They were viewed with alarm by old-line Americans. The immigration laws of the 1920's blatantly discriminated against their countries of origin.

But in the last two generations or so, the legal and social situation has changed dramatically. The change can be summed up as a formal commitment to what I have elsewhere called plural equality.[49] The great black-white split has of course not been healed, and race relations remains a fundamental and nagging problem of politics and the social order. But since the 1950's, a strong civil rights movement has led the way to dramatic changes in formal law and in social life in general.

This movement of black liberation became the model, in terms of ideology and strategy, for other identity groups that considered themselves suppressed. Such groups ranged from feminists to the so-called sexual minorities and the handicapped. None of these movements has had a smooth and easy path. There are plenty of examples of backlash and resistance to demands for legal and social equality; and the final chapter, needless to say, has not been written. Still, the great mass of the general public seems on the whole more ready to accept some of the basic premises of civil rights and civil liberties, than has been true at any prior point in American history. Here, as is always the case in the legal system, changes in general culture bring about changes in legal culture, which bring about changes in law; and these changes, in turn, loop back and affect the general culture.

Thus the historical argument can be summed up roughly as follows: traditional authority weakened in a mobile, pluralistic immigrant country. A society of the American type has fewer cultural brakes on litigation. Litigation also takes places among persons who do not have intimate, face-to-face relationships; and this is the basic characteristic of modern mass society. The United States was also the first truly middle-class society: the first society in which *masses* of families, not just a small elite, owned land, had some sort of property, and had, as well, the right to vote for their leaders.[50] Thus millions of people had a capital stake in society—something to sue about, which was never true of feudal societies, or of subsistence societies in general. Rights-consciousness, and individualism, flourished under these circumstances, in the nineteenth century, at a time when European societies were still, relatively speaking, traditional and extremely hierarchical. The traits have become even more salient in the last two generations or so—they have expanded and, in some ways, shifted gears. In any event, the elements of social structure which produced these traits have gotten stronger and more pronounced. Americans are as shiftless and restless as ever—indeed more so. And American pluralism is sharper and more salient.

The dramatic escalation in civil rights *cases* in the United States, which we have already mentioned, illustrates the dynamic at work. The factors mentioned produce changes in the legal culture, which make civil rights litigation possible. The frame of mind created demands which then pushed courts and legislatures to create new legal structures; and these structures—doctrines, agencies, laws—turned rights into realities. Congress passed a series of civil rights *laws* which explicitly produced new causes of action. The causes of action were tools to be used by people who felt victimized. Congress also created institutions to enforce these rights—and gave courts the power to monitor, review and enhance the rights.

There has also been a certain snowball effect. The civil rights law of 1964 prohibited sex discrimination, along with race discrimination, and discrimination on the basis of religion and ethnicity. Another series of statutes addressed the issue of age discrimination.[51] Very notably, in recent years, Congress passed a massive statute protecting the job rights of Americans with disabilities—the millions of people who are blind, deaf, in wheel chairs, or otherwise handicapped.[52] The laws produce cases, the cases produce stories in the newspapers; word gets around; knowledge (sometimes distorted) is communicated to the public, or pieces of the public; and the whole legal culture shifts in a particular direction—toward sensitivity to claims, toward willingness to assert certain claims. Businesses, too, change their behavior—and, possibly, their attitudes. Businesses hate to be sued; it costs them time, money, and reputation. They do not like the new laws, perhaps, and their reactions are, in part, purely defensive. But they adapt; and in some ways, the whole climate of business behavior also may shift, in the direction mapped out by the laws.[53]

The Lonely Americans; and their Groups

It is a cliché to describe American society as individualistic; but clichés, like stereotypes, are not *necessarily* wrong. Modern law (and modern culture) a reflect strongly individualistic culture—domi-ated by the concept of free choice. Yet, oddly enough, American individualism seems to coexist with a sense of group identity; and the age of individualism turns out to be also the age of rampant, militant groups. I have even argued that the two phenomena are related.[54] Group identity is a vehicle through which people assert their individualism. It is a mechanism for putting forward claims of individual worth and equality.

This looks like a paradox. But is it? Feminists, for example, want to gain, for women, the same opportunities and life-chances that men have always enjoyed. Many women would like to crack open the cage of roles into which women have been traditionally placed; they want to destroy whatever is ascriptive about the position of women in society. They therefore exalt the idea of choice; a woman can and should be able to be whatever she chooses to be. "Choice" means the right to decide whether to have children or not; to marry or not; to choose any occupation or not. It includes the right to be a militant feminist. It also includes the right to act like a traditional woman. In either event, many women feel that they can reach the goal of individual choice only *through* organization, through the power of an organized interest group. The seductive idea of individual choice also leads women to struggle against those aspects of women's lives that deny them choice or make their choices hollow. Some feminists, to be sure, think the ideology of choice is a snare and a delusion,[55] but if so, it is a powerful one. A similar observation—about the relationship of individualism and group rights—also holds true, I believe, with regard to groups that speak on the behalf of blacks, sexual minorities, the handicapped, the elderly, and so on. These "group" movements all rest on a base of individualism, but all exalt as well the ideology of free choice.

Private Law

Parallel changes have taken place in fields of private law as well—in the law of personal injury, for example, where there has been a gigantic expansion in the scope of liability in the 20th century. I have argued elsewhere that the liability "explosion" reflects a fundamental shift in legal culture: the emergence of what I have called the general expectation of justice.[56] For various reasons, which I tried to trace historically and socially, Americans no longer acquiesce fatalistically when calamity punches its way into their lives.[57] They expect "justice," that is, some form of payment or recompense; some recognition of wrong done to them, and some way of making it up.[58] This occurs in field after field of law.

One can also avert here to an apparent shift in the nature of a very different kind of litigation—litigation *between* businesses. One useful starting point is the classic article on business behavior by Stewart Macaulay.[59] Macaulay studied the contractual habits and attitudes of businessmen in Wisconsin. He found, among other things, that businessmen did not place enormous stock in the legal enforceability of contracts. They tended to shy away from litigation. They were not litigious and pugnacious; they did not, in general, "stick up for their rights." There was nothing mysterious about this behavior; and nothing inconsistent with competitive, aggressive, business behavior. Litigation is terrifically disruptive;

66 *Lawrence M. Friedman*

business people were loath to break off valuable long-term relationships with other businessmen—suppliers and the like—and drag them into court. The subjects Macaulay interviewed were convinced that litigation would, on the whole, do more harm than good; they tried to avoid it, if they could possibly do so; and for the most part they succeeded.

Recently, some scholars have detected a change in the business climate.[60] The competitive game became much rougher, in the years through the late 1980s. Business became, by some accounts, more volatile; there was less emphasis on long-term relationships, on personal ties, on getting along. (Similarly, the practice of law became more "transactional," that is, based upon one-time "deals" or legal matters. Relationships between attorneys and their clients were correspondingly less long-term and intimate.)[61] As a result, these scholars detected a real increase in certain kinds of business litigation. This is the flip-side of the Macaulay thesis: Macaulay sketched out conditions that *discourage* business litigation, but the clear implication was that litigation would in fact *rise*, if these conditions ceased to exist.

What accounted for these changes in the business environment? Globalization may have been one source. Global competition is tough competition; the world of international business is so rapid, unsettling, unstable, that only the most nimble and perhaps the most ruthless survive. American business can no longer rely on protected domestic markets; companies have to be "lean and mean;" and this may imply some sacrifice of comfortable, old-shoe relationships, in pursuit of "the bottom line." The changes may have something to do with the nature of American capital markets. In any event, it seems unlikely that business *culture* has changed radically; we may be in the presence of another set of *structural* inducements to "adversarial legalism." These structural elements, such as they are, are not distinctively American; they belong, rather, to the global world of the transnational corporation.

The Victim Society

There is another aspect to legalism that should be mentioned here. Plaintiffs—people who sue—are by definition claimants; they are people making demands, asserting rights. But they are also victims—or people who insist that are victims. Plaintiffs are people who are involved in auto accidents, or who have lost their jobs, or businessmen whose suppliers broke a contract, or creditors trying to squeeze money out of a bankrupt firm. Most of them, in their view, have suffered in some way; or been mistreated, whether by fate or (more likely) by somebody else's bad deeds or neglect. So, behind many or most claims is a sense of victimization, as well as a sense of right. For this reason, perhaps, a claims-conscious society is or becomes a society of victims as well; a society of people who feel aggrieved in life, for one reason or another.

The social psychology of modern life permits and indeed fosters this sense of victimization. A truly fatalistic or traditional society does not produce people who think of themselves as victims. Rather, it produces people who shrug their

Are We A Litigious People? 67

shoulders and accept their fate. Such a society might be, in fact, full of people we would classify as victims—victims from *our* point of view. But they may or may not define themselves that way. "Victims" in the subjective sense arise in societies that are free, open, individualistic, societies that stress personality, uniqueness, self-development. These societies are made up of people who do not accept chance, destiny, the will of heaven, or the role of hierarchy, as factors that are or should be crucial in molding human lives.

Of course, beyond a certain point groups or individuals can be so victimized, so downtrodden, so oppressed, that there is simply no way for them to assert claims, enjoy rights, or use their status to advantage, whether they feel oppressed or not. This is an all-too-common situation in totalitarian societies; it was and is the common fate of many minorities, in all sorts of societies (not all of them dictatorial); it was the fate of slaves in the Americas in the early 19th century, and so on. The contemporary era, in the West, has a sharply different edge to it. These societies include (of course) a host of victims; but these are victims who (often, or mostly) believe they have a chance to get back at those who are victimizing them.

But all this leads to a situation in which victimization becomes, in a sense, highly prized, a situation which in turn creates a "culture of complaint."[62] I hope this point is not misunderstood. It is not cynical or callous to observe that there is, today, in the United States, a certain cachet to victim status. For some members of victim groups, there are positive economic benefits—that is, programs of "affirmative action" or "benign discrimination." There is feverish debate about the value or justice of such programs; nonetheless, they are common in government, industry, and the academy. On the other hand, no scholarships are set aside for victims of child abuse, no job quotas for rape survivors or recovering alcoholics. The cachet is broader and subtler and more widespread then the "official" list of victims.

Nor do I pin the blame (if blame is the right word) on the civil rights crusades in the United States, and the analogous movements in other countries. Certainly, the *ethos* behind the civil rights movements has had an important impact on law and culture. Formally and doctrinally, the struggle against race discrimination influenced feminists and other groups in their own search for "liberation." The civil rights movement was a strategic model for action, a blueprint for the groups that came afterward. Yet in some sense, the civil rights movement was itself an *effect* of broad cultural change, rather than a cause. I would argue that these broad cultural changes—changes in the texture of American society—gave birth to a culture of expressive individualism, which in turn spurred on the movements to liberate submerged and suppressed minorities.

When minorities revolt, they demand equal rights and equal opportunities; but they also shout out that their condition is honorable, valuable, worthy of respect. In the United States, we began to hear (for example) that "black is beautiful." Some feminists have also been quick to claim for women a superior moral status: more sensitive, more caring, more morally attuned than men. It would be easy to find comparable statements coming from the sexual minorities, the elderly—even from some of the handicapped. To be deaf, it turns out, can also be beautiful. Minority status has also usually included an element of suffering; and hence, to a degree, the new movements spread the idea—or were fed by the idea—that suffering can be itself a badge of honor. This in turn makes vindication, redemption, and recompense pretty honorable causes in themselves; and reduces whatever stigma attaches to (say) filing a law suit complaining against discrimination.[63]

All this produces dramatic changes in American pluralism. On the one hand, pluralism (heterogeneity) implies coexistence; all of the groups cabinned inside America's borders have got to live together, one way or another; and hence there is a certain strength to the tradition of live and let live. This tradition is, for example, particularly evident in the history of American religion. Generally speaking, the culture has displayed considerable religious tolerance. There are to be sure quite a few blots on the record—Quakers hung for their beliefs in 17th century Massachusetts; convents burned and other 19th century outrages against Irish Catholics, the 19th century crusade against the Latter Day Saints[64]—but America has had relatively little religious strife compared to other countries, even though it is religiously diverse, and the people on the whole take religion quite seriously.[65] Religious wars have torn apart any number of countries; but not the United States.

On the other hand, nobody could seriously argue that pluralism and heterogeneity *necessarily* lead to tolerance; quite the contrary seems more and more to be the case. Diverse, heterogeneous countries are racked with internal conflict. It is enough to mention Bosnia or Northern Ireland. Why, then, has this not happened in the United States? In part, affluence may be part of the answer; conflicts tend to rub people most raw when they are competing for a shrinking or shrunk stock of goods. But partly it is (I think) because of the strength of American individualism, which has reconceptualized religion as an intensely *personal* matter. For most Americans, there is no "true" religion, in the traditional sense of the word; there may a religion which is truest, or best, for *them*; but that is an extremely personal choice.[66] Thus, the most rapidly growing, and most vital, religious movements in America, at the present time, are those that stress personal religious experience.[67] It would be absurd, after all, to persecute somebody else for having a different personal experience, or failing to have a personal experience at all. Different people follow different paths to salvation. This cliché applies very dramatically to sex in America—but it applies to religion as well.

Pluralism, we know, comes in various shapes and forms, and leads to various consequences. It can easily degenerate into a condition of nationalism inside a nation; a splintering of the framework; a clannishness, a sense of war of all against all. The world is, alas, full of examples of nations that have fallen into this pit of darkness. Religious pluralism in the United States seems to avoid this pit. But religion may be a special case. A home and a job—things that really matter—do not usually turn on religion. They may turn on race and ethnicity. Hence, for these, the situation is more complex, more touchy, more dangerous. The stakes are higher, the passions greater, the sense of victimhood much deeper. Some major victim groups have violent or extreme fringes. Many observers feel that the sense of commonality in this country, if there ever was one, has been declining, or slipping away. This lack of mutual trust has, perhaps, an influence on litigiousness, claims-consciousness, and the like. This is because the culture has defined the goals and methods in legal terms—in terms of "rights" that produce causes of action; the courts are a forum in which these rights can be pursued. They are the arena of choice for advocates who represent the underdog.[68] From the advocates, the word spreads to the members.

In one sense, "legalism" seems the very antithesis of the dynamic we have just described. "Legalism" refers to a kind of cold, bureaucratic, formalistic, logic-chopping style; it appears far removed from the "hot" phenomenon of group struggle. Indeed, in one sense, "adversarial legalism" is almost a kind of self-cancelling phrase; if a process is adversarial, can it be truly legalistic? One answer, of course, is that legalism is a weapon or tool of adversaries; but even so, it is a curiously bloodless tool. What is adversarial, however, about American society is not "legalistic" in the usual sense; it is struggle that uses legal weapons, but it is very far removed from formal rationality in Max Weber's sense. Indeed, it is tempting to connect litigiousness to the American tradition of violence, the propensity for fighting and biting; the macho culture that has (it is said) produced high rates of homicide and other crimes of fury and invasion; the tendency to fight for one's rights, the idea that no one had better get the better of you, that it is cowardly and weak to turn the other cheek.[69] Of course, the connection between violence and litigiousness is, to say the least, rather tenuous. Even the historical issue is hotly controverted—that is, whether American crime, violence, and the like can be derived from some particular historical tradition or not.[70] After all, many countries—including Japan—have had violent traditions, which they seem to have overcome.[71] Issues of personality and culture are, typically, subtle, ambiguous, and difficult to measure, and the influence of history or tradition no less so.

Pluses and Minuses

There are, obviously enough, terrible dangers in the proliferation of litigation, on specific issues; in the intransigence of victim groups; in what seems to be a growing mentality of nationalism abroad and clannishness at home. But is litigation—or indeed, adversarial legalism in general—really the incarnation of evil, as it has been sometimes described? In some ways, litigation is the antithesis of the "adversarial." Litigation is in some ways *always* a form of compromise. It is, of course, far different—and most people would say far better—than riots and street fighting; or apathetic retreat, for that matter. Are we ignoring the positive merits of litigation, as a strategy, as a safety valve, as a social substitute for less desirable forms of battle?

The legal system is one of the social arenas in which struggles over position, power, status take place; and, in American society, it is one of the most important of those arenas. Conflicts between groups play themselves out in the law courts, to an astonishing degree. De Tocqueville pointed this out over a century ago; but he himself would no doubt be amazed at what has happened since he wrote. There is something paradoxical about the use of litigation. It is taken as a sign of decay in community; and formal law is, indeed, a substitute for informal norms and consensus. Then, too, some litigation arises out of deep mistrust of government; some is a symptom of revolt against authority; some represents a revolt against major institutions—business corporations, universities, churches. Litigation, in general, is often a sign of some degree of disaffection; and a sign that people are willing to fight for their rights. Yet litigation is also a vote of confidence in at least *one* institution—the courts. Some deep trust, some strong faith in the courts themselves must underlie the waves of protest litigation—and litigation in general. People who bring lawsuits, risking time and money, expect *justice* from the judges. Otherwise they would not bother.

There is a curious ambivalence at work here. The courts are esteemed, in part, because they are forums of justice, because they seem to be above and beyond politics. At the same time, they must reflect the community, and what the community wants. Most American judges, in fact, are elected—a device to keep them (in theory) responsive to the popular will. But "reflecting the community" goes far deeper than elections. It is built into the very marrow of the system. The jury survives (for example) in more vigorous form in the United States than in almost any other country; and it survives as the voice of the community. Indeed, a jury is not considered truly fair unless it "represents" the community—this is now coming to mean something almost akin to proportional representation.[72]

The historical and social roots of adversarial legalism are extremely important, even though the message is murky and ambiguous. The record suggests that cures for this disease (if it is one) will not be easy to come by. The ailment is embedded, so to speak, in the very flesh and bones of American culture. And, as we have mentioned, it is not at all self-evident that adversarial legalism is as bad as claimed. The costs are easy to see. The benefits are more elusive. I have already mentioned one—and an important one—that is, the fact that people may be using law as a substitute for more dangerous forms of dispute-settlement (or non-settlement). Litigation is disruptive, to be sure; but riots are far more disruptive.

There are other benefits as well. Any business can tote up the expenses and the red tape that civil rights laws impose on the company. The gains are harder to measure, but are equally real. To begin with, the civil rights laws help specific individuals get and keep job. There is also, one hopes, a net increase in social justice. This benefit too is exceedingly real (and exceedingly important); but it cannot be expressed in terms of dollars. The "liability explosion," too, has benefits—"vindication," investments in safety, and the deterrence of "undesirable behavior."[73]

Convergence

In the pages above, I have assumed that adversarial legalism may well represent something real, something actually occurring; and something which, if not distinctively American, may be particularly strong in the United States. I have offered a word of two by way of explanation—historical and social. But the explanations are not, on the whole, expressed in terms that are uniquely American. This country may be an exaggerated case—or an *early* case—of the "disease" of adversarial legalism; but other societies seem to share some of the social conditions, and are subject to the same influences. We would expect, therefore, that they are evolving in the same general direction.

There are great similarities between *all* the Western societies; and especially between European societies and America. They have all developed into various permutations of the welfare-regulatory state; they share many legal and economic institutions, from stock exchanges to the income tax to unemployment compensation. What is more significant, they are all mobile societies, with a lot of *internal* migration; and often a good deal of external migration as well.

Anyone can see heterogeneity of a certain type—blacks and Muslims on the streets of Paris, for example. Less patent is the vast amount of movement *within* European countries and Japan. The big cities of the continent are bursting at their seams; the millions who live in London or Paris or Milan are mostly the great-grandchildren of rural villagers.[74] The process that sent them flying from their traditional homes into the heart of the mega-cities is a process of modernization. It is a process that dissolves, as well, many of the old restraints on litigation, and the inherited rules of deference and family respect.

Politically speaking, the immigrants that are "different" evoke the most interest (and controversy): Algerians in Paris, Pakistanis and West Indians in London, Turks everywhere in Germany; Yugoslavs, Spaniards, Sri Lankans, Ethiopians, and others in substantial force, all over the continent. Even in cities once as compact and uniform as Oslo and Helsinki, black and brown faces appear on the streets, whether as refugees, foreign guest-workers, or simply as what appears to be exotic intrusions.[75]

All this is a form of convergence, or an engine of convergence. There are other mechanisms as well. The global reach of business has already been noted. Big companies invariably have factories and laboratories all over the world, sell all over the world, buy all over the world. The same logos, the same brand names, are seen on the streets of every major city; the same neon signs are in the sky. Coca-Cola recently opened a plant in Albania—the "197th country where Coca-Cola is made."[76] Many major American and foreign law firms have also gone international, with branches in other countries as well as at home. The result is a kind of legal convergence, which Wiegand has labelled a "reception" of American law.[77]

There is a kind of uniculture, too, common to the whole Western world (and perhaps the rest of the world as well); satellites, TV, radio, instruments of transport and communication, bind everyone together into a single cognitive knot. McDonald's and rock music girdle the world. People talk different languages, but they dress much the same, listen to the same repetitive noises, watch many of the same TV programs (dubbed or with subtitles), pursue the same fashions and fads.

The developed nations, therefore, come to share many aspects of legal culture. American tort law may be unique; but if I am correct about the general expectation of justice, then certain aspects of the European welfare state may be a reflex of the same cultural shift that produced lawsuits against doctors and manufacturers in the United States. In the light of all this, American exceptionalism (if it is real) should be gradually fading out of the picture; and Japanese exceptionalism, too, ought to be passing away, or at least moderating, at the other end of the spectrum. In fact, Japanese society does seem to be changing in the same direction as European or American society. After all, Japan is much more "Western" today than it was, say, at the end of the second World War. One would expect, then, a degree of "convergence" in legal cultures and legal systems, despite the diverse historical traditions. That is, the systems and cultures would become more like one another, over time, in societies travelling down the same general road.[78]

It is an empirical issue how much divergence remains; how far convergence has gone. Americans are still often struck by differences between American society and other advanced societies in Europe, the far East, and elsewhere. There is much less street crime and violence in Japan and most European countries, compared to the United States. Their cities are not jungles (or do not seem to be). There is less police brutality.[79] Fewer intrusive, homeless beggars pester passersby or lie about on the streets and heating grates and in doorways, in Frankfurt and Rome, compared to New York or San Francisco. Families seem stronger and more cohesive in European societies; people move about less, and also less often; old formalities and hierarchies have survived in much better shape, well into the modern era. Japan, in particular, remains stubbornly resistant to ethnic pluralism; and nurtures a sense of specialness, a sense of difference.[80] There is virtually no (legal) immigration. There is a Korean minority, to be sure, and a handful of Ainu in the far North, and a certain number of illegal foreign workers; but basically the permanent population is Japanese, plain and simple.

Arguably, too, Japanese culture stresses group loyalty and identity, rather than individualism; and there are the old disputes about whether and why the Japanese shun litigation. According to John Braithwaite, Japan is the only major country in which the crime rate has *declined* since the Second World War. He explains this in terms of the Japanese emphasis on "reintegrative shaming," and a "culture in which duties to the community . . . overwhelm the rights of individuals."[81] This kind of shaming has lost whatever bite it had in the rest of the Western world. The Western world seems more impersonal, mobile, shiftless—and incurably rights-conscious. It lacks the tight neighborhood structure, the sense of clan, the firm family controls of Japanese society.

The debate goes on. Some scholars think too much has been made of Japanese exceptionalism; that the same forces are at work in Japan as elsewhere in the developed world. Japanese who want to sue, however, have to filter their complaints through a tough and resistant structure. And Japan remains a society "ordered more by . . . community and group controls" than by law or government power.[82] Still, the argument goes, a basic evolution is in fact taking place, away from Japanese " exceptionalism," and parallel to what is happening and has happened in the United States. It is hard to know where the truth lies. Much depends on the way a scholar looks at Japan; whether she wants to emphasis sameness or difference.[83] In any event, though it is always rash to predict the future, more convergence is likely be in store.

But we will have to leave the questions unresolved; all we can do, at this juncture, is to point our fingers back to the tough issues of structure and culture. And the conclusion has to be, with regard to litigation and litigiousness in America, that there is both sameness and difference. Adversarial legalism may well be in some manner distinctively American. But what is "distinctively American" is itself a product of concrete social forces; and these particular factors seem to be fairly general in the developed world, or at least to be spreading throughout that world—though not always evenly or at a regular pace. Whether America will stay ahead of the pack (so to speak) remains to be seen.

Notes

1. Robert M. Hayden, "The Cultural Logic of a Political Crisis: Common Sense, Hegemony and the Great American Liability Insurance Famine of 1986," in 11 *Studies in Law, Politics and Society* 95 (1991).

2. Marc Galanter, "Reading the Landscape of Disputes: What We Know and Don't Know (and Think We Know) about our Allegedly Contentious and Litigious Society," 31 *UCLA Law Review* 4(1983).

3. Robert A. Kagan, "Adversarial Legalism and American Government," 10 *J. Policy Analysis and Management* 369 (1991).

4. Barbara A. Curran and Clara N. Carson, *The Lawyer Statistical Report: The U.S. Legal Profession in 1988* (1991 Supplement p. 1); see also Robert L. Nelson, "The Futures of American Lawyers: A Demographic Profile of a Changing Profession in a Changing Society," 44 *Case Western Reserve Law Review* 345 (1994).

5. Michael J. Powell, "Professional Innovation: Corporate Lawyers and Private Lawmaking," 18 *Law and Social Inquiry* 423 (1993).

6. John Flood, "Doing Business: The Management of Uncertainty in Lawyers' Work," 25 *Law & Society Review* 41 (1991).

7. Mark S. Suchman, "On the Role of Law Firms in the Structuration of Silicon Valley," unpub'd paper, ann. meeting, Law & Society Association, Chicago, Illinois (1993).

8. John P. Heinz, Edward O. Loumann, Robert L. Nelson, and Robert H. Salisbury, *The Hollow Core: Private Interests in National Policy-Making* (1993).

9. Of course, the lawyers, in their role as information brokers, have the power to distort the message and modify the rule. For a case study of this process at work, see Lauren B. Edelman, Steven E. Abraham, and Howard S. Erlanger, "Professional Construction of Law: The Inflated Threat of Wrongful Discharge," 26 *Law and Society* Review 47 (1992).

10. Charles P. Epp, "Do Lawyers Impair Economic Growth?" 17 *Law and Social Inquiry* 585 (1992).

11. Marc Galanter, "Predators and Parasites: Lawyer-Bashing and Civil Justice," 28 *Georgia Law Review* 633 (1994).

12. Robert A. Kagan, "Do Lawyers Cause Adversarial Legalism? A Preliminary Inquiry," 19 *Law & Social Inquiry* 1 (1994).

13. Marc Galanter, "Law Abounding: Legalization around the North Atlantic," 55 *Modern L. Rev.* 1 (1992).

14. Richard H. Sander, "Elevating the Debate on Lawyers and Economic Growth," 17 *Law and Social Inquiry* 659 (1992). Another estimate is 75 billion, see Nelson, "The Futures of American Lawyers," supra, at 345.

15. See for example, Erhard Blankenburg, ed., *Prozessflut? Studien zur Prozesstätigkeit europäischer Gerichte in historischen Zeitreihen und im Rechtsvergleich* (1988).

16. See Galanter, "Reading the Landscape of Disputes," supra, n. 2; Lawrence M. Friedman, *Total Justice* (1985).

17. José Juan Toharia, *Cambio Social y Vida Jurídica en España* (1974).

18. Lawrence M. Friedman and Robert V. Percival, "A Tale of Two Courts: Litigation in Alameda and San Benito Counties," 10 *Law and Society Review* 267 (1976).

19. State Court Caseload Statistics: Ann. Report 1991, pp. 3-4.

20. State Court Caseload Statistics, 1991, p. 15.

21. Other kinds of litigation are *less* common; some aspects of debt collection, for example, have been "routinized" and have almost vanished from court dockets, see Robert A. Kagan, "The Routinization of Debt Collection: An Essay on Social Change and Conflict in the Courts," 18 *Law & Society Rev.* 323 (1984); Friedman and Percival, supra, n. 18.

22. A certain number of sex discrimination cases are brought by men as well.

23. David M. Engel, "The Oven Bird's Song: Insiders, Outsiders, and Personal Injury in an American Community," 18 *Law and Society Review* 551 (1984).

24. Toharia, supra, n.17.

25. See Lawrence M. Friedman, "Limited Monarchy: The Rise and Fall of Student Rights," in David L. Kirp and Donald N. Jensen, eds., *School Days, Rule Days: The Legalization and Regulation of Education* (1986), p. 238.

26. See Lawrence M. Friedman, *Total Justice* (1985).

27. On the data, see Marc Galanter, "Reading the Landscape of Disputes: What We Know and Don't Know (and Think We Know) about our Allegedly Contentious and Litigious Society," 31 *UCLA Law Review* 4 (1983).

28. On Australia, see J. FitzGerald, "Patterns of 'Middle Range' Disputing in Australia and the United States," 1 *Law in Context* 15 (1983); on England see Robert A. Kagen, "What Makes Sammy Sue?" 21 *Law & Society Review* 717 (1988); see also Basil Markesinis, "Litigation-Mania in England, Germany and the USA: Are We So Very Different?", 49 *Cambridge L.J.* 233 (1990).

29. Günter Bierbrauer, "Toward an Understanding of Legal Culture: Variations in Individualism and Collectivism between Kurds, Lebanese, and Germans," 28 *Law and Society Review* 243 (1994).

Are We A Litigious People? 75

30. In 1986, there were only 1,483 attorneys in the Republic of Korea, which had a population of more than 41,000,000; Dae-Kyu Yoon, *Law and Political Authority in South Korea* (1992) p. 129.

31. On Japan, see Robert L. Kidder and Setsuo Miyazawa, "Long-Term Strategies in Japanese Environmental Litigation," 18 *Law & Social Inquiry* 605 (1993); for the general argument, using a comparison of Germany and Holland as the basis, see Erhard Blankenburg, "The Infrastructure for Avoiding Court Litigation: Comparing Cultures of Legal Behavior in the Netherlands and West Germany," 28 *Law & Society Review* 789 (1994).

32. And the numbers are growing, in country after country; for examples, see the essays in Richard L. Abel and Philip S. C. Lewis, eds., *Lawyers in Society. Vol. 2: The Civil Law World* (1988).

33. Blankenburg, ed., *Prozessflut?* (1988).

34. See David S. Clark, "Civil Litigation Trends in Europe and Latin America Since 1945: The Advantage of Intracountry Comparisons," 24 *Law & Society Rev.* 549 (1990).

35. Yoon, *Law and Political Authority in South Korea*, p. 129.

36. The rate of passage seems to be rising, however: some 11 percent passed in 1991; also a somewhat larger number of lawyers have been admitted informally—through "connections," rather than through passing the bar exam; Jane Kaufman Winn, "Relational Practices and the Marginalization of Law: Informal Financial Practices of Small Businesses in Taiwan," 28 *Law and Society Review* 193 (1994) pp. 203-204.

37. The largest Canadian firm in 1961 had 39 lawyers; in 1989, the largest firm had 225; David A. A. Stager, *Lawyers in Canada* (1990) p. 176.

38. Richard Abel, *The Legal Profession in England and Wales* (1988) pp. 199-302, 406.

39. Robert A. Kagan, "Adversarial Legalism and American Government," 10 *J. Policy Analysis and Management*, 369 (1991).

40. This makes "customary law" something of a paradox, which would surprise anthropologists, and which calls for a bit of explanation. The subject of this essay is the law of Westernized, industrial, regulatory states, not tribal societies or pre-modern societies. It is precisely in these "modern" societies that the contrast between "custom" and "law" become most sharp. I do not mean to suggest that the broad definition of "law" used in anthropological literature—for example, in E. Adamson Hoebel, *The Law of Primitive Man: a Study in Comparative Legal Dynamics* (1954)—is wrong; it is only different.

41. Kenneth Karst, *Belonging to America. Equal Citizenship and the Constitution*(1989) p.193.

42. Gordon S. Wood, *The Radicalism of the American Revolution* (1992).

43. Thomas J. Archdeacon, *Becoming American: an Ethnic History* (1983).

44. Lawrence M. Friedman, "Crimes of Mobility," 43 *Stanford Law Review* 637 (1991).

45. But the relationship between "community", tradition and legal culture is complex; and may differ as between urban and rural societies; see David M. Engel, "The Oven Bird's Song" (1984), supra.

46. There are, of course, the native "tribes," officially called "nations." There are some hundreds of these, but they were long ago driven into "reservations;" and most of them are of small size. The largest, the Navajo nation, is the only native American group with more than 100,000 population. To be sure, claims of something like sovereignty have been asserted by the native peoples with great force—and some success—in recent years.

47. Milton Gordon, *Assimilation in American Life: The Role of Race, Religion and National Origins* (1964).

48. See Bill Ong Hing, *Making and Remaking Asian America Through Immigration Policy, 1850-1900* (1993).

49. Lawrence M. Friedman, *The Republic of Choice: Law, Authority and Culture* (1990).

50. Of course, it is also important to point out that most *people* did not vote or own land in, say, 1850; these benefits were conferred on white men only, for the most part. But in comparison to Europe—to England or France or Spain—this was already a mass society in the 19th century, a middle-class society.

51. Lawrence M. Friedman, *Your Time Will Come: The Law of Age Discrimination and Mandatory Retirement* (1985).

52. 42 U.S.C. sec. 12101ff; 104 Stats. 327 (act of July 26, 1990).

53. Lauren B. Edelman, "Legal Environments and Organizational Governance: The Expansion of Due Process in the American Workplace," 95 *Am. J. of Sociology* 1401 (1990).

54. Lawrence M. Friedman, *The Republic of Choice: Law, Authority and Culture* (1990).

55. Joan Williams, "Gender Wars: Selfless Women in the Republic of Choice," 66 *New York University Law Review* 1559 (1991).

56. Lawrence M. Friedman, *Total Justice* (1985).

57. I tried to explain the shift partly in terms of real changes in science and technology, which reduced the sense of the precariousness of life; along with the growth of the welfare state, which attacked other forms of precariousness. All this, I argued, led to a cycle of demand and response, which fed the appetite of the state—and the citizenry, as well.

58. See Marc Galanter, "Righting Old Wrongs," (unpub'd, 1993), on, for example, reparations to the Japanese-American survivors of internment camps; official apologies to victims of injustices suffered long, long ago; and other instances in which there is an attempt to pay victims at least some token amount, or with the coin of symbolism.

59. Stewart Macaulay, "Non-contractual Relations in Business: A Preliminary Study," 28 *Am. Sociological Rev.* 55 (1963).

60. Marc Galanter and Joel Rogers, "The Transformation of American Business Disputing? Some Preliminary Observations," Paper for 1988 Ann. Meeting, Law and Society Association, Vail, Colo., June 1988; see Lawrence M. Friedman, "Litigation and its Discontents," 40 *Mercer Law Review* 973 (1989).

61. Robert L. Nelson, *Partners with Power: The Social Transformation of the Large Law Firm* (1987).

62. Robert Hughes, *The Culture of Complaint* (1993).

63. The statement in the text is *relative*, not absolute. It is still very costly in all sorts of ways to file a complaint or to put oneself forward as a victim; see, for example, the treatment of the subject in Kristin Bumiller, *The Civil Rights Society: The Social Construction of Victims* (1988).

64. And of course, there has been plenty of anti-Semitism, coming to the surface in an ugly way from time to time, for example, in the Ku Klux Klan movement of the 1920's, which was also anti-Catholic.

65. John Wilson, *Religion in American Society: The Effective Presence* (1978).

66. Thomas Luckmann, *The Invisible Religion* (1967); Friedman, *The Republic of Choice: Law, Authority and Culture* (1990) pp. 164-169.

Are We A Litigious People?

67. American history is dotted with massive religious revivals, which amount on the whole to personal reinventions of religious experience; the society has also been a fruitful source of *new* religions—Christian Science and Mormonism, for example.

68. See David Vogel, "The Public-Interest Movement and the American Reform Tradition," 95 *Pol. Sci. Q.* 607 (1980-81).

69. So, for example, in American law, there is "no duty to retreat;" that is, a man (it was almost always a man) had the right to stand his ground and fight to the death when threatened, even if he could have run away to safety. The issue arose in homicide cases, where defendant claimed to have killed in self-defense; see Richard Maxwell Brown, *No Duty to Retreat: Violence and Values in American History and Society* (1991).

70. See, for example, Roger D. McGrath, *Gunfighters, Highwaymen & Vigilantes: Violence on the Frontier* (1984); Lawrence M. Friedman, *Crime and Punishment in American History* (1993).

71. Japan, indeed, with its samurai past, its "feudal wars," and its acts of "brutal subjugation" in China and Korea, illustrates "how rapid social change can influence attitudes toward physical aggressiveness," Edward Green, *The Intent to Kill: Making Sense of Murder* (1993), pp. 34-35.

72. Jeffrey Abrahamson, *We, the Jury: The Jury System and the Ideal of Democracy* (1994).

73. Galanter, "Predators and Parasites," at 655.

74. This would, of course, even be true of "homogeneous" Japan; the explosive growth of the big cities must come at the expense of village life.

75. The debris of modernization is also readily visible. You do not have to look very far to find people living in cardboard boxes in London—not as many as in New York, to be sure; but they exist; and the numbers seem to be growing.

76. *New York Times*, May 20, 1994, Nat'l Ed., p. C1.

77. Wolfgang Wiegand, "The Reception of American Law in Europe," 39 *Am. J. Comp. Law* 225 (1991).

78. John Merryman, "On the Convergence (and Divergence) of the Civil Law and the Common Law," 17 *Stanford J. of International Law* 357 (1981).

79. Although it is not always easy to be sure; on Japan, see Setsuo Miyazawa, *Policing in Japan: A Study on Making Crime* (1992).

80. On Japanese legal culture, see Frank K. Upham, *Law and Social Change in Postwar Japan* (1987); John O. Haley, *Order Without Authority* (1992).

81. John Braithwaite, *Crime, Shame and Reintegration* (1989) p. 65.

82. Haley, *Authority Without Power*, p. 200.

83. For a good example of an argument for "sameness" see J. Mark Ramseyer and Minoru Nakazato, "The Rational Litigant: Settlement Amounts and Verdict Rates in Japan," 18 *J. Legal Studies* 263 (1989).

4

The Assault on Civil Justice:
The Anti-Lawyer Dimension[1]

Marc Galanter

Introduction

For over a decade the reigning public view of the United States' legal establishment has been a negative one. In many quarters the civil justice system is viewed as a miasma of opportunistic self-seeking and a menace to America's economic well-being. Much of the animosity is focussed on lawyers as the authors, proprietors and chief beneficiaries of that system.

When it comes to lawyer-bashing, there is not much new under the sun. Hostility toward lawyers is a perennial. Yet its expressions vary greatly. There is a great cultural repertoire of anti-lawyer observations and sentiments.[2] At any time one or another grievance may gain prominence. The changes in fashion are not random, but are part of wider changes in sensibilities. I propose to examine the distinctive anti-lawyerism of the present to see what it tells us about our legal system, our society, and ourselves.

I. A Taxonomy of Anti-Lawyer Themes

Before taking up the current discontent with lawyers, let me set out a very crude taxonomy of anti-lawyer themes. I have organized some of the common themes into four clusters of related complaints: that lawyers are (1) corrupters of discourse; (2) fomenters of strife; (3) betrayers of trust; or (4) economic predators.[3]

Corrupters of Discourse: The first of my four clusters blames lawyers for corrupting discourse by promoting needless complexity, mystifying matters by jargon and formalities, robbing life's dealings of their moral sense by recasting them in legal abstractions, and offending common sense by casuistry that makes black appear white and vice versa.

> [C]asuistry is one of the diseases of a decadent order. . . . It is lawyers who can take a plain recitation of facts, turn it upside down, shake it, marinate it with doubts, and trundle it upstairs to a higher court for reconsideration.[4]

Fomenters of Strife: A second cluster portrays lawyers as aggressive, competitive hired guns, unprincipled mercenaries who foment strife and conflict by encouraging individual self-serving and self-assertion rather than cooperative problem solving. Examples are legion:

> The entire legal profession . . . [has] become so mesmerized with the stimulation of the courtroom contest that we tend to forget that we ought to be healers—healers of conflicts. . . . Healers, not warriors. . . . Healers, not hired guns. . . .[5]

> Lawyers have an economic interest in generating and prolonging conflict.[6]

> [Lawyers] encourage their clients to think with selfish defensiveness, to imagine and prepare for the worst from everyone else.[7]

And then there is the old joke about the town with one lawyer who was starving, but when a second lawyer settled there, they both prospered.

Betrayers of Trust: A third cluster damns lawyers as betrayers of trust: they are opportunistic, manipulative, self-serving deceivers who, under color of pursuing large public responsibilities, take advantage not only of hapless opponents but of clients who entrust their fortunes to them.

> An ancient, nearly blind old woman retained the local lawyer to draft her last will and testament, for which he charged her two hundred dollars. As she rose to leave, she took the money out of her purse and handed it over, enclosing a third hundred-dollar bill by mistake. Immediately the attorney realized he was faced with a crushing ethical question:

> Should he tell his partner?[8]

Economic Predators: Finally, lawyers are economic predators; they are greedy, money-driven monopolists, who levy a tariff on matters of common right. They are parasitic rent-seekers who do not really produce anything, but merely batten on the productive members of society, often in alliance with the undeserving—opportunistic malingerers in some versions, the privileged and powerful in others.

> There's a reason people hate lawyers. . . . It's because they have a monopoly on what rightfully belongs to everyone.[9]

These clusters overlap and reinforce each other: for example, mystification helps lawyers manipulate the unwary and shield their monopoly. Lawyers betray their clients by fomenting needless conflict, and the resulting economic burdens directly benefit lawyers. And so on.

Each of these clusters is a composite, consisting of a number of specific and partially overlapping complaints. In each cluster, there is a range from complaints about mistreatment of specific individuals (clients, opponents) to wrongdoing that in the aggregate has larger public consequences. Thus, a lawyer can be accused of hoodwinking a client by mystification, or propelling that client into an unnecessary fight, or betraying that client's interest for self-serving reasons, or charging that client excessively for his services. These grievances are the private, individual versions of the four clusters. On the other hand, the complaint might be that lawyers' jargon and mystification obscure public understanding and diminish citizen participation; or that lawyer-induced excessive adversariness makes public life nasty and wasteful; or that lawyers misuse their authority to sustain illegitimate privilege and power; or, finally, that lawyers' exploitation of their monopoly is a drain on the economy, reducing growth and decreasing competitiveness. These are the aggregate, public, and systemic versions of the four clusters.

Each of these clusters points to the dark side of things that may otherwise appear as virtues or at least useful qualities of lawyers. In the sins of discourse we can recognize the inventiveness of lawyers and their obsession with precision and relevance. Fomenting conflict mirrors the lawyer's zealous advocacy and insistence on vindicating rights. In economic predation, we see appreciation of the lawyer's prowess as an agent of redistribution. The betrayal complaint proclaims regard for the lawyer as an ally coupled with fear and resentment that he is an undependable ally. The things for which lawyers are despised are closely related to the things for which they are esteemed.[10]

II. The "Public Justice" Critique

To appreciate the distinctiveness of the current discourse about lawyers, it is useful to look back to years before the Reagan presidency. In 1978, President Jimmy Carter took the occasion of the 100th Anniversary dinner of the Los Angeles Bar Association to deliver a critique of the legal system.[11] Beginning with an excerpt from *Bleak House*, President Carter excoriated delay, "excessive litigation and legal featherbedding,"[12] and chastised lawyers for aggravating rather than resolving conflict. We have heard much in recent years about these lawyer vices, but in Carter's critique these complaints were interwoven with another set of themes that have been notably absent from more recent presidential rhetoric about the legal system. President Carter declared that legal services were, more than any resource in our society, "wastefully [and] unfairly distributed."[13] Lawyers were particularly to blame for failing to make justice "blind to rank, power and position."[14] He deplored that "lawyers of great influence and prestige led the fight against civil rights and economic justice."[15] Devoted to the service of dominant groups, lawyers had failed to discharge their "heavy obligation to serve the ends of true justice."[16] He called upon them to release "the enormous potential for good within an aroused legal profession."[17] In short, lawyers had fallen woefully short of their calling to be votaries of justice in an imperfect world. He called on them to embrace the theme of "Access to Justice," which was the official theme of the American Bar Association for 1978.[18] Although the tones were critical, the song was one of optimism and hope: rededication to their high calling combined with institutional redesign could vindicate the promise of connecting law to pursuit of a just society.[19] Needless to say, the President's observations did not get a warm reception from the bar.[20] The general press was quite unfavorable.[21] But the President's criticism of the bar met with general public approval.[22]

The organizing theme of the Carter critique was betrayal of trust. President Carter's speech was the culmination of a decade of attacks on lawyers for self-serving alliance with the powerful, attacks that acquired added credibility from the heavy representation of lawyers among the Watergate villains.[23] Let me mention just a few of the landmarks of that trail. In a much cited 1967 article entitled "The Practice of Law as a Confidence Game," Abraham Blumburg indicted criminal lawyers for allowing themselves to become co-opted by the court organization so that they became "double agent[s]" cynically manipulating their clients.[24] In his 1968 best seller, *The Trouble With Lawyers*, Murray Teigh Bloom recounted the various ethical lapses of lawyers who abuse their clients by self-serving behavior.[25] In a 1977 Law Day address, the Chief Judge of New York's Court of Appeals warned that lawyers were increasingly motivated by "self interest rather than social responsibility."[26]

Other critics recast the betrayal theme in terms of large public interests rather than individual lawyer-client relations.[27] In his highly regarded 1976 history, *Unequal Justice*, Jerold Auerbach condemned the elite of the legal profession for its subservience to the powerful and privileged, and its failure to implement equal justice.[28] That year at the American Bar Association convention, Secretary of Transportation William T. Coleman, Jr. "accused the organized bar . . . of having 'failed the American public' by turning its back on people unable to afford high-priced lawyers."[29] In response, Chesterfield Smith, a former ABA president, called for a system of dues going to public interest law; and a change in the profession's ethical canons to require at least some public interest work by each lawyer.

"You need someone who can represent the general interest," he said.[30]

Ralph Nader attacked the "endemic malaise" of lawyers' acquiescing in a maldistribution of their services that fortified powerful interests.[31] Lawyers evaded the duties to the broader public that flowed from their status as officers of the court and evaded their obligation to secure justice by hiding behind canons of behavior that protected their self-interest.[32] Similarly, Jethro K. Lieberman's 1978 critique argued that the "unethical ethics" of the legal profession undermined its role as a "public profession."[33]

The "public interest law"[34] and "access to justice"[35] movements that flourished during the 1970s, seeking to give voice to unrepresented groups and to enlarge the modalities for securing justice, called for lawyers to embrace these neglected responsibilities. Some adherents of the public justice critique called for formation of a "National Legal Service" to make legal services freely available to all.[36]

The public justice critique culminated in the work of the Kutak Commission, set up in 1977 to revise the rules of ethical conduct for lawyers.[37] The major theme of the new Model Rules proposed by the Commission was enlargement of the public duties of lawyers and limitation of their license for adversary combat.[38] The Commission sought to accentuate the duties of lawyers that transcended their responsibilities to clients—for example, by limiting confidentiality to enable lawyers to blow the whistle on client wrongdoing, imposing a duty of fairness in negotiations by requiring disclosure of material facts, and requiring lawyers to devote a portion of their time to *pro bono publico* work.[39] The Commission's proposals aroused fierce opposition from various sectors of the bar and were vitiated at a series of ABA meetings in 1982 and 1983.[40] Notwithstanding, echoes of the public justice critique are audible from time to time in bar precincts.[41]

The dominant pre-Reagan critique was that lawyers were blameworthy for failing to meet their professional obligations. The relatively apolitical Murray Teigh Bloom focused on the failure of lawyers to fulfill their obligations to clients. The broader, more political versions of Carter, Auerbach, and Nader emphasized lawyers' deflection from promotion of justice due to their co-optation by the powerful. In each case, it was lawyers' misdeeds and omissions that attracted reproach, not the legal enterprise as such.

III. Contemporary Lawyer-Bashing

At the very time that the notion of justice underserved by its disloyal servants was being elaborated, other currents were reshaping attitudes toward the state of the civil justice system. Eminent judges, lawyers, and academics opined that American society was suffering from an excess of law in the form of "legal pollution" or a "litigation explosion." The popular press echoed this concern, reporting that "Americans in all walks of life are being buried under an avalanche of lawsuits."[42] The Chief Justice of the United States criticized lawyers for commercialism, for incompetence, and for excessive adversariness that produced court congestion and runaway litigation.[43] He mounted a broad attack aimed at curtailing litigation and replacing adversarial confrontation by a "better way."[44]

Concern about mounting costs and expanding frontiers of liability led to sustained campaigns for "tort reform."[45] The thrust for increased "access to justice"[46] was transformed from a desire to multiply the paths to justice to a movement to curtail litigation by diverting disputes into alternative dispute resolution.[47] Typically, the performance of these alternatives was assessed in terms of efficiency rather than superior justice.

By the mid-1980s, the discourse about lawyers and civil justice in America was dominated by what I call the "jaundiced view." Our civil justice system was widely condemned as pathological and destructive, producing untold harm. A series of factoids or macro-anecdotes about litigation became the received wisdom: America is the most litigious society in the course of all human history; Americans sue at the drop of a hat; the courts are brimming over with frivolous lawsuits; resort to courts is a first rather than a last resort; runaway juries make capricious awards to undeserving claimants; immense punitive damage awards are routine; litigation is undermining our ability to compete economically.[48]

Although a litigious populace and activist judges were blamed, lawyers, as the promoters, beneficiaries, and protectors of this pathological system, were prominent among the culprits. Then, in the early 1990s, attacks on lawyers escalated sharply. Older themes of suspicion of and disdain for lawyers reappeared in new guises.

A. Too Many Lawyers

It is widely believed that the United States is cursed with a population of lawyers that is vastly disproportionate to any possible usefulness. This notion achieved extraordinary prominence in August 1991, when Vice President Quayle ended his speech on the wrongs of our legal system with the rhetorical question, "Does America really need 70% of the world's lawyers?"[49]

The origins of this seventy percent figure are mysterious. The notion that the United States had "two thirds of the world's lawyers" had surfaced a decade earlier, although it had no ascertainable origin in research—scholarly, journalistic or otherwise.[50] This item was retailed by Chief Justice Burger as part of his indictment of litigious America, and was repeated by a few judges and law school deans, but gained no currency in wider circles.[51] A few years later, in contrast, the Vice President's seventy percent figure was immediately parroted by many political figures and media experts.[52] It was eventually inscribed in the 1992 Republican platform, reappeared in Vice President Quayle's acceptance speech, and surfaced during the presidential campaign.

Counting lawyers cross-nationally is a daunting undertaking, plagued by poor data and a bushel of apples and oranges problems. However these problems are resolved, it is clear that the seventy percent figure is very far from the mark. An informed guess would be something less than half of that. Counting conservatively, American lawyers probably make up somewhere between twenty-five and thirty-five percent of all the world's lawyers, using that term to refer to all those in jobs that American lawyers do (including judges, prosecutors, government lawyers and in-house corporate lawyers).[53]

The Assault on Civil Justice: The Anti-Lawyer Dimension 85

But "seventy percent" is not just a matter of mistaken statistics. Seventy percent is an accusation of monstrous disproportion. It suggests that America has departed from the normal model of development and that the national body is disfigured by a cancerous excrescence that requires to be excised.[54] America needs to be "de-lawyered."[55]

B. The Drag on the Economy

Why is having all these lawyers such a bad thing? Contemporary critics concur on one central charge: these lawyers are a drag on the economy. This takes several forms. First, legal careers simply divert high grade talent into unproductive work.[56] Second, not only are these scarce talents squandered, but they are transformed into enemies of productivity. The principal intellectual foundation for the view that lawyers hurt the economy is the work of University of Texas finance professor Stephen Magee. Magee has tried to show that the countries with the highest lawyer populations[57] suffer from impaired economic growth. Magee's conclusion is wrong; its first version was shown to be false,[58] and its latest version is no stronger. The best research on the topic reaches entirely different conclusions.[59]

In Magee's first take on this issue, he claimed that all lawyers are economically destructive.[60] Apart from being silly on its face, that conclusion resulted from an empirical analysis containing major methodological errors. His analysis compared the lawyer populations and economic growth rates of thirty-four countries and concluded that the more lawyers a country has, the lower is its rate of growth.[61] That analysis is shot through with problems. First, Magee relied on poor lawyer data—his lawyer figures for several countries were substantially incorrect. Second, he employed a peculiar research design that used lawyer data in 1983 to predict economic growth from 1960 to 1985—even though his own figures showed that the number of lawyers in 1983 bore little relation to the number in 1960. Third, Magee's research did not take into account ("control for") any other known influences on economic growth, including such powerful influences as a country's level of political instability. Finally, the conclusion resulted in large part from the coincidence of low economic growth rates and high lawyer populations in two "outliers" (Argentina and Nepal), whose legal systems and economies bear little relation to our own.

After critics pointed out those failings, Magee refurbished his research and now claims that only lawyers above a certain optimal number hurt an economy.[62] Stated that simply, the view has an intuitive plausibility: surely if all Americans were lawyers and did nothing else, our economy would have problems. Magee's leap to the conclusion that there are, in fact, too many lawyers in the United States is a different matter.

Like the first version, Magee's latest research is deeply flawed, and probably would not merit discussion were it not getting so much publicity. In attempting to determine the economic effect of lawyers, he now takes into account known influences on economic growth.[63] But his conclusions still rely primarily on 1983 lawyer data to predict prior economic growth, and they still rest on flawed lawyer data. For example, he estimates that there are 43,100 lawyers in West Germany; but if we include not only lawyers in private practice but also government lawyers, corporate lawyers, judges and law teachers—all included in the United States lawyer count—the total number of German lawyers in 1985 was 115,900.[64] That produces a lawyer-to-white-collar worker ratio of twenty-nine per thousand, not the eleven per thousand that Professor Magee asserts. Inaccuracies of this magnitude are not minor details. In his most recent response to these criticisms, he declares that lawyer data corrected for such errors still support his conclusion.[65] But that is true only if the lawyer data are used to "predict" prior economic growth—an unjustifiable research strategy; the same data contradict Magee's results when they are employed to analyze subsequent economic growth.[66] In addition, Magee's latest conclusion, like his earlier one, rests on the coincidence of slow growth and high lawyer populations in a few idiosyncratic countries, now Uruguay and Chile.

As a corollary, Magee claims that lawyers have captured the United States political system, evidenced by the fact that forty-two percent of United States Representatives and sixty-one percent of Senators are lawyers.[67] But that hardly means the legal profession has captured the political system: those lawyers in Congress are Democrats and Republicans, liberals and conservatives, proponents of regulation and enemies of regulation. As a bloc, they share no discernible interest; a range of studies finds no difference between the voting patterns of lawyer-legislators and those of nonlawyer-legislators.[68]

Careful analyses of the effect of lawyers on the economy find no support for the Magee hypothesis; indeed, they find that lawyers have no significant effect at all on overall economic growth.[69] The Magee analysis rests on many of the familiar but unproven contentions about the civil justice system. He assumes that the presence of "excess" lawyers is evidenced by the presence of "predatory" litigation, as distinguished from justified or beneficial litigation. But he provides no evidence of the frequency of bad litigation that is independent of the conclusion that there are too many lawyers.

Notwithstanding the absence of reliable evidence, Magee—or at least his point about the economic predation of lawyers—is widely believed by those who should know better. Thus a former chair of the President's Council of Economic Advisors, lamenting slow growth, says:

> Law schools have been flooding the nation with graduates who are suffocating the economy with a litigation epidemic of bubonic plague proportions.[70]

His successor as chair of the Council of Economic Advisors told the National Economists Club that our legal system has become:

The Assault on Civil Justice: The Anti-Lawyer Dimension *87*

an albatross around productivity . . . we spend more time and more resources actively suing each other or taking defensive actions to prevent lawsuits that could be generated toward or diverted toward productive social uses. . . . And I think we badly need to do that. I think part of the problem lies in the nature of our civil justice system, and everything from malpractice reform to product liability reform to changing the basic nature of our civil justice system, some of these economic incentives, that we get more of a balance into our civil justice system to stop some of the frivolous lawsuits.[71]

The thrust here is that lawyers impair America's economic competitiveness and the principal means by which they do so is by promoting bad litigation. "With 70% of the world's lawyers, it is not surprising that America has experienced a litigation explosion."[72] In the words of Vice President Quayle:

[T]he American people sense that something is wrong with our legal system. They believe there are too many lawsuits, . . . too many excessive damage awards. They believe there is too much litigation and this is hurting the American economy. They believe too much litigation is costing American jobs. They believe that too much litigation is driving up the cost of financing federal and state and local government, that it's driving up the cost of liability insurance and the key factor, is driving up health care.[73]

President Bush told the American Business Conference in April 1992:

Over the last several years, dead weights have begun to slow the engine of growth, inefficiencies a competitive economy simply cannot tolerate. . . . Let me begin with the crying need to reform our country's civil justice system. Every American has heard stories of bizarre or frivolous lawsuits. But most of you have lived with them, tales that could have been torn from the pages of Kafka.[74]

Implicit in much of this talk is a folkloric image of plaintiffs' lawyers working for contingency fees, seeking immense damages on behalf of malingering or opportunistic clients, bringing frivolous lawsuits based on "junk science" against deep pocket defendants, and goading capricious juries to award excessive damages—especially immense and arbitrary punitive damages.[75] Litigation explosion lore gives top billing to this figure of the "tassel-loafered" lawyer.[76] But complaints about the number and increase of lawyers make no distinctions. All lawyers are inculpated for promoting adversarialism, fostering complexity and uncertainty, and sharing in the vast and undeserved profits generated by this excessive litigation.[77] This broader indictment is given clear expression in a critique by Richard Weise, General Counsel of Motorola: "America is awash with lawyers who make mischief. . . . They are forced to innovate, to develop new legal products so they can usefully fill their time, that usually means thinking of ways to separate American corporations from their money."[78] He includes not only securities class actions, but cases about wrongful termination and employee-benefit fraud. "The drain on corporate assets and energy is tremendous. . . . While cases are being litigated, corporate America often can't do anything innovative because executives are too absorbed in and exhausted by the legal process."[79]

This portrays the lawyer as a parasite, feasting on productive corporations. In its simple form, the "parasite" critique is that lawyers do not "make" anything; but then neither do bankers, insurers, accountants, diversified financial services companies, police, pollution inspectors, etc. The spectacle of economists, journalists, senators, and executives disparaging lawyers because they do not *make* anything exposes a deep vein of anxiety about the meaning of productivity in our information age. Beneath this anxiety lies a genuine question: Do "services"—particularly those that are concerned with the regulation and facilitation of transactions—contribute anything of value to society?

As the Weise quotation above indicates, it often is assumed that the regulatory regime that envelops these corporations, manifested in laws, administrative enforcement, litigation, and preventive lawyering, imposes costs but engenders no benefits to society. The estimates of costs that have figured prominently in the "too much lawyering" discourse have been based on unsubstantiated conjecture, have vacillated about just what is being measured, and have conflated costs and transfers.[80]

Beyond these infirmities, exclusive concentration on costs has distracted the critics from looking at the benefits that might offset or even surpass those costs. Our accounts should reflect not only the costs but also the benefits of enforcing such transfers, which afford vindication, induce investments in safety, and deter undesirable behavior. For instance, the sums transferred by successful patent infringement litigation not only are not lost, but maintain the credibility of the patent system, which in turn has powerful incentive effects. To put forward estimates of gross costs—even ones that are not make-believe—as a guide to policy displays indifference to the vital functions that the law performs. America's institutions of remedy and accountability and the lawyers that staff them are portrayed as burdensome afflictions. They are viewed as costs and thus as deadweight losses.[81]

It is much more difficult to measure benefits than costs. But several studies suggest that the presence of lawyers does confer real benefits on their societies. Lawyers, concluded Robert Clark, are specialists in normative ordering, and the increased demand for their services is attributable to more intense and diverse interaction, greater diversity, changes in wealth levels, and the burgeoning of formal organizations.[82] Stephen Bundy and Einer Elhauge argue that lawyers' advice to clients results in an overall improvement in the working of tribunals.[83] Frank Cross argues that, in addition to promoting significant non-market benefits such as civil liberties and political democracy, the presence of lawyers promotes efficient allocation by helping to internalize externalities and by facilitating transactions among dispersed, interdependent, productive units.[84] Ron Gilson argues that business lawyers create value by acting as "transaction cost engineer[s]."[85] In a pioneering field study of business lawyering, Mark Suchman and Mia Cahill found that:

> By virtue of their distinctive location within the Silicon Valley community, lawyers quite literally produce and reproduce the social structures underpinning the local high-risk capital market. Through their relations with both entrepreneurs and investors, they identify, create, transmit and enforce the emerging norms of the community. In doing so, Silicon Valley lawyers absorb and control some of the central uncertainties in encounters between venture capitalists and entrepreneurs, facilitating what might otherwise be prohibitively costly, complex and unpredictable transactions.[86]

A full assessment of the benefits, testing hypotheses about linkages between what lawyers do and the occurrence of these favorable things, must wait for another day. My point is that the parasite argument is not closely dependent on evidence and that it resonates with a deeper resentment of lawyers. Even if our system of civil justice does produce benefits that outweigh its costs, critics ask, why should lawyers be able to "farm" it for their personal advantage? Here we turn to earlier polemicists who articulated this theme.

C. The Justice Tariff

Some 150 years ago, Georgian John W. Pitts published a little book that both anticipates and illuminates current discontents.[87] Pitts thinks lawyers are driven by self-interest both to make laws prolix and complicated and to "excite strife, confusion and debate."[88] Lawyer legislators make law complex and generate a need for lawyers to vindicate rights.[89] These rights are then diminished, however, by the very need for professional lawyers, who extract fees for securing these rights for their clients. The justice they secure is thus flawed and incomplete, for a portion of the clients' entitlement is diverted to the lawyers, who add no value. Thus, for Pitts, every legal entitlement is diminished by the presence of an occupational group that is paid for vindicating it. This "justice tariff" (my phrase, not his) is an affront to liberty, which is "the power of enjoying rights without paying for them."[90]

> Fees at the bar, from their first institution up to this hour, have been the source of more numerous and more malignant evils in the countries where they have been tolerated than all the wars, pestilences, famines, tornadoes & earthquakes that ever harassed these lands.[91]

Beneath Pitts's bluster lie some of the deep roots of resentment of lawyers, growing from the necessity of using and paying lawyers to secure what people regard as already rightfully theirs.

Max Radin discerns an ancient theme that "justice is a man's right. That is what society is for. It should be free as air."[92] Reviewing "antilawyer sentiment in the early Republic," Maxwell Bloomfield reports widespread suspicion of the lawyer as an intruder who inserts himself into a self-regulating, harmonious community, displacing substantive justice with artificial formality, self-interest, and high fees.[93] As an influential anti-lawyer tract of the early 19th century complains:

> God never intended his creature man, should be under the necessity to carry a written book in his pocket, or a lawyer by his side, to tell him what is just and lawful; he wrote it on his mind.[94]

As one contemporary critic puts it, "There's a reason people hate lawyers .... It's because they have a monopoly on what rightfully belongs to everyone."[95] A long tradition holds that the need for lawyer intermediaries is not natural, but is itself an outgrowth of the lawyers' corruption of legal discourse. It is because lawyers have made law complex and mysterious that they can levy the justice tariff.

D. The Law Trap: Entanglement in Legal Myth

So the charge of economic predation has led us back to the sins of discourse, for the justice tariff is supported by lawyers' successful mystification of the law. In a famous polemic, Yale law professor Fred Rodell decried the law as a pretense, a fraud, a hoax, mumbo-jumbo, "a scheme of contradictory and nonsensical principles built of inherently meaningless abstractions" that exercises a superstitious hold over the populace.[96] "The legal trade . . . is nothing but a high-class racket."[97] Lawyers are soothsayers, modern medicine men,[98] "purveyors of streamlined voodoo," priests of mystification.[99]

Rodell thinks that most business affairs "run off smoothly of their own accord."[100] By introducing legalities, lawyers "no doubt increase, instead of decreasing, the number of transactions that end up in dispute and litigation."[101] Yet lawyers can be narrowly useful. The law tends to favor the rich and powerful because its fraudulent character can be manipulated by lawyers:

> It makes it worth-while for those with money enough to afford it to buy the court services and the pre-court advice of those mumbo-jumbo chanters and scribblers who can best wring desired results out of legal language and legal principles.[102]

Rodell vacillates on the culpability of lawyers for this state of affairs. At times he portrays them as self-deceived: "[T]he lawyers, taken as a whole, cannot by any means be accused of *deliberately* hoodwinking the public. . . . They, too, are blissfully unaware that the sounds they make are essentially empty of meaning."[103] Yet elsewhere they are portrayed as knowing conspirators:

> For the lawyers know it would be woe unto the lawyers if the non-lawyers ever got wise to the fact that their lives were run, not by The Law, not by any rigid and

impersonal and automatically applied code of rules, but instead by a comparatively small group of men, smart, smooth, and smug—the lawyers.[104]

Rodell has his technocratic version of that abiding faith in a simple, natural, accessible system of social regulation. He would abolish law and replace it with a practical, comprehensible system of common-sense decisionmaking by experts.[105] Where critics like President Carter portrayed lawyers as errant priests of the true church of social justice, Rodell portrays them as the idolatrous priests of a false religion, which he thinks can be dismantled by eliminating lawyers.

This dark vision of law as fraudulent mystification runs from Pitts to Rodell to contemporary anti-lawyer polemicists,[106] and reappears as a component of the new "economic" anti-lawyerism that dominates current discourse about lawyers. Rodell's portrayal of lawyers as the source of the mythic reification of legal rules and as captives of the law's empty mysteries makes important empirical claims about the beliefs and behavior of lawyers and lay people, claims that I suspect are at least incomplete and very likely seriously mistaken. Forty years ago, David Riesman observed that lawyers

> are feared and disliked—but needed—because of their matter-of-factness, their sense of relevance, their refusal to be impressed by magical "solutions" to people's problems. Conceivably, if this hypothesis is right, the ceremonial and mystification of the legal profession are, to a considerable degree, veils or protections underneath which this rational, all too rational, work of the lawyer gets done.[107]

Jethro Lieberman suggests that lawyers are not votaries of illusory certainty, but rather technicians of indeterminacy:

> The only secret that the lawyer really possesses about the law is that no one can ever be certain of what the law is. . . . The lawyer is accustomed to the ways of bending and changing rules to suit his (or his client's) purposes, to dance in the shadows of the law's ambiguities. Rules hold no particular terror for the lawyer, just as the sight of blood holds no terror for the surgeon. Because he operates a system of rules, the lawyer becomes indifferent to them in the way that a doctor becomes indifferent to the humanity of the body that is lying on the operating table.[108]

These observations raise the question whether it is lawyers' bloody-mindedness that irks people rather than, or along with, their penchant for mystification. Answering that question requires close analysis of professional and popular perceptions of the law, how these views shape and are shaped by lawyer-client interaction,[109] how this varies from setting to setting, and how it has changed over time. Whether the public perceives lawyers as genuine or bogus votaries of the law's mysteries and the extent to which it subscribes to those mysteries is deeply problematic.[110]

IV. The Distribution of Views About Lawyers

The new economic anti-lawyerism is closely connected to what I have called the "jaundiced view" of our civil justice system expressed by political, media, and business elites. How does this strain of anti-lawyer feeling relate to the array of attitudes toward lawyers in American society? Unfortunately, we do not have a comprehensive profile of the attitudes and beliefs of the public regarding lawyers; nor do we know how these views have changed over time. A scatter of public opinion data, however, enables us to get a sense of the general contours and some inkling of recent trends.[111]

Most Americans who have used lawyers think well of them. In a 1986 *National Law Journal* (NLJ) poll, almost half of American adults reported professional contact with a lawyer within the preceding five years.[112] Well over half of these users reported themselves "very satisfied" with the lawyer's performance and another quarter were "somewhat satisfied."[113] By 1993, the number who had used a lawyer had risen to 68%.[114] In comparison, 67% of the respondents in the 1993 ABA survey reported using a lawyer in the last ten years.[115] Even with all these novice customers, the level of dissatisfaction was only slightly higher.[116] About two-thirds of the ABA respondents who used lawyers were satisfied.[117]

But when asked about lawyers in the aggregate, the public views them less favorably. Lawyers' ethical standards and practices are thought to be middling by most people, with a much larger contingent regarding them as poor (21%) than as excellent (3%).[118] Those who thought lawyers less honest than most people rose from 17% in 1986 to 31% in 1993.[119] The ABA poll reports that "[h]alf the public thinks that about one-third or more of lawyers are dishonest, including one in four Americans who believe that a *majority* of lawyers are dishonest."[120] Over the past decade, general estimations of lawyers' ethical standards have fallen-- especially since 1991.[121] In the 1993 NLJ survey, 36% of the respondents said their image of lawyers had "gotten worse" and only 8% said it had "improved."[122]

Disapproval of lawyers is not distributed uniformly, and there is a pronounced pattern to the disparities:

> By and large, those who see lawyers in a more favorable light than average tend to be downscale, women, minorities, and young. . . .
>
> . . . Americans who are more critical than average tend to be more establishment, upscale, and male. The higher the family income and socioeconomic status, the more critical the adults are. Pluralities of college graduates feel unfavorably toward lawyers, while pluralities of non-college graduates feel favorably.[123]

More and more Americans believe that there are too many lawyers. In 1986, 55% of the NLJ respondents believed that there were too many lawyers; in 1993 this number had increased to 73%.[124] The ABA survey asked people to volunteer criticism of lawyers: only five percent volunteered that they were too numerous.[125]

The Assault on Civil Justice: The Anti-Lawyer Dimension

This sense of the superfluity of lawyers is more intense among "top" people.[126] While 55% of all respondents to the 1986 NLJ survey agreed that the country had too many lawyers, this sentiment was shared by 69% of college graduates, 68% of those earning over $50,000 annually, and 64% of the occupational category made up of professionals, executives, and managers.[127]

A 57% majority thought lawyers had "too much influence and power in society."[128] Again, distribution was skewed with more prosperous and powerful groups high (college graduates, 64%, professionals, 60%) and outsider groups low (blacks, 39%).[129]

"Top" groups were also the most likely to attribute to lawyers principal responsibility for a litigation explosion in the United States.[130] Curiously, however, the members of these categories were at least as highly satisfied with the performance of their own lawyers as were respondents overall.[131]

This profile of elite concern is reflected in a 1992 survey of executives by *Business Week*, which found that 62% felt "that the U.S. civil justice system significantly hampers the ability of U.S. companies to compete with Japanese and European companies."[132] Over 80% believed that the fear of lawsuits was growing.[133] Elites, including lawyers, seem to hold exaggerated views of the prevalence of litigation, the size of awards, and the incidence of punitive damages.[134] More generally, perceptions of the menace of product liability litigation have intensified during a period in which many indicators suggest that the world of product liability is contracting rather than expanding.[135] Folklore about the spectre of runaway litigation abounds, augmented and amplified by a small but vigorous industry.[136]

But the broad public subscribes to much of the jaundiced view. Over half thought it a fair criticism of *most* lawyers that "[t]hey file too many lawsuits and tie up the court system."[137] And when asked whether it was a fair criticism that lawyers' "excessive costs and lawsuits make America less able to compete against foreign countries," only 31% thought it was an unfair criticism—although another 28% thought it should be confined to a minority of lawyers.[138] A resounding 74% agreed that "the amount of litigation in America today is hampering this country's economic recovery."[139] But only 25% thought lawyers "played the largest role" in contributing to the liability crisis, trailing insurers (34%).[140] (In spite of falling estimations of lawyers, the public attribution of the litigation explosion and the liability crisis to lawyers declined slightly from 1986 to 1993, while rising slightly for insurers and manufacturers.) Traces of the public justice critique surface in these broad public soundings: "The public contends that lawyers have suffered the greatest decline in the areas of defending the underdog, providing leadership in the community, and seeking justice."[141]

It appears that the jaundiced view, which sees lawyers as fostering a civil justice system that is devouring American business, is most intense and most widespread among elites—i.e., among those with more wealth, education, and power. For all their misgivings about lawyers, other survey evidence suggests that most Americans (also) hold very different views of the legal system. Although they do not express a high degree of confidence in the legal system, their qualms do not seem to involve the system's oppression of business. When asked whether "[t]he justice system in the United States mainly favors the rich" or "treats all Americans as equally as possible," 57% of respondents chose the "favored the rich" response and only 39% the "equally" response.[142] Similarly, 59% of a national sample agreed that "the legal system favors the rich and powerful over everyone else."[143] In early 1995, amid agitation about "tort reform" and reported outrage at lawyers and the legal system, a *U.S. News & World Report* survey asked how the access of "average Americans" to the legal system compared with that of "rich people:" 13% said average Americans had less access and 62% said "much less."[144] When asked which types of people were "not apt to be treated fairly by the law," respondents identified the poor (54%), uneducated (47%), and blacks (33%); only 5% thought "top business executives" were treated unfairly.[145] Indeed, when asked which types of persons "the courts are too lenient with," government officials and top business executives ranked, along with heroin users and frequent offenders, just below dope peddlers.[146]

The survey evidence indicates that the grievances of ordinary people are quite different from those that constitute the jaundiced view. For example, respondents to a recent poll split evenly on whether tort reform should "tilt things a little more in favor of those injured in accidents" (39%) or "keep pretty much the same balance we have now" (39%). Only 7% favored "tilt[ing] things a little more in favor of the insurance companies."[147] An examination of the publications of HALT, a reform organization founded in 1977, indicates the kind of issues that engage that small section of the public that devotes attention and energy to challenging lawyers' practices.[148] They are concerned about excessive fees, particularly exactions like fixed percentage probate fees. They are concerned with t"he weakness of lawyer discipline and call for the abolition of self-regulation and the establishment of an open public procedure for grievances against lawyers. They want plain language, do-it-yourself provisions, and higher small claims court limits—all to permit citizens to pursue their legal business without lawyers; they oppose the lawyer monopoly, enthusiastically urging nonlawyer practice. It is a consumerist perspective in which access is a major theme: they want a system that is user-friendly for ordinary people. Overall, problems are visualized as impositions on individual users rather than in the aggregate perspective that is part of the jaundiced view.

The gulf between the jaundiced view and this more consumerist take on lawyers is revealed by the response of HALT leadership to Dan Quayle's campaign against the civil justice system. HALT officials welcomed Quayle's ABA speech as a boost "for the visibility of the legal reform movement" and for putting reform on the front burner, but criticized the Quayle proposals as "either too superficial or too one-sided."[149] Invoking the access theme, the organization's Executive Director took a cool view of the Council on Competitiveness reforms, which "tend to be aimed at reducing litigation for the sake of reducing litigation, without addressing the impact these proposals will have on obtaining justice."[150] A few months later, comparing the reform proposals of the ABA and the Bush administration, HALT's Deputy Director criticized the ABA proposal as "too lawyer-dominated—it equates access to justice with finding an attorney—and fails to take into account the consumer perspective."[151] The administration's legislation, on the other hand, "is too one sided and is aimed more at reducing litigation than ensuring justice."[152] There is no indication here of any objection to the substantive justice afforded by the system—what is wanted is expanded access to it. If the HALT view is at all reflective of what ordinary people want, then we can understand how the anti-lawyer strategy of the 1992 Bush campaign mistakenly conflated distinct kinds of anti-lawyer sentiment. Attacks on the litigation explosion, which caught fire with elite audiences, were expected to ignite the grievances and resentments of the wider public.[153] But the wider public's concern about the legal system includes the theme of access to the remedies and protections of the legal system.

To business people, who feel accused of responsibility for America's flagging economic performance and lack of competitiveness, it is reassuring to know that the fault is not theirs and that they are the victims of predatory lawyers, activist judges, and biased jurors.[154] But the evidence that the liability system actually impairs the economic competitiveness of American corporations is vanishingly thin.[155] The focus on lawyers and civil liability as a major source of business distress does not seem to be the product of calculating examination of balance sheets. Instead it seems to proceed from, or at least implicate, the resentments of lawyers discussed earlier.

V. American Exceptionalism

A. Only in America?

In the jaundiced view, America's legal malaise is not an expression of its essential character, but is part of a falling away from the true America. The jaundiced view mourns the loss of a time when society was benignly self-regulating, law was clear, certain and reasonable, judges applied it dutifully and eschewed activism, lawyers were upright paragons of civic virtue, and litigation was rare.[156] Nostalgia for this normal, orderly world flourishes in many sectors of American life.[157] Within the legal profession itself, many share the sense that law has declined from a noble profession infused with civic virtue to commercialism.[158] This sense of decline has been a recurrent theme for at least a hundred years. Distress about lost virtue has been a constant accompaniment of elite law practice since the formation of the large firm a hundred years ago.[159] The time when virtue prevailed is just over the receding horizon of personal experience. Lawyers' sense of decline reflects the gap between practice and professional ideology: in the flesh, working life is experienced as more mundane, routine, business-like, commercial, money-driven, client-dominated, and conflict-laden than it is supposed to be. It is easy to believe that the way it is supposed to be is the way that it used to be.[160]

This nostalgia is fused to a sense that America has taken a wrong turn. The contemporary critique of lawyers as economic predators is pervaded by a sense of the uniqueness of the American predicament. Vice President Quayle's "seventy percent" probed a sensitive spot precisely because it served as shorthand for the sense that we are radically different and have departed the trodden path along a perilous detour. While other industrial democracies flourished with few lawyers and less litigation, we carried a crushing legal burden. Japan was Exhibit A, supposedly displaying the inverse relation of lawyers to economic vigor.[161] As fortunes change and the United States is again regarded as outperforming its economic rivals,[162] it remains to be seen how many of those who were so outspoken about the deleterious effect of lawyers will retain their conviction of the close linkage of legal activity to economic performance.

A media pundit tells us, "It's an 'only in America' spectacle that we have here where products that are later proven to be perfectly safe are driven off the market by lawyers."[163] President Bush, lamenting the debilitating effects of litigation against corporations, stresses that "[o]nly the United States has seen the number of lawyers double over a 20 year period."[164] Actually, lawyer populations have been growing even faster elsewhere. Between the years 1965 and 1985, the number of lawyers in the United States roughly doubled. But the rate of growth of the legal profession was higher in Canada, England, France, and Germany, to take only a few places for which data is readily available.[165] In other respects as well, other industrial democracies seem less different from the United States. All have taken part in a tremendous enlargement of the legal world: the amount and complexity of regulation; the frequency of litigation; the amount of authoritative legal material; the number, coordination, and productivity of lawyers; the number of legal actors and the resources they devote to legal activity; the amount of information about law and the velocity with which it circulates—all of these have multiplied several times over.[166]

Comparisons with supposedly less legalistic and contentious populations elsewhere do not invariably show Americans to be more litigious and legalistic.[167] Several recent and detailed comparisons place more emphasis on the similarities that interlace the differences in litigation patterns. A study comparing tort litigation in the United States, Britain, and Germany concludes with the surmise that "the differences that exist between the systems are much less spectacular than they are commonly believed to be once allowance has been made for differences in cost of medical care, standard of living and the cost and method of funding litigation."[168] A study of medical malpractice claims in the United States, Canada, and England takes up the "similar growth in malpractice litigation during the 1970s and 1980s" and takes this "parallelism [to] suggest . . . that this growth must arise less from isolated doctrinal changes in one country than from changes in medical practice and social mores, which occur roughly simultaneously in most Western countries."[169] These convergences are more remarkable because the other countries place far less reliance on courts and litigation to deal with compensation for injury than is the case in the United States.[170]

Swift and incessant currents of American influence are flowing through the legal systems of the industrialized world and spilling over into ex-second and third worlds. As one European observer sums it up, "almost all fundamental and far-reaching changes in European law and understanding of law during the post-war period have started from America."[171] American styles of structuring business relations, drafting contracts, regulating financial markets, and protecting injury victims have infiltrated into European legal practice.[172] There is massive borrowing of American institutional devices from constitutionalism and judicial review[173] to the large business law firm,[174] alternative dispute resolution,[175] and public interest law.[176] The lopsided infusion of procedural and substantive law, of general concepts and perspectives, of new images of lawyering, and of new organizational forms has provoked European observers to compare the contemporary wave of Americanization to the transformative reception of Roman law that produced modern European law.[177]

B. Characterizing American Distinctiveness

When we discount for exaggerated notions of American uniqueness and for the enticements of cultural nostalgia, America *is* different and some things *have* changed. Beneath the illusion and caricature of these "only in America" and "good old days" fantasies lie genuine and serious questions about the distinctive character of American legal life.

The nostalgic component of the jaundiced view points to real changes as well as imaginary ones. Before World War II, American law in practice provided little remedy for have-nots against dominant groups. Lawrence Friedman described the late nineteenth century tort system as a "system of non-compensation" in which few claims were brought and plaintiffs faced an array of doctrinal, practical, and cultural barriers to recovery.[178] Studying personal injury cases in New York City over a forty-year period, Randolph Bergstrom concludes that "[t]he injured had few reasons to think that lawsuits would offer a ready source of sustenance in 1870, less still in 1910."[179] My own review of pre-World War II disasters shows that compensation was uncertain and meager.[180] Successful claims by those in subordinate positions—workers, minorities, prisoners—against bosses and authorities were few and far between.

In this respect, law has changed. Compensation for many of life's troubles has become routine, through social insurance (ranging from social security disability payments to federal insurance of bank deposits) and through use of the litigation system.[181] Expectations of remedy and compensation have risen.[182] Legal representation of victims is more available and more competent.[183] There is more "litigation up" by outsiders and clients and dependents against authorities and managers of established institutions. The leeways and immunities from legal accountability of the powerful have shrunk, and there is a sense of enhanced and oppressive exposure. It is this exposure that excites much of the reproach of our litigious society. To many members of the elite, lawyers are no longer pillars of the established order but are recast as enemies of established interests. Thus a *Wall Street Journal* columnist observed that "lawyers are replacing trade unions as the main scourge of the business community."[184] In a situation where many elite groups feel threatened by social and legal changes, the underlying and ineradicable themes of hostility toward lawyers are available to decipher and explain these troubling developments.

Enlarged responsiveness to the concerns of ordinary people does not imply a lessening of legal attention to the concerns of dominant groups. The system is more inclusive, but all parts of it have grown. During the era of expanding responsiveness to victims and outsiders, there was even greater growth in legal activity on behalf of dominant groups: litigation by businesses increased more rapidly than litigation by individuals;[185] legal expenditures by businesses and government increased more rapidly than expenditures by individuals;[186] the large firm sector of the legal profession that provides services for corporations and large organizations grew and prospered more than the small firm sector that services individuals.[187]

America is a society that absorbs huge amounts of law and lawyering—both absolutely and compared to other industrial democracies. Even when we adjust for the different occupational structure and nomenclature of providers of legal services, it is clear that the United States supports far more lawyers per capita than do other industrial democracies.[188] I would argue that this reliance on lawyers is the effect, rather than the cause, of a decentralized legal regime in which any activity is subject to multiple bodies of regulation; where the application of those rules depends on complex and perhaps unknowable states of fact; where decision-makers produce not definitive and immutable rulings but contingent temporary resolutions that are open to further challenge; where outcomes are subject to contestation in multiple forums by an expanding legion of organized and persistent players who invest increasing amounts in more technically sophisticated legal services. The allegiance of the lawyers that provide these services is less to their guild than to their clients, whose views they absorb and whose interests they champion. Mark Osiel points out that American lawyers are different not only in their "unqualified partisanship" but also in the kind of knowledge that comprises their expertise.[189] They provide not only technical mastery of legal texts but "practical judgement: discernment in predicting how courts will balance, in light of underlying policy and principle, the relative significance of particular features of a complex factual configuration."[190] The distinctive scope and role of American lawyers underlies their prominence in the American political and cultural scene. As the myth of lawyers undermining American competitiveness attests, they are seen as major actors responsible for major problems.

Through this decentralized, endlessly receptive, and very expensive system, we attempt to pursue our multiple and colliding individual and social visions of substantive justice.[191] We want our legal institutions to yield both comprehensive policy embodying shared public values and facilities for the relentless pursuit of individual interests. But we are suspicious of the concentrated authority required for the former and reluctant to support the elaborated public machinery required to provide the latter routinely to ordinary citizens. We prefer fragmented government and reactive legal institutions with limited resources, so that in large measure both the making of public policy and the vindication of individual claims are delegated to the parties themselves who are left to fend according to their own resources. In such a complex system, lawyers form a major component of these resources. But lawyers, each attached to her own client, cannot fulfill the fatally divided promise of substantive justice.[192]

Does this more capacious and more complex law bring with it more justice? Surely, yes, but paradoxically it is simultaneously accompanied by an increase in injustice. Injustice is something bad that someone ought to do something about. As the risks of everyday life have declined dramatically, there is a widespread sense that science, technology, and government can produce solutions for many of the remaining problems.[193] As more things are capable of being done by human institutions, the line between what is seen as unavoidable misfortune and what is seen as imposed injustice shifts.[194] The realm of injustice is enlarged. Hurricanes are misfortunes; but inadequate warning, insufficient preparation, and bungled relief efforts may be injustices. Once, having an incurable disease was an unalterable misfortune; now a perception of treatment withheld or insufficient vigor in pursuing a cure can give rise to a claim of injustice. As the scope of possible interventions broadens, more and more terrible things become defined by the incidence of potential intervention. Thus, poverty, disease, and disability are not unalterable fate, but a matter of appropriate interventions. Our consciousness of injustice increases, not because the world is a worse place, but because it is in important ways a better, more just place.

Just as our longer and healthier lives call for more medical attention, every addition to human capacity for control and remedy enlarges the legal world. It can safely be predicted that health care delivery, genetic engineering, and the information superhighway—to pick just a few matters from today's headlines—will, at the same time that they address old needs, spawn vast thickets of new law and create new needs. As resources increase and expectations rise and new claims for remedy are vindicated, new vistas of injustice unfold.

The American legal setting—in which decisions responding to claims based on our competing commitments are fragmented among multiple regulators, superintended but not controlled by independent courts—gives full play to the ambiguities and strains in the lawyer role. As lawyers devise more complex public structures and embellish innovative pursuit of conflicting client interests within and around those public structures, the inevitable tensions of the lawyer's role are accentuated. Lawyers seem to be ushering us ever further from the legal idyll of substantive justice that is direct, simple, and accessible. It comes as no surprise that they are blamed for both a surfeit of law and a shortage of justice.

How distinctive are these American developments? Is America on an idiosyncratic detour, or is it launched on a pioneering excursion into territory that will soon be common ground? Will this fluid, flexible, ubiquitous law, responsive to enhanced expectations for justice, prove to have a general and transforming appeal in other societies in the way that the (now transnational) consumer culture has? Or will these American formations turn out to be just one of the legal idioms through which the life of modern societies can be conducted?

Some would take the extensive borrowing of American institutions and devices as an indication that America is leading the way to a convergent transnational legal culture. But legal cultures, like languages, can absorb huge amounts of foreign material while preserving a distinctive structure and flavor. Yet even as the various legal cultures remain distinct, they seem to be driven by similar demands to address many of the same problems and increasingly they draw upon a common repertoire of responses.

The enlargement of the legal world is not an exclusively American phenomenon, but a general one.[195] Other nations seem to be moving toward this soft, pluralized, participative, expensive law, with more lawyers who play a more central and expansive role.[196] As these lawyers become more adaptable and more useful to an enlarged cast of legal actors, they may well join their American counterparts as targets of discontent.

Anti-lawyer feeling varies in both intensity and focus. Of course, episodes of elevated anti-lawyer feeling are never entirely new; they draw on old themes. But they are never just reruns. Such episodes are about more than lawyers: they are about people's responses to the legal system and the wider society in which it is set. The level of discontent with lawyers may be sharply elevated and intensified by groundless panic about the legal system. The most recent round of American lawyer-bashing exhibits elite reaction to the pervasiveness and expense of law and to its new inclusiveness and accountability. This "too much law" critique supplanted the earlier "not enough justice" critique that focused on lawyers' betrayal of their public duties. To my knowledge, no prescient analyst predicted this shift in the most visible and vehement critique of the legal profession. This should induce modesty about imagining that we know what is coming next. None of the basic themes of criticism is going to disappear, since they are rooted in the lawyer's role. As we expect ever more of the law and become ever more aware of its shortcomings,[197] the focus of discontent with lawyers may shift once again, but there is little reason to think that its intensity will abate more than temporarily.

Notes

1. This is an expanded version of the John A. Sibley Lecture, delivered at the University of Georgia School of Law, March 17, 1993. I would like to thank Dean C. Ronald Ellington, Associate Dean Paul Kurtz, and their colleagues for their gracious hospitality. In addition to presenting this material at the conference on Legal Cultures and The Legal Profession, from which this volume has been published, I had presented variants of the paper at the Legal Profession Workshop at Stanford Law School, and at a panel on adversarial legalism at the June 1993 meetings of the Law and Society Association. I am

grateful to the participants in these exchanges and to Richard Abel, Robert Gordon, John Lande, and Robert Post for challenging responses and helpful advice. Chris Burke provided able research assistance and the law libraries at Stanford and the University of Wisconsin provided indispensible and dedicated support. I am indebted to Herbert Jacob for sharing his collection of public opinion data, to Mark Osiel for permission to quote from his unpublished work, and to Doreen Weisenhaus for making available unpublished data from the 1986 *National Law Journal* survey.

2. *See, e.g.*, Max Radin, "The Ancient Grudge: A Study in the Public Relations of the Legal Profession," *Virginia Law Review* 32:734, 740-52 (1946) (summarizing historical sources of lawyer-bashing from Ancient Greece to present).

3. These four clusters summarize most of the prevalent substantive gripes about lawyers. However, the public discourse about lawyers includes several more general themes of condemnation that focus not on their deeds but on their character and standing. One brands lawyers as morally obtuse, lacking common decencies and deficient in common sentiments. Another identifies them as objects of scorn, to be despised precisely because they are such objects. While many of the prevalent anti-lawyer jokes refer to specific grievances about lawyers, there are others that allude to their general moral deficiency or celebrate the shared contempt for them (e.g., Q. "What do you call sixty thousand lawyers at the bottom of the sea?" A. "A good start.").

4. William F. Buckley, Jr., "Nobody Loves Lawyers Any More," *Washington Star*, 27 October 1977, A15.

5. Warren E. Burger, Annual Message on the Administration of Justice at the Midyear Meeting of the American Bar Association 13 (12 February 1984) [hereinafter Burger, Annual Message] (transcript on file with author).

Robert J. Samuelson, "Hustling the System," *Washington Post*, 23 December 1992, A17.

7. Charles Peters, "How Your Lawyer Does It," *Washington Monthly*, February 1974, 33, 37.

8. Versions of this story may be found in virtually any collection of lawyer jokes. This one is taken from Blanche Knott, *Truly Tasteless Lawyer Jokes*, 73 (1990).

9. Michael Castleman, "Just Say Nolo," *California Lawyer*, August 1992, 182, 184 (quoting Nolo Press founder Jake Warner).

10. *See generally* Robert C. Post, On the Popular Image of the Lawyer: "Reflections in a Dark Glass," *California Law Review* 75:379 (1987) (exploring the organization of "profoundly contradictory" popular attitudes toward lawyers). *See also* Marvin W. Mindes, "Trickster, Hero, Helper: A Report on the Lawyer Image," *American Bar Foundation Research Journal* 1982:177, 211 (empirically documenting tension among contradictory images of lawyers) ("[T]he lawyer finds himself in a conflicted world in which one must be both Tricky and Helpful to maximize admiration, while being Helpful requires that one is not Tricky and being Tricky requires that one is not Helpful.").

11. President James E. Carter, Address at the 100th Anniversary Dinner of the Los Angeles Bar Association (4 May 1978), reprinted in "President Carter's Attack on Lawyers, President Spann's Response, and the Chief Justice Burger's Remarks," *American Bar Association Journal* 64:840 (1978) [hereinafter "Carter's Attack on Lawyers"].

12. "Carter's Attack on Lawyers," 842.

13. Ibid.

14. Ibid., 843.

15. Ibid., 842.

16. Ibid.

17. Ibid.

18. Ibid., 844.

19. Ibid., 846. Carter's address is the direct descendant of an unheralded Law Day speech at the University of Georgia School of Law, delivered four years earlier, when he was Governor of Georgia. In that speech, he traced his understanding about justice and "what's right and wrong in this society" to reading Reinhold Neibuhr and listening to the songs of Bob Dylan. Governor James E. Carter, Address at The University of Georgia School of Law, Law Day (1975) in *Addresses of Jimmy Carter (James Earl Carter), Governor of Georgia 1971-1975*, 261 (Ben W. Fortson, Jr., Sec. of State, ed., 1975). Cataloging the injustices of the legal system, he chastised lawyers for tolerating injustice, lacking fire to improve the system of which they were part, avoiding the obligation to "restore equity and justice and to preserve or enhance it," and being distracted from the pursuit of justice into self-serving concern for their own well-being and authority. Ibid. He closed with the reflection, echoed four years later, that the State could be transformed if the body of attorneys were deeply committed to abolish the inequities of the system. Ibid. Apparently the speech was from notes and there is no text. The version that appears in his book of addresses was apparently reconstructed from a tape recording.

Fortuitously, the audience that day included gonzo journalist Hunter Thompson, who reports Carter telling him in 1976, "[T]hat was probably the best speech I ever made." Hunter S. Thompson, "Fear and Loathing on the Campaign Trail '76, Third Rate Romance, Low Rent Rendezvous," *Rolling Stone*, 3 June 1976, 54, 64. Viewing it as "the heaviest and most eloquent thing I have ever heard from the mouth of a politician," Thompson extended an enthusiastic endorsement of Carter's candidacy for the Democratic presidential nomination. Ibid.

20. Tom Goldstein, "Carter's Attack on Lawyers'" *New York Times*, 6 May 1978, 11 ("[L]eading lawyers around the country reacted with anger, bitterness, frustration and sadness yesterday to President Carter's assertion that the legal profession has been an impediment to social justice.") On behalf of the American Bar Association, its President, William B. Spann, responded that "we disagree sharply with the implications of the president's remarks" and accused him of "tak[ing] the popular course of attacking the professions" to distract attention from foreign problems, inflation, and his political vulnerability. "Carter's Attack on Lawyers," 841. In President Spann's view, Carter's speech was a simplistic distraction from the ceaseless and constructive efforts of lawyers to solve the problems of the justice system. Ibid.; *see also Congressional Record* 124:H13939 (daily ed. 16 May 1978) (statement of Rep. Kastenmeier) (characterizing President's remarks as harsh and inaccurate).

21. *E.g.*, "The Law's Delay," *Wall Street Journal*, 10 May 1978, 24 (noting that since "Washington itself has become the fountainhead of unnecessary laws and litigation," the President should spend "less time lashing out at lawyers in general and more time asking the government's lawyers just what it is they are trying to do"); "Mr. Carter's Class Struggle," *Washington Post*, 7 May 1978, C6 (dismissing President's remarks as "unfocused resentment").

22. Two-thirds of a national sample of registered voters polled by Yankelovich, Skelly and White thought the President's criticism of the legal profession was fair. Roper Center, Public Opinion Online, 1989, *available in* LEXIS, NEWS, ARCNWS Library (accession no. 0132789). A Roper poll of a national sample of adults found 53% who thought his criticisms were justified and another 16% who thought them partly justified. Ibid. (accession no. 0116933). The public was equally critical of doctors, whom Carter criticized

The Assault on Civil Justice: The Anti-Lawyer Dimension

in responding to questions the day after his lawyer speech, as of lawyers. *Ibid.* (accession no. 0132788).

Carter was not entirely lacking in elite support. In addition to the figures discussed below, his critique was defended by his Secretary of State, who called for "innovative approaches for making justice available for all." Peter Kihss, "Vance, at Fordham Law Graduation, Calls for 'Innovative' Justice," *New York Times*, 29 May 1978, 9. Admiral Hyman J. Rickover also supported the President, attacking lawyers for "making a great negative contribution to our defense." Bernard Weinraub, "Rickover Asserts Lawyers' Tactics Hinder Military," *New York Times*, 31 March 1979, 22.

23. *See, e.g.*, John W. Sheppard, "Ethics," *Florida Bar Journal* 49:184 (1975) ("With the overflow of Watergate and the revelation that a great majority of the offenders were members of the legal profession, the public image of the Bar seems to have reached a low ebb. . . . There seems to be a rising tide of resentment to the entire profession who [sic] guides the legal system in our country.").

24. Abraham S. Blumberg, "The Practice of Law as a Confidence Game: Cooptation of a Profession", *Law and Society Review* 1:15 (1967).

25. Murray Teich Bloom, *The Trouble With Lawyers* (1968).

26. Linda Greenhouse, "Breitel Tells Lawyers that Greed is Undermining Their Profession," *New York Times*, 3 May 1977, 1 (quoting New York State Court of Appeals Chief Justice Charles Breitel).

27. *See* Marvin E. Frankel, *Partisan Justice* (1980) (critiquing public justice and faulting lawyers for serving their clients with such obdurate partisanship as to eclipse their duties to the wider system of justice). Frankel was a member of the Kutak Commission, discussed in note 38.

28. 29. Jerold S. Auerbach, *Unequal Justice: Lawyers and Social Change in Modern America* (1992).

29. Lesley Oelsner, "Coleman Asserts Bar Fails Public," *New York Times*, 8 August 1976, 25 (quoting Secretary of Transportation William Coleman).

30. Ibid. (quoting former ABA President Chesterfield Smith).

31. Ralph Nader, *Overview to Verdicts on Lawyers* vii, viii, ed. Ralph Nader and Mark Green (1976).

32. Ibid. at ix.

33. Jethro K. Lieberman, *Crisis at the Bar: Lawyers' Unethical Ethics and What to Do about It* (1978).

34. *See generally* Burton A. Weisbrod, Joel F. Handler and Neil K. Komesar, *Public Interest Law: An Economic and Institutional Analysis* (1978) (providing economic and institutional analysis of public interest movement); *Council for Public Interest Law, Balancing the Scales of Justice: Financing Public Interest Law in America* (1976) (discussing potential approaches to funding public interest law).

35. *See generally* the multi-volume *Access to Justice*, ed. Mauro Cappelletti (1978); *Access to Justice and the Welfare System*, ed. Mauro Cappelletti (1981).

36. *E.g.*, Frankel, *Partisan Justice*, 124; Philip M. Stern, *Lawyers on Trial*, 199 (1980).

37. The American Bar Association's Special Commission on Evaluation of Professional Standards was known as the Kutak Commission. The impetus for a new ethics code came in part from the damage to the bar's public image occasioned by Watergate. *See* William B. Spann, Jr., "The Legal Profession Needs a New Code of Ethics," *Bar Leader*, November-December 1977, 2 (relating ABA President's charge to Kutak Commission).

38. Ted Schneyer, "Professionalism as Bar Politics: The Making of the Model Rules of Professional Conduct," *Law and Social Inquiry* 14:677 (1989).

39. Ibid.

40. Gerald J. Clark, "Fear and Loathing in New Orleans: The Sorry Fate of the Kutak Commission's Rules," *Suffolk University Law Review* 17:79, 85 (1983). Ted Schneyer points out that, although a number of the Commission's major innovations were jettisoned, the Model Rules in many ways accommodated elements of the public justice critique:

> They . . . invite lawyers . . . to take their own values into account. They permit lawyers to refuse on moral grounds to represent would-be clients; authorize lawyers to "limit the objectives" of representation by excluding aims they find "repugnant or imprudent"; and in a remarkable concession to lawyers' sensibilities allow them to withdraw whenever "a client insists upon pursuing an objective the lawyer considers repugnant or imprudent"—even if the client's interest will be "adversely affected" by the withdrawal!

Schneyer, *Professionalism as Bar Politics*, 736 (footnotes omitted).

41. Thus, in the mid-1980s, the ABA's Commission on Professionalism recommended:

> A far greater emphasis must be placed by the Bar on the role of the lawyer as both an officer of the court and, more broadly, as an officer of the system of justice. . . . [L]awyers must avoid identifying too closely with their clients.

ABA Commission on Professionalism, In the Spirit of Public Service (1986) [hereinafter *Stanley Report*] (known as the *Stanley Report*, for Chair Justin Stanley).

42. "Why Everybody is Suing Everybody,"*U.S. News & World Report*, 4 December 1978, 50.

43. Chief Justice Warren E. Burger, *Agenda for 2000 A.D.—A Need for Systematic Anticipation*, Address delivered at the National Conference on the Causes of Popular Dissatisfaction with the Administration of Justice (7-9 April 1976), in *F.R.D.* 70:79 (1976) [known as the Pound Conference, after Roscoe Pound's 1906 address of the same title. Like Pound, his 1976 successors propounded "popular" perceptions unaided by any discernable consultation of the broader public].

44. These concerns antedate Carter's 1978 speech. Burger's Address to the 1976 Pound Conference contains faint echoes of the public justice critique in the Chief Justice's observation of "the loss of public confidence caused by lawyers' using the courts for their own ends rather than with a consideration of the public interest." Ibid. But the predominant theme of the Chief Justice's address is not a shortage of justice, but surfeit of law. Ibid. at 91. Just a year later, the Chief Justice was warning that "unless we devise substitutes for the courtroom processes—and do so quickly—we may well be on our way to a society overrun by hordes of lawyers, hungry as locusts, and brigades of judges in numbers never before contemplated." Chief Justice Warren E. Burger, *Remarks at the American Bar Association Minor Disputes Resolution Conference* (27 May 1977).

45. *See generally* Joseph Sanders and Craig Joyce, "'Off to the Races': The 1980s Tort Crisis and the Law Reform Process," *Houston Law Review* 27:207 (1990); Eliot Martin Blake, Comment, "Rumors of Crisis: Considering the Insurance Crisis and Tort Reform in an Information Vacuum," *Emory Law Journal* 37:401 (1988).

46. See generally *Access to Justice, supra* note 36; *Access to Justice and the Welfare System, supra* note 35.

The Assault on Civil Justice: The Anti-Lawyer Dimension

47. "Alternatives" were very much part of the *Access to Justice* repertoire. The General Report of the great multi-volume compendium on *Access to Justice* includes a section on "Devising Alternative Methods to Decide Legal Claims" that discusses arbitration, conciliation, and settlement. Mauro Cappelletti and Bryant Garth, *Access to Justice: The Worldwide Movement to Make Rights Effective, A General Report*, in *Access to Justice, supra* note 45, 1:3, 59-107; *see also* Richard Danzig, "Toward the Creation of a Complementary, Decentralized System of Criminal Justice," *Stanford Law Review* 26:1 (1973) (analyzing concept of decentralized criminal justice system as means to provide access to justice); Richard Danzig and Michael J. Lowy, "Everyday Disputes and Mediation in the United States: A Reply to Professor Felstiner," *Law and Society Review* 9:675, 685-87 (1975) (calling for supplementation of ineffective court system by informal, non-coercive "community moots").

Although these themes of enlarging justice occasionally surface in current discourse on alternatives, they are vastly overshadowed by concerns to expedite case processing, deflect institutional burdens, and curtail exposure to liability. *See* Carrie Menkel-Meadow, "Pursuing Settlement in an Adversary Culture: A Tale of Innovation Co-opted or The Law of ADR," *Florida State University Law Review* 19:1 (1991) (providing eloquent response to this shift in concerns).

48. These larger assertions about the civil justice system were embodied in oft-related atrocity stories about outrageous claims and monstrous decisions. *See* Stephen Daniels, "The Question of Jury Competence and the Politics of Civil Justice Reform," *Law and Contemporary Problems* 52:269, 292-97 (1989); Robert M. Hayden, "The Cultural Logic of a Political Crisis," *Studies in Law, Politics and Society* 95, 104-08 (1991); Steven Brill and James Lyons, "The Not-so-Simple Crisis," *American Lawyer*, 1 May 1986, 1; Fred Strasser, "Tort Tales: Old Stories Never Die," *National Law Journal*, 16 February 1987, 39.

49. The Council on Competitiveness did not include the 70% figure in its *Agenda*, President's Council on Competiveness, Agenda for Civil Justice Reform in America (1991), but apparently there had been some consideration of it in the preparation of the Vice President's August 13 speech, for a week earlier "a Quayle spokesman" was reported as having "noted that the United States has 70 percent of the world's lawyers, and that the rising tide of litigation 'is a burden on our economy.'" Saundra Torry, "BCCI Scandal a Windfall for Attorneys Unlike Any Other," *Washington Post*, 12 August 1991, F5. The drafters of the Council's *Agenda* had reason to be aware that seventy percent was a falsehood. On page one of the *Agenda*, there is an approving reference to, but not citation for, "a recent report by a Professor of Finance at the University of Texas . . . [that] estimated that the average lawyer takes $1 million a year from the country's output of goods and services." The report referred to is chapter eight of Stephen P. Magee et al., *Black Hole Tariffs and Endogenous Policy Theory* 111-21 (1989). That source contains an incomplete listing of the number of lawyers in some 34 countries as of 1983. Ibid., 120-21. Even this inadequate enumeration showed American lawyers as just 45% of the total. Ibid. One can conclude that the Council staff either did not examine the source they approvingly cite, or that they were aware that there was good reason to believe the seventy percent figure was spurious.

50. Among the earliest sightings was a news magazine report that "[t]he U.S. has 610,000 lawyers, two thirds of the world's total . . . . About 70 percent are in private prac-

tice." "The Pervasive Influence of Lawyers," *U.S. News & World Report*, 1 November 1982, 55. (Could this be the origin of the 70% figure?) A few months earlier, James Spensley, a lecturer at the University of Denver Law School, was quoted as saying "[T]he U.S. has become the world's most litigious society, employing over two thirds of the world's lawyers." David F. Salisbury, "Colorado's Quality of Life Fades in a Changing West," *Christian Science Monitor*, 30 July 1982, 4.

51. *See* Burger, Annual Message. The Chief Justice stated: "[I]t has been reported that about two-thirds of all the lawyers in the world are in the United States and of those, one-third have come into practice in the past five years." Ibid. A very similar item appeared a few months earlier in a contribution to *Legal Times* by New York lawyer Peter Megargee Brown, who stated that "two-thirds of all the lawyers in the world are in the United States. One-third of all lawyers in this country have been in practice less than five years." Peter Megargee Brown, "Profession Endangered by Rush to Business Ethic," *Legal Times*, 26 September 1983, 10.

The Chief Justice's "two-thirds" observation was taken as factual by a sympathetic *Washington Post*. "Bench to Bar: Shape Up," *Washington Post*, 14 February 1984, A18. It was subsequently used by Justice O'Connor and others. Milly McLean, UPI, 9 April 1984, *available in* LEXIS, News Library, UPSTAT File. Similarly, a law school dean noted in an op-ed in the *Wall Street Journal* that "two-thirds of the world's lawyers now practice in this country, and one-third of these were graduated during the past five years." Ernest Gellhorn, "Too Much Law, Too Many Lawyers, Not Enough Justice," *Wall Street Journal*, 7 June 1984, 28. This item became part of the speeches of Governor Lamm of Colorado about America's descent to doom. *See, e.g.*, Richard W. Larsen, "Time to Restore Logic to Public Policies," *Seattle Times*, 14 October 1990, A18; John J. Sanko, "Governor Addresses Businessmen," *UPI*, 3 November 1983, *available in* LEXIS, News Library, UPSTAT File.

52. For example, cabinet members Mossbacher and Sullivan, and Senators Dole, McConnell, and Grassley, among many others. *See* Marc Galanter, "News from Nowhere: The Debased Debate on Civil Justice," *Denver Law Review* 71:77 (1993) [hereinafter Galanter, "News from Nowhere"]. This figure was also solemnly reported as fact by several media experts, such as David Gergen. David Gergen, "America's Legal Mess," *U.S. News & World Report*, 19 August 1991, 72. Likewise, William Buckley noted that Quayle's speech "reminded us that 70 percent of the lawyers in the world are American." William Buckley, "Invisible Hand Tripped Up by Burden of Lawyer Glut," *Austin Am.-Statesman*, 30 October 1991, A19. In the May, 1992 issue of *Commentary*, Francis Fukuyama wrote that "there is something wrong with an economy that employs 70 percent of the world's lawyers." Paul L. Berger et al., "Is America on the Way Down? (Round Two)," *Commentary*, May 1992, 20, 21.

53. *See* Galanter, "News from Nowhere," 79, n.10 (presenting calculation and documentation).

54. "I don't think it is healthy for the United States to have 70 percent of the world's lawyers. We have only 5 percent of the world's population. There ought to be a more equitable balance between population and the number of lawyers." Press Conference with Vice President J. Danforth Quayle, Federal News Service, 4 February 1992, *available in* LEXIS, News Library, FEDNEW File [hereinafter Vice President Quayle, Press Conference].

55. Gergen, "America's Legal Mess," 72. "Clearly, we need to de-lawyer our Ibid. Governor Lamm had various proposals to "de-lawyer" the American system. *See* Larson, "Time to Restore Logic to Public Policies," A18.

The Assault on Civil Justice: The Anti-Lawyer Dimension

56. The nuanced version of this diversion argument was put forward in 1983 by Derek Bok. Derek C. Bok, "A Flawed System," *Harvard Magazine* 85(5):38 (1983). He spoke of "a massive diversion of exceptional talent into pursuits that often add little to the growth of the economy, the pursuit of culture, or the enhancement of the human spirit." Ibid., 41. Like Carter and unlike many later critics, Bok was also concerned with issues of maldistribution of law: "[T]here is far too much law for those who can afford it and far too little for those who cannot." Ibid., 38-39. The "other great problem of our legal system [is] lack of access for the poor and the middle class." Ibid., 41.

57. In Magee's research, the lawyer population is measured as a ratio to either doctors or white collar workers, which are both taken as to reflect the size of the productive work force of a society. See note 60.

58. Frank B. Cross, "The First Thing We Do, Let's Kill All the Economists: An Empirical Evaluation of the Effect of Lawyers on the United States Economy and Political System," *Texas Law Review* 70:645 (1992) [hereinafter Cross, "First Thing"].

59. Charles R. Epp, "Do Lawyers Impair Economic Growth?" *Law and Social Inquiry* 17:585 (1992) [hereinafter Epp, "Do Lawyers"]; Charles R. Epp, "Toward New Research on Lawyers and the Economy," *Law and Social Inquiry* 17:695 (1992) [hereinafter Epp, "New Research"]; Cross, "First Thing."

60. Stephen P. Magee, "The Invisible Foot and the Waste of Nations: Lawyers as Negative Externalities," in Stephen P. Magee et al., *Black Hole Tariffs and Endogenous Policy Theory: Political Economy in General Equilibrium* (1989).

61. Ibid.

62. According to Magee's calculations, the optimal number in 1983 was 23 lawyers per 1,000 white collar workers; the U.S. had about 38/1,000 in that year. Stephen P. Magee, "Letter to the Editor," *Wall Street Journal*, 24 September 1992, A17.

63. Ibid.

64. David S. Clark, "The Selection and Accountability of Judges in West Germany: Implementation of a Rechtsstaat," *Southern California Law Review* 61:1795, 1807 (1988).

65. Stephen P. Magee, "The Optimum Number of Lawyers: A Reply to Epp," *Law and Social Inquiry* 17:667 (1992). In that article, Magee also presents statistical results using lawyer data for a number of countries from 1975. Epp shows that those results are very tenuous, depending on one outlier (the United States); if that outlier is removed from the sample of countries, Magee's discovered relationship between lawyers and growth disappears. Yet one country cannot justifiably be used as the basis for statistical conclusions. Epp demonstrates that Magee's 1975 lawyer data are "largely his own creation" and are "no better than a guess." Epp, "New Research," 702.

66. *E.g.*, Epp, "Do Lawyers"; Epp, "New Research."

67. Magee, "The Optimum Number of Lawyers," 675.

68. The research on lawyers in legislative bodies is cited by Epp. He finds "[t]he most persuasive explanations for the overrepresentation of lawyers in U.S. legislatures have nothing to do with the legal profession's ostensible interest in capturing the legislative process. Those explanations relate to the structure of political recruitment in the United States, where parties are weak and not class-based, and where entrepreneurial skills are important for political office, and to the advantage legislative service provides for lawyers seeking to advance their careers within the legal bureaucracy." Epp, "Do Lawyers," 590.

69. *E.g.*, Epp, "Do Lawyers"; Epp, "New Research"; Cross, "First Thing."

70. Paul W. McCracken, "The Big Domestic Issue: Slow Growth," *Wall Street Journal*, 4 October 1991, A12.

71. Michael Boskin, Remarks to the National Economists Club, Washington, D.C., Federal News Service, 31 March 1992, *available in* LEXIS, News Library.

72. The White House, Office of the Press Secretary, Fact Sheet: Access to Justice Act of 1992 (4 February 1992).

73. Vice President Quayle, Press Conference.

74. President George Bush, Remarks to the American Business Conference, Washington, D.C., Federal News Service, 7 April 1992, *available in* LEXIS, News Library, FEDNEW file [hereinafter President Bush, April 7, 1992 Remarks].

75. "[T]he civil justice reform is aimed at taking away the incentives that contingency fee plaintiff lawyers have to bring cases based on junk science." L. Gordon Crovitz, "Legal Limits: Prescription for Change; Historical Roots," on *MacNeil-Lehrer News Hour* (PBS television broadcast, 10 February 1992).

76. "[M]y opponent's campaign is being backed by practically every trial lawyer who ever wore a tasseled loafer." George Bush, "Acceptance Speech at the Republican National Convention," *in New York Times*, 22 August 1992, 9.

77. Crovitz, Legal Limits. The centrality of the plaintiffs' lawyer as demon is preserved by the theory that the bad sort of lawyers are the source of a spreading contamination of professional life. Thus Walter Olson speaks of the way that "the influx of contingency-fee lawyers into commercial and family litigation has begun to transform the style of practice in those fields." Walter Olson, *The Litigation Explosion: What Happened When America Unleased the Lawsuit*, 232 (1991). Olson seems unaware that corporate litigators need little instruction in hardball lawyering from "contingency-fee lawyers." For one of many possible examples, see the account of Thomas Austern, whose scorched earth tactics delayed inssuance of an FDA order on the labelling of peanut butter for twelve years. Mark J. Green, *The Other Government: The Unseen Power of Washington Lawyers*, ch. 6 (1975). Nor does Olson offer reliable guidance on the onset of such practices. He presents an excerpt from one of the classic accounts of hardball lawyering, referring to events half a century ago, as if it were evidence of novel conditions. Cravath litigator Bruce Bromley told Stanford law students in 1958:

I quickly realized in my early days at the bar that I could take the simplest antitrust case . . . and protract it for the defense almost to infinity.

Bruce Bromley, *Judicial Control of Antitrust Cases*, 23 F.R.D. 417, 417 (1958). Olson borrows an excerpt of the Bromley talk from a 1978 *Time Magazine* article, omitting the date of Bromley's talk. Olson, *The Litigation Explosion*, 231, 366.

78. Ronald E. Yates, "Lawyers Not Exempt from Quality Crusade," *Chicago Tribune*, 1 December 1991, (Business), 1 (quoting Richard Weise, General Counsel of Motorola). Weise also noted: "The root of America's penchant for litigation can be found in the nation's prolific law schools, which are admitting students and turning out lawyers at a rate well in excess of the nation's ability to employ them." Ibid.

79. Ibid.

80. Galanter, "News from Nowhere." A significant portion of the wealth that flows through the litigation system is justified compensation delivered to creditors and wronged parties. The Institute for Civil Justice estimated that the net compensation to plaintiffs in tort cases in 1985 was roughly half of the dollars spent on tort litigation. But the portion received by plaintiffs varied with the type of litigation: it was 52% in automobile torts, 43% in non-automobile torts, and only 37% in asbestos cases. Deborah R. Hensler et al., *Trends in Tort Litigation: The Story Behind the Statistics*, 29 (1987). I know of no data about the ratio of recoveries to total expenditures in non-tort litigation. This half (or more) of the

supposed cost is a cost to defendants, but it is not a cost of the system or a cost to the country, for the wealth is not lost, but only transferred to different hands. Controlling these inordinate transaction costs is a worthy project that should not be confounded with reducing the rights of claimants.

81. The costs attributable to present institutional arrangements are made to loom menacingly large by ignoring the costs of alternative arrangements for obtaining equivalent benefits. For example, if we were to forego the tort system's contribution to accident prevention, presumably people and businesses would make other expenditures to prevent and minimize injury. The savings from completely abolishing the tort system would not be all the billions that flow through it—nor even all the billions spent on it—but only that increment beyond what would be spent on the alternative means of protection. Therefore, a genuine assessment of the legal system would have to consider not only its costs, but both the benefits it produces and the cost of producing such benefits by alternative means. *See* Neil K. Komesar, "Injuries and Institutions: Tort Reform, Tort Theory, and Beyond," *New York University Law Review* 65:23 (1990); *see also* Peter L. Kahn, "Pricing the U.S. Legal System," *Christian Science Monitor*, 11 September 1992, 19.

82. Robert C. Clark, "Why So Many Lawyers? Are They Good or Bad?" *Fordham Law Review* 61:275 (1992).

83. Stephen McG. Bundy and Einer Richard Elhauge, "Do Lawyers Improve the Adversary System? A General Theory of Litigation Advice and Its Regulation," *California Law Review* 79:313 (1991).

84. Cross, "First Thing."

85. Ronald J. Gilson, "Value Creation by Business Lawyers: Legal Skills and Asset Pricing," *Yale Law Journal* 94:239 (1984).

86. Mark C. Suchman and Mia L. Cahill, "The Hired-Gun as Facilitator: Lawyers and the Suppression of Business Disputes in Silicon Valley," *Law and Social Inquiry* (forthcoming).

87. John W. Pitts, *Eleven Numbers Against Lawyer Legislation and Fees at the Bar* (n.p., 1843).

88. Ibid., 11, 13.

89. Ibid., 42. His argument that "lawyer legislating" is a major cause of bad policy anticipates Magee's concern. For a discussion of Magee's research, see *supra* notes 58-71 and accompanying text.

90. Pitts, *Eleven Numbers*, 5.

91. Ibid., 33.

92. Radin, *The Ancient Grudge: A Study in the Public Relations of the Legal Profession*, 748.

93. Maxwell H. Bloomfield, *American Lawyers in a Changing Society, 1776-1876* (1976).

94. Jesse Higgins, *Sampson Against the Philistines* (2d ed. 1805), 92, *quoted in* Bloomfield, *American Lawyers in a Changing Society, 1776-1876*, 48.

95. Castelman, *Just Say Nolo*, 182, 184 (quoting Jake Warner, one of the founders of Nolo Press, a leading publisher of do-it-yourself legal material).

96. Fred Rodell, *Woe Unto You, Lawyers!* (2d ed. 1957), 166.

97. Ibid., 16.

98. This characterization was particularly appealing to Rodell's most recent admirer: Rennard Strickland, "The Lawyer as Modern Medicine Man," *Southern Illinois University Law Journal* 11:203, 208 (1986).

110   *Marc Galanter*

99. Rodell, *Woe Unto You, Lawyers!*, 19.

100. Ibid., 121.

101. Ibid.

102. Ibid., 164.

103. Ibid., 131. *But see* ibid., 16 (accusing lawyers of being part of a "racket").

104. Ibid., 108.

105. Rodells' prescriptions for change are found in Chapter XI. The following passages give a sample of their flavor:

> The answer is to get rid of the lawyers and . . . run our civilization according to practical and comprehensible rules, dedicated to non-legal justice, to common-or-garden fairness that the ordinary man can understand, in the regulation of human affairs.
>
> . . . .
>
> A mining engineer could handle a dispute centering around the value of a coal-mine much more intelligently and therefore more fairly than any judge, untrained in engineering, can handle it. A doctor could handle a dispute involving a physical injury much more intelligently and therefore more fairly than any judge. . . .
>
> . . . .
>
> As a matter of fact, abolition of the lawyers and their Law might eventually lead to the virtual disappearance of courts as we know them today. Every written law—written, you remember, in comprehensible language—might be entrusted to a body of technical experts, to administer and apply it and make specific decisions under it. . . . [E]ach state would have, say, a Killing Commission to apply its laws about what are now called murder and manslaughter. Moreover, the decision of the technical experts who make up each commission would be final. There would be no appeals . . . .

Ibid., 167, 169-70, 176.

106. For example, the contemporary Texas anti-lawyer polemicist Alfred Adask states:

> Our entire judicial system has become an extortion racket designed to enrich lawyers at the expense of productive members of society. Almost every licensed, practicing lawyer is a beneficiary and co-conspirator in that extortion racket. . . .Lawyers are "political racketeers," "economic cannibals," and "social parasites" who "help . . . destroy America for a buck." Lawyers are: 98% bad people, lousy Americans, ethical cowards, professional socio paths who are almost certainly the primary cause of the social and economic decline of this nation.

Alfred Adask, "Daddy, Why Doesn't the Vice President Like You?," *Anti-Shyster*, January 1992, 12-13.

107. David Riesman, "Toward an Anthropological Science of Law and the Legal Profession," in *Individualism Reconsidered and Other Essays* (1954), 450. Compare Sally Engel Merry's observation in a contemporary urban court:

> If a case progresses to a pretrial conference or to a trial, the prosecutors and defense attorneys play a critical role in translating complex, emotional problems

The Assault on Civil Justice: The Anti-Lawyer Dimension *111*

> into narrow legal cases. They serve as the front line, cleansing problems of their emotionally chaotic elements and reducing them to cold rational issues.

Sally Engel Merry, *Getting Justice and Getting Even: Legal Consciousness Among Working-Class Americans* (1990), 148 [hereinafter Merry, *Getting Justice*].

 108. Lieberman, *Crisis at the Bar: Lawyers' Unethical Ethics and What to do About it*, 208-09.

 109. In at least some settings, lawyers spend considerable effort reducing their clients' sense of the determinacy and predictability of the law. For a contemporary example, see Austin Sarat and William L.F. Felstiner, "Law And Strategy in the Divorce Lawyer's Office," *Law and Society Review* 20:93 (1986).

 110. For example, most Americans believe that "[t]he legal system favors the rich and powerful over everyone else" and that "[l]awyers will (not) work as hard for poor clients as for clients who are rich and important." Barbara A. Curran, *The Legal Needs of the Public: The Final Report of a National Survey* (1977), 234. Sally Merry observes that her working class American court-users

> do not accept that the system is always fair, just, or even-handed. Experience in court leads them to think that the institution is erratic, unreliable, and sometimes ineffectual. For many, a sense of legal entitlement coexists with cynicism about power and influence within the government and the court system.

Merry, *Getting Justice*, 170. A comparable skepticism is displayed in surveys from Canada, where most respondents think of lawyers as manipulators who "are always finding loopholes to get around the law," Robert J. Moore, "Reflections of Canadians on the Law and the Legal System: Legal Research Institute Survey of Respondents in Montreal, Toronto and Winnipeg," *in Law in a Cynical Society? Opinion and the Law in the 1980s* (Dale Gibson and Janet K. Baldwin eds., 1985), 41, 53, and in England, where respondents think lawyers "[f]or a price . . . will use every trick in the book to help their clients," Brian Abel-Smith et al., *Legal Problems and the Citizen* (1973), 249-50.

 111. Much of the survey data reported in this section is derived from three national sample surveys, each conducted by telephone. Two of these surveys were conducted for the *National Law Journal*, the first in 1986 and the second in 1993. The third major survey was conducted for the American Bar Association in 1993.

The first of the *National Law Journal* surveys (n=1004) was published in David A. Kaplan, "The NLJ Poll Results: Take Heed, Lawyers," National Law Journal, 18 August 1986, S-2 [hereinafter Kaplan, "NLJ Poll"]. A second survey (n=815), which largely replicates the 1986 survey and thus provides a useful reading of recent changes, was conducted for the *National Law Journal* and the West Publishing Company by Penn & Schoen Associates, Inc. This survey was published in Randall Samborn, "Anti-Lawyer Attitude Up," *National Law Journal*, 9 August 1993, 1 [hereinafter Samborn, "Anti-Lawyer"].

The other 1993 survey (n=1202) was conducted by Peter D. Hart Research Associates, Inc., for the American Bar Association. It was reported in Gary A. Hengstler, "Vox Populi: The Public Perception of Lawyers: ABA Poll," *American Bar Association Journal*, Sept. 1993, 60 [hereinafter Hengstler, "Vox Populi"]. More extensive data can be found in Peter D. Hart Research Associates, *A Survey of Attitudes Nationwide Toward Lawyers and the Legal System* (Jan. 1993) [hereinafter *Hart Survey*].

 112. Kaplan, "NLJ Poll," Table 4.

113. Ibid., Table 6.

114. Samborn, "Anti-Lawyer," Graphs 4-5.

115. *Hart Survey*, 25.

116. Samborn, "Anti-Lawyer," (containing a steady number of "very satisfied" responses).

117. *Hart Survey*, 25.

118. ABC News/*Washington Post* Survey, May 1989 (on file with author).

119. Samborn, "Anti-Lawyer," 20. Samborn reviews figures from Gallup and Roper polls that suggest a downward trend in estimations of the ethical character of lawyers since the mid-1970s. Ibid.

120. *Hart Survey*, 5.

121. A useful summation of data for the period 1976-1993 is in American Bar Association, Commission on Advertising, *Lawyer Advertising at the Crossroads* (Chicago: American Bar Association, 1995), 64-65.

122. Samborn, "Anti-Lawyer," 1.

123. *Hart Survey*, 4-5.

124. Samborn, "Anti-Lawyer," 1.

125. *Hart Survey*, 13.

126. This pattern is not unique to present day America. In early modern England, antagonism to lawyers and blaming them for excessive litigation was highest among top people. C.W. Brooks, *Pettifoggers and Vipers of the Commonwealth: The 'Lower Branch' of the Legal Profession in Early Modern England* (1986), 136; Wilfred R. Prest, *The Rise of the Barristers: A Social History of the English Bar 1590-1640* (1986), 313.

127. Kaplan, "NLJ Poll," Table 9.

128. Samborn, "Anti-Lawyer," Question 4.

129. Ibid.

130. Ibid., Question 22.

131. Ibid., Table 6. They were among the most knowledgeable, least enthusiastic about mandatory pro bono service for lawyers, and most opposed to an elective federal judiciary. Ibid.

132. Mark N. Vamos, "The Verdict from the Corner Office," *Business Week*, 13 April 1992 66. This was a survey conducted by Louis Harris & Associates, in early 1992, of 400 senior executives drawn from the "*Business Week* Top 1000" companies. Ibid.

133. Ibid.

134. A survey of how the working of tort law was perceived by three elite groups in South Carolina (doctors, lawyers, and legislators) found that all of them overestimated the incidence of litigation, the percentage of cases that went to jury trial, the proportion of jury trials that were won by plaintiffs, and the size of judicial awards. Donald R. Songer, "Tort Reform in South Carolina: The Effect of Empirical Research on Elite Perceptions Concerning Jury Verdicts," *South Carolina Law Review* 39:585 (1988).

135. Fewer non-asbestos product liability cases are filed, plaintiffs have been less successful at trial, defendants have secured favorable opinions from the courts in an increasing number of cases, the number of punitive damage awards in product liability cases has decreased, and claims per dollar of product liability premium have fallen. *See generally* Galanter, "News from Nowhere."

136. In addition to eager consumers of folklore about litigation and lawyers, there are eager suppliers who have an interest in promoting lore about the litigation menace. *See, e.g.,* Daniels, *The Question of Jury Competence and the Politics of of Civil Justice Reform*

The Assault on Civil Justice: The Anti-Lawyer Dimension

(discussing insurance industry civil-justice campaign); Lauren B. Edelman et al., "Professional Construction of Law: The Inflated Threat of Wrongful Discharge," *Law and Society Review* 26:47 (1992) (finding exaggerated pessimistic lore about the dangers to corporations of employment discrimination suits promoted by personnel and legal professionals); Kenneth J. Chesebro, "Galileo's Retort: Peter Huber's Junk Scholarship," *American University Law Review* 42:1637, 1705-22 (1992-93) (regarding Manhattan Institute promotion of civil justice lore).

137.   *Hart Survey*, 16.

138.   Ibid.

139.   Samborn, "Anti-Lawyer," Question 23.

140.   Ibid.,Question 22.

141.   *Hart Survey*, 18.

142.   ABC News/*Washington Post* Survey, June 1985 (USACWP.196.R24) (on file with author).

143.   Curran, *The Legal Needs of the Public*, 234.

144.   The combined response is reported in the cover story, "How Lawyers Abuse the Law," *U.S. News & World Report*, 30 January 1994, 50, 52. The breakdown is from a news release by the magazine, dated 21 January 1995.

145.   Roper Report 87-7, July, 1987 (on file with author).

146.   Ibid.

147.   Yankelovich Partners and Talmey-Drake Research and Strategy, National Survey on Tort Reform: 1001 Registered Voters: Report and Percentages. Janaury 1995. Question 5.

148.   HALT was founded in 1977. The name was originally an acronym for "Help Abolish Legal Tyranny," but this was displaced by the less combative "An Organization of Americans for Legal Reform." In early 1988, it was reported that the organization had a staff of 26 and nearly 150,000 "members." "Help from HALT," *Washington Post*, 21 January 1988, B5. Since then, economic constraints have led to closing the field offices and cutting the staff to about a dozen; in 1992, membership was said to be about 100,000. Martha Middleton, "HALT: Rebels at a Crossroad," *Student Lawyer*, Sept. 1992, 21, 22. Grassroots and militant offshoots such as Justice for All and the National Congress for Legal Reform charged HALT with being unresponsive to its membership and too amicable with the bar. Ibid.

149.   "On the Front Burner," *The Legal Reformer* 12(1)1 (October-December 1991).

150.   Ibid.

151.   "White House, ABA Offer Tort Reforms," *The Legal Reformer* 12(3)6 (April-June 1992).

152.   Ibid.

153.   See Karen Riley, "Measure To Limit Product Lawsuits Shelved in Senate for this Session," *Washington Times*, 11 September 1992, C3 (stating President Bush's "attacks on the litigation system and on trial lawyers have consistently drawn some of the loudest cheers in his recent campaign stops").

154.   Business and other elites are not exempt from the current cultural style of finding solace and justification by displaying oneself as a victim. Popular strains of victimism are widely deplored. *See, e.g.*, Charles J. Sykes, *A Nation of Victims: The Decay of American Character* (1992); John Taylor, "Don't Blame Me: The New Culture of Victimization," *New York*, 3 June 1991, 26; Jesse Birnbaum, "Crybabies: Eternal Victims," *Time*, 12 August 1991, 16 (asserting that this is the "age of the victim"). Higher status

varieties are less celebrated. Sally Power, "They Did It!,"
Business Ethics, September/October 1993, 22 ("[O]ne might argue business itself has come to see itself as a victim, blaming the courts, the media, and the legal system for placing companies at risk.").

155.   This evidence is assessed in Galanter, "News from Nowhere," 90-99. The supposed bias of jurors against corporations is examined in Valerie P. Hans and William S. Lofquist, "Jurors' Judgments of Business Liability in Tort Cases: Implications for the Litigation Explosion Debate," *Law and Society Review* 26:85 (1992).

156.   In the most elaborated version of the jaundiced view, Olson, *The Litigation Explosion: What Happened When America Unleashed the Lawsuit*, there is recurrent reference to "the old legal system"—a normal orderly world in which the law was clear, judges were restrained, lawyers were upright, and litigation was rare. Ibid., 3; *see also* ibid., 142, 145, 155-56, 168, 216-19, 340. *See also* Peter Huber, *Liability: the Legal Revolution and Its Consequences* (1988). Huber's book is premised on the notion that "we are living in an altogether new legal environment, created in little more than twenty years, and profoundly different from what existed in this country and in England for six centuries before." Ibid. at 10. Huber makes references to the more rational and benign conditions that prevailed under "the old law." *E.g.*, ibid., 21, 23, 71, 96, 97, 116-19, 186.

157.   *See, e.g.*, David Engel, "The Oven Bird's Song: Insiders, Outsiders and Personal Injuries in an American Community," *Law and Society Review* 18:551, 551-52 (1984). Engel studied a small Illinois county in which concern about litigiousness was high, although there was relatively little litigation. Ibid. at 551. Although contract actions were almost ten times as frequent as personal injury cases, it was the latter that provoked concern because they controverted core community values of self-sufficiency and stoic endurance. Ibid. at 574-75. Engel concluded that denunciation of tort litigation was "significant mainly as a symbolic effort by members of the traditional community to preserve a sense of meaning and coherence in the face of social changes they found threatening and confusing." Ibid., 580.

158.   The literature is vast. The latest book-length entries are Mary Ann Glendon, *A Nation Under Lawyers: How the Crisis in the Legal Profession is Transforming American Society* (1994); Anthony T. Kronman, *The Lost Lawyer: Failing Ideals of the Legal Profession: Lawyering at the End of the Twentieth Century* (1994). Other recent contributors include Arlin M. Adams, "The Legal Profession: A Critical Evaluation," *Dickinson Law Review* 93:643, 652 (1989) ("[T]he . . . most pervasive manifestation of the change in the legal climate is the decline of professionalism and its replacement with commercialism."); Norman Bowie, "The Law: From Profession to a Business," *Vanderbilt Law Review* 41:741 (1988); Lincoln Caplan, "The Lawyers' Race to the Bottom," *New York Times*, 6 August 1993, A-29. A dyspeptic version of the declension theme is Peter Megargee Brown, *Rascals: The Selling of the Legal Profession* (1989). The bar's "official" account of the danger of commercialization is the *Stanley Report*.

159.   Marc Galanter and Thomas Palay, *Tournament of Lawyers: the Transformation of the Big Law Firm* (1991), 11, 36 ; Robert Gordon, "The Independence of Lawyers," *Boston University Law Review* 68:1 (1988).

160.   Lawyers are not the only legal actors beguiled by nostalgic reconstruction of the past. *See* Marc Galanter, "The Life and Times of the Big Six: Or, The Federal Courts Since the Good Old Days," *Wisconsin Law Review* 1988:921 (misperception by Supreme Court Justice of change in Federal Court Dockets.).

The Assault on Civil Justice: The Anti-Lawyer Dimension 115

161. Commending the relative absence of lawyers in Japan has long been a staple of purveyors of the jaundiced view. Some early examples are Warren Burger, "Agenda for 2000 A.D.—A Need for Systematic Anticipation," *F.R.D.* 70:83, 94 (1976); Laurence H. Silberman, "Will Lawyering Strangle Democratic Capitalism?," *Regulation*, March-April 1978, 15, 21 ("[P]erhaps some measure of the competitive advantage that Japan and some European nations seem to enjoy vis-a-vis the United States is attributable to their much less intrusive use of lawyers."); William Chapman, "Japan: the Land of Few Lawyers," *Washington Post*, 19 April 1981, C5 (noting comparatively few lawyers in Japan).

The paucity of lawyers in Japan reflects the way that the several legal occupations are structured rather than the absence of trained professionals who occupy themselves with legal matters. *See, e.g.*, Richard S. Miller, "Apples vs. Persimmons—Let's Stop Drawing Inappropriate Comparisons Between the Legal Professions in Japan and the United States," *Victoria University of Wellington Law Review* 17:201, 204 (1987); Robert Brown, "A Lawyer by Any Other Name: Legal Advisors in Japan," in *Legal Aspects of Doing Business in Japan* (1983), 201-05. Restrictive definitions that produce the illusion of lawyer-free Japan may exert an appeal on critics as well as admirers of the Japanese situation. For an ingenious but unconvincing attempt to preserve these definitions as sociologically coherent, see the questionaire, introduction and paper on Japanese lawyers in K. Rokumoto, ed., *The Social Role of the Legal Profession: Proceedings of the International Colloquium of the International Association of Legal Service* (Tokyo, 1993).

162. *E.g.*, Sylvia Nasar, "The American Economy: Back on Top," *New York Times*, 27 February 1994, § 3, at 1 (noting America's economic prosperity).

163. Crovitz, Legal Limits.

164. President Bush, April 7, 1992, Remarks.

165. Richard L. Abel, "Comparative Sociology of Legal Professions," in *Lawyers in Society* (Richard L. Abel and Philip S.C. Lewis eds., 1988), Table 3.2.

166. Marc Galanter, "Law Abounding: Legalisation Around the North Atlantic," *Modern Law Review* 55:1 (1992) [hereinafter Galanter, "Law Abounding"].

167. British respondents are more likely to seek legal assistance in connection with work accidents than are Americans. Deborah R. Hensler et al., *Compensation for Accidental Injuries in the United States* (1991), 129 (suggesting disparity might reflect fact that, in Great Britain, injured workers can sue employers, while in the United States they may not). Auto accident victims in Ontario were found "slightly more likely to seek professional legal help in dealing with compensation-related issues than are victims in the United States." Herbert Kritzer et al., *The Aftermath of Injury: Compensation Seeking in Canada and the United States* (Working Paper 10-4, Institute for Legal Studies, Disputes Processing Research Program, University of Wisconsin-Madison), 37. A comparison of Australian and American disputing found Australians to be "substantially more likely to complain of troubles than are their U.S. counterparts and somewhat more likely to engage in an actual dispute," but fewer of these disputes reached the courts. Jeffrey FitzGerald, "Grievances, Disputes and Outcomes: A Comparison of Australia and the United States,"*Law in Context* 1:15, 30 (1983).

Explanations for the observed differences range from incentives that derive from substantive or procedural rules to the general character of the compensation system to the wider culture with its views of adversity, misfortune, assertion, recompense, and so forth. Patrick Atiyah attributes the greater incidence of tort cases in the United States to more favorable law, higher awards, lower risks, and fewer alternatives to litigation. P.S. Atiyah,

"Tort Law and the Alternatives: Some Anglo-American Comparisons," *Duke Law Journal* 1987:1002, 1016-25. The focus on incentives is shared by Robert Pritchard, who emphasizes the primacy of rules about costs and fees. Robert S. Pritchard, "A Systematic Approach to Comparative Law: The Effect of Cost, Fee and Financing Rules on the Development of the Substantive Law," *Journal of Legal Studies* 17:451, 456-60 (1988). Herbert Kritzer argues that "the kinds of incentive-based factors advanced by Atiyah and Pritchard cannot explain more than a small part of the blaming and claiming gaps" and emphasizes the expectations that frame the legal activity, leaving open the question of how much these "arise from the compensation systems themselves and . . . [how much they are] much more deeply ingrained in the semiotic spiral that define[s] different cultures?" Herbert Kritzer, *The Propensity to Sue in England and the United States: Blaming and Claiming in Tort Cases* (1991) (Working Paper DPRP 10-5, Institute for Legal Studies, Disputes Processing Research Program, University of Wisconsin-Madison), 36. To Robert Kagan, who contrasts English legal culture that sees law as an authoritative ideal with American legal culture that takes a more instrumental and political view of law, these views reflect the organization of social and political life in the two countries. Robert A. Kagan, "What Makes Uncle Sammy Sue?" *Law and Society Review* 21:717 (1988).

168.   Basil Markesinis, "Litigation-Mania in England, Germany and the USA: Are We So Very Different?," *Cambridge Law Journal* 49:233, 273-74 (1990).

169.   Donald N. Dewees et al., "The Medical Malpractice Crisis: A Comparative Empirical Perspective," *Law and Contemporary Problems* 54:217, 250 (Winter-Spring 1991).

170.   See Werner Pfennigstorf and Donald G. Gifford, *A Comparative Study of Liability Law and Compensation Schemes in Ten Countries and the United States*, eds. Donald G. Gifford and William M. Richman (1991), 129 (noting less frequent resort to tort system in other industrialized democracies is due to presence of public entitlement systems or to public and private insurance). The authors point out that these "alternative compensation sources do much of the work that is accomplished under the tort system in the United States." Ibid. On the scantier coverage and lesser coordination of American social security schemes, see P.R. Kaim-Caudle, *Comparative Social Policy and Social Security: A Ten-County Perspective* (1973); John M. Grana, "Disability Allowances for Long-Term Care in Western Europe and the United States," *International Social Security Review* 36:207 (1983). *Cf.* Alfred Kahn, U.S. Department of Health, Education, and Welfare, *Social Services in International Perspective*, Table 2.2 (1976).

171.   Wolfgang Wiegand, "The Reception of American Law in Europe," *American Journal of Comparative Law* 39:229, 232 (1991). See also Chapter 5, *infra*.

172.   Ibid., 235-42.

173.   *See, e.g., Judicial Activism in Comparative Perspective*, ed. Kenneth M. Holland (1991); Alec Stone, *The Birth of Judicial Politics in France* (1992); Guido Calebresi, "Thayer's Clear Mistake," *Northwestern University Law Review* 88:269 (1993); Mauro Cappelletti, "Repudiating Montesquieu? The Expansion and Legitimacy of 'Constitutional Justice,'" *Catholic University Law Review* 35:1 (1985); Mary L. Volcansek, *Politics, Courts and Judges in Western Europe* (unpublished paper presented at the 1992 Annual Meeting of the American Political Science Association).

174.   *See, e.g.*, Yves Dezalay, "Territorial Battles and Tribal Disputes," *Modern Law Review* 54:792 (1991); Yves Dezalay, "The Big Bang and the Law: The Internationalization and Restructuration of the Legal Field," *Theory, Culture and Society* 7:279 (1990); John Flood, "Megalaw in the U.K.: Professionalism or Corporatism? A Preliminary Report,"

Indiana Law Journal 64:569 (1988-1989); R. G. Lee, "From Profession to Business: The Rise and Rise of the City Law Firm," *Journal of Law and Society* 19:31 (1992).

While the large business law firm is the most prominent organizational borrowing, there is also some borrowing of devices such as the formation of litigation groups by plaintiffs' lawyers in mass disaster cases. *See* Stuart M. Speiser, *Lawyers and the American Dream* (1993), 344-64 (discussing formation of litigation groups in United Kingdom).

175. *See, e.g., Beyond Disputing: Exploring Legal Cultures in Five European Countries,* eds. Konstanze Plett and Catherine Meschievitz (1991); Thomas E. Carbonneau, *Alternative Dispute Resolution* (1989); Mauro Cappelletti, "Alternative Dispute Resolution Processes within the Framework of the World-Wide Access-to-Justice Movement," *Modern Law Review* 56:282 (1993); Simon Roberts, "Alternative Dispute Resolution and Civil Justice: An Unresolved Relationship," *Modern Law Review* 56:452 (1993).

176. *See, e.g.,* Jeremy Cooper, *Keyguide to Information Sources in Public Interest Law* (1991).

177. *E.g.,* Wiegand, "The Reception of American Law in Europe," 230. *Cf.* J. Gillis Wetter, "The Case for International Law Schools and an International Legal Profession," *International and Comparative Law Quarterly* 29:206, 217 (1980) (suggesting that we are living in midst of a "singular movement," comparable to reception of Roman law in Europe, which is characterized by "the adoption and absorption throughout the world of a less clearly defined legal heritage in which many characteristic elements can be traced back to the common law, with an American flavour"). Wiegand elaborates his observations in Wolfgang Wiegand, *Reception of American Law in Europe—A Second Thought,* (unpublished paper presented at the Conference on Legal Cultures and the Legal Profession, Berkeley, California, 7-8 May 1993), now revised and published in this volume, Chapter 5 *infra.*

178. Lawrence M. Friedman, "Civil Wrongs: Personal Injury Law in the Late 19th Century," *American Bar Foundation Research Journal* 1987:351, 355 (1987); *see also* Lawrence M. Friedman and Thomas D. Russell, "More Civil Wrongs: Personal Injury Litigation, 1901-1910," *American Journal of Legal History* 34:295 (1990).

179. Randolph E. Bergstrom, *Courting Danger: Injury and Law in New York City, 1870-1910* (1992), 157.

180. Marc Galanter, "Bhopals, Past and Present: the Changing Legal Response to Mass Disaster," *Windsor Yearbook Access to Justice* 10:151 (1990) [hereinafter Galanter, "Bhopals"].

181. A reading of the magnitude of this change is provided by the analysis of Tillinghast, a firm of actuarial consultants, which has compiled data on the gross cost of the tort liability system and of other social systems from the 1930s to the present. Tillinghast found that "[u]ntil shortly after World War II, growth in both tort costs and the GNP ran fairly parallel. Only in the late 1940s and early 1950s did the two diverge. Tillinghast, *Tort Cost Trends: An International Perspective* (1992), 4. Tort costs have risen dramatically from 0.6% of gross domestic product in 1950 to 2.3% of gross domestic product in 1991. Ibid. at 13. This includes the cost of insurance and self-insurance. Only a fraction of this goes to victims; Tillinghast estimates 25 percent. Ibid., 10. The compensation received is only a fraction of the economic losses of victims, leaving aside all other forms of loss, pain and suffering, etc. For example, a study of recoveries by victims of air crash fatalities from 1970 to 1984 found that decedents recovered about one-fourth of their economic loss and survivors about one-half of theirs. Elizabeth M. King and James P. Smith, *Economic Loss and Compensation in Aviation Accidents* viii (1988).

182. Lawrence M. Friedman, *Total Justice* (1985), 42.

183. Galanter, "Bhopals," 164; Speiser, *Lawyers and the American Dream.*

184. Paul A. Gigot, "Bill Clinton Bellies Up to the Tort Bar," *Wall Street Journal,* 10 April 1992, A-16.

185. Marc Galanter and Joel Rogers, *A Transformation of American Business Disputing? Some Preliminary Observations* (1991) (Working Paper DPRP 10-3, Institute for Legal Studies, University of Wisconsin-Madison).

186. From 1967 to 1987, the portion of the receipts of the legal services industry contributed by businesses increased from 39% to 51% of a much enlarged total, while the share purchased by individuals dropped from 55% to 42%. U.S. Department of Commerce, Bureau of Census, Census of Service Industries: Legal Services Table 3 (1972); Table 9 (1977); Table 30 (1982); Table 42 (1987). Figures for 1967 are estimates from Richard Sander and E. Douglass Williams, "Why Are There So Many Lawyers? Perspectives on a Turbulent Market," *Law and Social Inquiry* 14:435, 441 (1989).

187. Galanter and Palay, *Tournament of Lawyers,* ch. 4; Sander and Williams, "Why Are There So Many Lawyers?"

188. Marc Galanter, *Adjudication, Litigation and Related Phenomena, in Law and the Social Sciences,* eds. L. Lipson and S. Wheeler (1986), 151, 166. A calculation that the U.S. has fewer "law providers" per capita than many other nations, Ray August, "The Mythical Kingdom of Lawyers," *American Bar Association Journal,* September 1992, 72, is seriously flawed. *See* Marc Galanter, "Re-entering the Mythical Kingdom," *American Bar Association Journal,* Nov. 1992, 118. Based on international data on enrollment in law courses, it makes insufficient adjustment for differential rates at which students in various countries graduate and graduates become and remain suppliers of legal services. Ibid.

189. Mark Osiel, *Historical Roots of Adversarial Legalism* (May, 1993) (unpublished remarks at Annual Meeting of the Law and Society Association, Chicago). Mark Osiel observes that "The especially stringent duties of client loyalty now widely taken for granted by American lawyers, and embodied in their ethics codes, developed from the alliance struck in the late 19th century between large law firms and large companies." Ibid.

190. Ibid. *See also* Mark J. Osiel, "Lawyers as Monopolists, Aristocrats and Entrepreneurs," *Harvard Law Review* 103:2009, 2056-64 (1990).

191. Atiyah and Summers regard the quest for substantive justice as a characteristic distinguishing American law from English law. P.S. Atiyah and Robert S. Summers, *Form and Substance in Anglo-American Law* (1987). *Cf.* Robert A. Kagan, "Adversarial Legalism and American Government," *Journal of Policy Analysis and Management* 10:369, 392 (1991) (observing the inherent mismatch of attempting "to articulate and implement the socially transformative policies of an activist, regulatory welfare state through the legal structures of a reactive, decentralized, nonhierarchical governmental system").

192. Post, *On the Popular Image of the Lawyer: Reflections in a Dark Glass.*

193. Friedman, *Total Justice,* 42.

194. Judith N. Shklar, *The Faces of Injustice* (1990), 5.

195. Galanter, "Law Abounding."

196. Ibid.

197. *See Hart Survey,* 4-5 (reporting that those most knowledgeable about the system are most negative toward lawyers).

5

The "Globalization" of Judicial Review

Martin Shapiro

Too Much

The leitmotif of much current legal discussion is "too much." There are allegations about that there is too much of something legal: too much law, too much litigation, too much judicial intervention in public affairs, too many lawyers. It appears that there are four major vectors of complaint. The first is about the proliferation of legal rules, and thus rigidities, governing matters both public and private. These matters, it is argued, would be better left to discretion, bargaining and markets, that is to flexible, piecemeal and non-uniform decision making by private and public executives. The second is about the transfer of decision making authority from the private to the public sector that occurs when more legal rules governing private conduct are introduced. In part this is just another form of the rigidity complaint—the private sector is flexible, the public rigid because rule-bound. But in part it is a complaint about the concentration of power in the hands of government law makers and implementers. They cannot be trusted to, or are inherently incapable of, using it wisely. The third complaint is simply one of transactions costs. Too many laws and too much litigation raise transaction costs more than is justified by whatever good the laws do. In particular, there is a kind of multiplier effect in which three good laws bearing on the same action increase by ten-fold the transactions costs that would have occurred if there had been only one good law. And there is also the suspicion that where there are a large number of lawyers, they artificially raise transaction costs far above those that even too many laws would otherwise generate. The final complaint has to do more specifically with judges and judicial policy-making. There is the suspicion that those defeated in the electoral, party, legislative and executive processes that form the "normal" or "correct" or "democratic" route to public policy choice turn to litigation. They seek to lure judges into giving them the policies that they have failed to achieve "at the ballot box." The objection here is largely couched in terms of democracy but in part also in terms of the judges' low capacity to make substantively good policy choices.

In spite of flurries of enthusiasm for deregulation, we probably would not be so alarmed if the major concern was too much law and, therefore, too much rigidity, too much government authority and too high transaction costs. In fact the regulatory state is accepted by nearly everybody. Indeed in the newest world religion, environmentalism, regulation has reached its pinnacle of perceived grace. It is not too much law, but too much litigation and too much judicial policy making that are the real burrs under our saddle. And while they may be tangled together, they are not one burr but two. Even presided over by judges who were modest, loyal followers of preexisting legal rules made by non-judges, excessive litigation or adversary legalism would be troublesome both because of transaction costs and the loss of substantive rationality that flows from adversariness. When judges do "too much law making" a second set of objections arise. Judicial policy making involves a transfer of decision making from the private to the public sector—to more government because judges are themselves part of government. It involves transfer from "democratic" parts of government to "nondemocratic" parts. And it involves transfers from competent private and public decision makers to incompetent judicial decision makers. Here again, however, the crux of the matter does not seem to be the transfer from the private to the public sector but the transfer within the public sector. Complaints are heard everywhere about the "judicialization" of politics, that is the "excessive" part that judges are coming to play in public policy making.

Judicialization

I want to focus on this alleged judicialization of politics, that is on the supposed evils of the judges themselves rather than the evils of adversary legalism or excessive litigation as such. There certainly is a widespread perception that judges do more than they used to. In part this perception is a result of the relative growth of public law over private. Both common and civil law judges had erected a marvelous, technical screen behind which they enacted enormous new bodies of private law in ways that were impenetrable by the public. These screens are not nearly so effective where the law is not a series of rules about private conduct but a set of directives about the conduct of public authorities.

Certainly the current, global vogue in American-style, constitutional, judicial review contributes in a major way to the perception of increased judicial involvement in public policy.[1] The power of a court to veto a law duly enacted by the legislature is a dramatic, and undeniably political, one. And in most nations of the world where it exists today, it is a very recently acquired one. This novelty is further accentuated by the growth of such review powers in a transnational court, the European Court of Justice, which adds the newness of transnational review to the newness of constitutional review.[2] Indeed to most people "big" constitutional decisions—race and gender discrimination, abortion, rights of accused, property rights, free economic movement among the member states of federal systems, constitutional powers of the Executive—are at the center of concerns about the judicialization of politics. Who said that handfuls of non-elected judges should decide the fate of the nation, or the transnation, while pretending to settle merely "legal" questions?

Administrative Judicial Review

Constitutional judicial review may be the glamour trade, but if major transfer of policy making authority from elsewhere to courts has occurred, administrative judicial review rather than constitutional review is the far more likely vehicle of transfer. In the modern regulatory state far less of the law is to be found in statutes that can be found unconstitutional than in administrative regulations that can be found unlawful. Surely it can be argued that such judicial findings of the unlawfulness of administrative regulations and decisions involves as much policy judgment as does constitutional review.[3] That all public administration involves not merely policy implementation but policy making is widely acknowledged. Less widely acknowledged, but increasingly so, is the policy making role of judges engaged in review of administration. A judge seeking to review an administrative regulation for lawfulness must go through the same policy analysis as did the administrator in order to determine whether to judicially uphold the administrative action.[4] The same thing is true of a judge who reviews a discretionary administrative decision for abuse of discretion or arbitrariness. If there is "too much" judicial policy making, it is most likely to have occurred in this area of judicial review of administrative action.

Delegated Legislation

A series of interacting factors that appear to be operating in all industrialized states give rise to the suspicion that increased judicial policy making is occurring in the realm of administrative review. In such states, legislatures confronted with the need to generate vast, complex, highly technical and rapidly changing regulatory regimes have passed much of their law making authority to administrative agencies. As their very name implies, such a transfer creates vast principal-agent problems. How can legislatures be sure that the agencies are wielding the legislative authority passed to them in the way the legislative donors would desire? One answer is to set judges to watch the agents on behalf of the principals.[5] That is, of course, precisely what judges are supposed to do when they engage in administrative review. They determine whether the agency has used its delegated authority in the ways that the statute delegating the authority directs. Unfortunately there is no way of setting judges to watch administrators on behalf of legislators that does not entail investing some additional policy making authority in the judicial watchdogs themselves. So if more delegated legislation leads to more judicial review, then it will also lead to the opportunity for more judicial policy making.[6]

Yet legislatures need not choose to seek solutions to principal-agent problems by encouraging more judicial review. Nor need judges seize the opportunity to make more policy that acquiring more judicial review powers would offer them. Legislatures have other ways of checking their agents. Particularly in parliamentary regimes, the illusory parliamentary control over administration through the cabinet has often been claimed to make it unnecessary to adopt other means of legislative control over administrative law making. Moreover even where extensive judicial review is formally mandated, courts may either openly or covertly refuse to do judicial review, and thus judicial policy making, by entirely deferring to administrative decisions. Most of the world's courts that have administrative review powers do not have the direct authority to invalidate a rule or regulation, that is delegated legislation made by an agency. Most only have the authority to invalidate a particular agency action as applied to a particular individual. Moreover most of the world's courts with administrative review powers almost automatically approve anything the administration does. Generally they require only that certain niceties of legal language be observed. The outstanding example is the French Council of State which on paper is the most powerful administrative court in the world. At least as far as an outsider can tell, the Council of State appears to trouble the ministries not one bit except to provide the proper linguistic embroidery. So massive delegation of law making authority to administrative agencies does not, in and of itself, necessarily suggest more judicial policy making.

Distrust of Technocracy

Other factors, when combined with this massive delegation, may move us further. The first is distrust of technocracy. The great appeal of bureaucracies to the modern regulatory state is that industrial and post-industrial regulation requires high levels of technical expertise. The administrative agencies are repositories of such expertise. Because "we" defer to such expertise, courts defer to such expertise even when they are given extensive review powers. For various reasons, however, "we" and a rather world-wide we, have come to distrust expertise. The government expert is seen as gripped by professional deformation—that distortion of perspective that comes from knowing too much about one thing and not enough about everything else. The expert is also seen as entangled with the particular special interests to which his expertise is relevant. If we suspect experts, courts may be less willing to defer to them.[7]

Transparency and Participation

Connected to this distrust of technocracy is a growing interest in the democracy of administrative, regulatory government. There is a widespread desire for more transparency and more outsider participation in bureaucratic decision making. The technocrats should allow the people to see what they are doing and allow the people to participate in their decision making processes. Transparency and participation themes obviously fueled the enormous growth of administrative law and administrative judicial review in the United States in the 70s and 80s.[8] They have been the central slogans, if not the real moving forces, of the overthrow of the Leninist states. They are becoming the central themes in the debate over the further evolution of the European.

Transparency is, of course, the weaker of the two themes. Even if they won't let us have a voice in their decisions, at least the bureaucrats ought to let us know what they have decided and how and why they decided it. In this form even the most servile industrial populations and judiciaries, such as the British, have begun to make demands. To tell technocrats, "You may do what you please, but you must tell us your reasons for doing it" appears to be the mildest form of self-enforcing restraint. Those who must give reasons are likely to be less arbitrary and capricious than those who needn't. They are not substantively constrained in any way in their choices, but the knowledge that they must ultimately rationalize their choices publicly is likely to make them slightly more careful in making those choices. There are strong reasons to believe, however, that once a legal system and its judiciary start down the transparency road, a great deal more will almost inevitably follow after.[9]

First there is the simple power of the negative. If a technocracy simply issues its fiat or rule with nothing else, there is no basis at all for any outsider to claim the technocrats were wrong. The more record accompanies a rule, the more an outsider is enabled to fault the rule. Demands for transparency, beginning with the simplest reasons giving requirement, tend to grow into demands for a complete record. (How can we understand the reasons given if we don't know the facts and goals on which the reasons are based?) Once a public record is required, the moves toward public participation on the one hand and activist judicial review on the other are almost inevitable. When records are examined it becomes clear that the ability of government technocracies to generate facts on their own is severely limited. Outside participation is necessary to complete the factual record. And once judges see a record, it is hard for them not to second, guess the agencies. Giving reasons, which seems such an innocuous requirement, eventually strips the technocrats of their strongest armor, the total ignorance of all outsiders about what the bureaucrats are doing.

If transparency leads to participation, the independent desire for participation also leads to transparency. You can't participate unless you know. Furthermore, how can anyone know whether outsiders have really been allowed to participate in the process of decision making unless the ultimate decision makers have to demonstrate how the views of outsiders were taken into account? Thus the famous "dialogue" requirement in American administrative law.[10] Unless the agency presents a record of each issue raised by outsiders and how the agency responds to each issue raised, how can we know that the insiders paid any attention to the outsiders? Participation must be more than the opportunity to talk to a brick wall. So here again, a demand, this time for participation, leads to a record, and the presence of a record allows judges to second-guess agencies in ways they could not do if the judges had no access to the facts.

"Globalization" in reality usually means what is happening in the most developed countries. In that sense we can speak of the globalization of administrative law making and of demands for transparency and participation.[11] Then we can look for a globalization of demands that there be a public record of agency decision making. And we can anticipate a globalization of activist judicial review of agency action made possible by the generation of these records and aimed at perfecting transparency and participation. As a side effect we may anticipate a global increase in the propensity of judges to themselves intervene in the substance of policy as they immerse themselves in substantive records. If judges see all the facts and analysis that the technocrats do, can they really resist correcting the technocrats when it is clear on the record that the technocrats have acted like damned fools?

If we confront a post-industrial segment of nations that are demanding that their bureaucracies explain and defend what they are doing, rather than raising the opaque shield of expertise, then we should also expect a "global" concern for what constitutes a good explanation and defense. And we should anticipate judges' participation in that global concern.

Scientific Perfection

At this point grave difficulties and a central paradox are encountered. Traditionally the defense of every act of bureaucratic policy discretion has been a flat assertion of technical expertise. If that flat assertion is now met with doubts, the natural response is not to abandon technological claims to legitimacy but to prove out those claims, to offer a full technical explanation of the decision reached. This tendency is accelerated by the environmental, health and safety orientation of much recent regulation. Regulation in these areas rests on highly complex scientific data and modes of analysis. At the same time that rapidly advancing science and technology both cause and appear to offer the regulatory cures for many dangers, economics has become an increasingly central tool of policy analysis. Cost-benefit analysis is now central to regulatory policy making and thus to its explanation and defense.[12] In the United States at least, reviewing courts

The "*Globalization*" *of Judicial Review* 125

which began with demands for transparency and participation have ended by demanding that agencies demonstrate that their rules are scientifically correct.[13] Moreover, agencies cannot justify achieving a particular level of benefit by a means more costly than some other means that would achieve the same level of benefit. In most spheres of government, policies must be "least cost" even if not "cost justified." This demand is made by legislatures, executives and courts alike.

The difficulties of scientific and economic justification of bureaucratic decision are myriad because science and economics both promise and demand more than they can deliver. Scientific and economic canons of proof are high and require highly accurate data. Yet the data needed often cannot be collected. Often the level of accuracy of the data is unavoidably low. Frequently the projections of current findings into the future, where the policy adopted now must work, is mostly a guess. Subjective probability assessments abound. Modes of analysis which combine painstaking accuracy in some segments with highly speculative estimates in others are typical. The tendency for data collection and analysis to match the pre-existing policy preferences of the investigators is notorious. So is the impossibility of accurately quantifying intangible benefits and indirect costs.[14]

Thus a paradox is created. When reviewing courts demand that agencies show that their decisions are scientifically and economically correct, and the state of the data and available modes of analysis will simply not allow such a demonstration, the agencies are impelled to lie. The demand for correctness undermines the demand for transparency. Agencies throw up huge smoke screens of science and accounting to hide the gaps and guesses in their own analyses. They do so because others demand that there be no gaps and guesses, that a bureaucracy that justifies itself by expertise actually demonstrates it to the nth degree. Thus the agency is reluctant to present a transparent record of where its science and accounting are very certain, and of where gaps exist and high and low end estimates must be chosen among. Instead of explaining why one guesstimate rather than another has been chosen, the agencies obscure their uncertainties and the policy guesses used to resolve those uncertainties. They pretend to the certainties demanded of them but which are unattainable. In the process they make it increasingly difficult for reviewing judges and other outsiders to understand what has actually gone on in the administrative decision making process.

Thus the first proposed cure of our suspicion of scientific expertise—the demand for more scientific expertise—has been partially self-defeating. I say "partially" because the demand for more and better agency science and economic analysis has no doubt yielded a lot of better agency science and economic analysis. The trick is to get perfect science where it is attainable. When it is not, we want the agencies clearly to label their unavoidable uncertainties and show us why they resolved those uncertainties in the ways that they did. The defeats come in this latter portion of the trick. The demand for perfect science inevitably leads to agency overclaiming about how perfect their science is. And at its most perverse, the demand for perfect science leads to the condemnation of agencies that frankly and openly label their own uncertainties and confess to what they really have done

Deliberation

Growing awareness of this paradoxical relationship between demands for transparency and demands for substantive correctness, and no doubt a set of much deeper and wider currents in contemporary Western thought, have led to increasing interest in a mode of policy justification somewhat different from the scientific and cost-benefit mode. The label "deliberation" may be given to this mode, although it must be confessed from the outset that it is very difficult to specify clearly just what we mean by deliberation.[15] The call for deliberation might at first glance appear to be more easily met by legislatures than by their bureaucratic agents. We are accustomed to speaking of legislative deliberations by which we have customarily meant parliamentary-style debate. But the identification of debate with legislative deliberation is somewhat illusory. In many legislatures the key discussions of proposed legislation occur in legislative committee rooms rather than on the floor. And in other legislatures the key discussions are either among party leaders outside of all formal legislative channels or in the ministries where the initial drafts of proposed laws are prepared. Just what variety, style, location and range of participation in communication would constitute true deliberation is unclear. Moreover legislative deliberations on the floor end with a vote. It is the vote, not the debate, that makes the law. Typically there is no way of knowing whether the debate influenced the vote. Indeed in parliamentary bodies with strong party discipline, we are often quite sure that floor debate had no influence on the vote. It will eventually run along straight party lines no matter what is said in debate. Of course the parties may have reached their voting positions as a result of intra-party and/or interparty deliberations, but often we have no way of knowing. Long parliamentary debates may be deliberative in the sense of providing each party a chance to fully expose its reasoning and final policy position to public scrutiny. But that is not quite the same thing as saying that legislation following debate is actually the product of parliamentary deliberation.

If deliberation is not an easy thing to identify even in "deliberative bodies" like parliaments, how much harder to know whether it is there in administrative agencies. The call for deliberation seems to incorporate calls for transparency, participation and substantive rationality. Of course, without transparency of agency processes, we could not tell whether deliberation had occurred. If we do not trust agency technicians merely to certify that they have done their technical work properly, how much less we would trust their certificate of deliberation. Furthermore the notion of deliberation seems somehow to imply full knowledge on the part of all the deliberators. That would require great agency transparency.

The problem of participation is more complex. In order for there to be true deliberation, need everyone who wishes be allowed to participate? Or is it enough to follow the town meeting rule that talk will proceed until everything that needs to be said has been said but not until everyone who wishes to speak has done so.[16] Clearly the easiest way to insure that everything necessary has been said is to allow everyone to speak. Unlike town meetings, agency deliberations involve a wide variety of interested parties not routinely in face-to-face contact. Unlike the town moderator, the agency cannot know what someone will say until he or she has said it and so can not easily cut off repetitive or extraneous statements. Deliberation seems to run along with conventional modern standards of participation. All interested parties should have their say. There is a point, however, at which each can be told to stop repeating itself, and some standard of relevancy is applied.

Could we say then that the modern "dialogue" requirement imposed on agencies by American reviewing courts is the equivalent of the deliberation requirement at least along the participation dimension? If the agency must listen to and respond to every interested party before it makes a decision, hasn't deliberation taken place? Not necessarily. The dialogue requirement more or less assumes that each participant comes to proceedings with a fixed position, explains that position to the agency and then departs. The agency hears all of these individual, fixed positions and then announces its own. At one extreme, the agency may be conceived as a mere summator of the various policy positions of the participants. Or at the other it may come into the proceedings with a fixed position that it is simply required to defend against all comers. In the middle it comes in with a tentative position that it is prepared to modify in response to what it hears. The dialogue requirement may imply some level of compromise or integration of opposing positions, but it does not seem to imply any real meeting of the minds. Nor does it imply that any of the participants, except perhaps the agency, learn anything or modify its definition of its own interests as a result of the process. Deliberation seems to imply something more than the struggle of predetermined interests in front of and with the help of a government observer-participant.

What more it appears to imply is substantive rather than procedural. That is, the same observable bare bones of procedure seem applicable to dialogue as to deliberation. All the interested parties get a chance to interact with the agency. But the quality of the interaction called for appears to be different. Parties to deliberation ideally would be prepared to change their positions as they learned from deliberation, not only in the sense of incorporating new facts presented by other deliberators but also in the sense of actually changing their preferences. True deliberation implies a collaborative search for a better set of preferences or a better truth than the sum or lowest common denominator of the values and preferences the various deliberators initially brought to the deliberation. Indeed in one sense deliberation is dialogue without adversary legalism. It seeks to arrive at a better common understanding rather than merely the compromising of inter-group conflict. The agency is neither coat holder for the struggling groups nor policy entrepreneur conceding whatever is necessary to get the investors on board, but rather a fellow participant in reaching this common understanding.

Deliberation also implies a resolution of the paradox of transparency and correctness we noted earlier. It seeks best policies but not policies that masquerade themselves as scientifically correct. Presumably deliberators will do the best science and the best economic analysis that can be done. Where we can be certain of things we should be. But the true deliberator will also carefully and openly confess uncertainties, state probabilities as accurately as possible, and clearly label weak or entirely subjective probabilistic estimates. The deliberator will clearly state what reasons of interest, value or policy have led to the choices of probabilities made in the construction of future policy scenarios. Deliberators will indicate why they have not chosen other plausible probabilities that would have led to other scenarios. True deliberation would entail not the masking of uncertainties but their clear statement and clear statements of why the policy maker has proceeded as it has in the face of those uncertainties.

All of this seems rather wonderful; open covenants openly arrived at and a meeting of the minds in a far, far better place than the hell of clashing interests and opinions. All of this assumes, however, that ordinary, interest-laden mortals are capable of the very opposite of adversary legalism, of reasoning together to achieve a policy position better for everybody and better than any of the initial, interest-laden, policy proposals.

What we are encountering here is the image of politics as philosophy seminar. In the 19th and early 20th century the dominant ethics or moral philosophy was utilitarianism, the greatest good for the greatest number. Cost-benefit analysis and indeed the whole ideal of "rational" policy analysis is obviously the descendant of that utilitarianism. To argue that a policy is good whose benefits are greater than its costs, and/or whose benefits are achieved at the lowest possible costs is merely to restate the utilitarian calculus. So, at least initially, is the quest for participation. Each individual or group of individuals is the best judge of its own interest. It follows that if all interests participate in a government decision, then the final policy is most likely to achieve the optimal satisfaction of all the interests, that is the greatest good of the greatest number. This interest, group pluralism, which dominates American administrative law and is now attracting Europeans, and whose most obvious manifestation is adversary legalism, is really late blooming utilitarianism.

Yet paradoxically, as utilitarianism has generated or at least ethically rationalized, adversary legalism, it has lost most of its support as a "global" ethics, that is as the generally dominant moral philosophy of the industrialized world. The great ethical weakness of utilitarianism is, of course, that what is good for the greater number may be absolute disaster for the lesser number. The great advantage of utilitarianism is that it proposes a definition of the good, and a procedure for discovering it, always the greatest hurdles in moral philosophy. What you want is what is good. What the greatest number want most is what is best. The

The *"Globalization" of Judicial Review* 129

procedure for attaining the good is majoritarian democracy. Or it is democratic pluralism once it is recognized that for many purposes group political action rather than individual voting is the central mode of political expression of what people want. Concern for minority interests plus a growing discontent with the notion that the good is no more than the sum of selfish individual preferences have undermined the persuasiveness of utilitarianism.

What is replacing utilitarianism is a post-utilitarian philosophy which is a kind of pragmatism. Few of us have the nerve to assert some set of universal moral truths or goods to replace utilitarianism as utilitarianism replaced the earlier natural law universal moral truths. Instead modern moral philosophers tend to argue that at least we can get beyond mere statements of individual preferences and their summation to agreements that some moral propositions are more true than others. These propositions are not absolutely or universally true, but they are better for this particular situation than other alternative propositions. Although no final truths are ever arrived at, we achieve more moral truth by constantly searching for the better than by despairing of finding the best and retreating to simply what each of us perceives himself as wanting. The image often employed for this always incomplete constituting of moral truth as we go along is that of building the boat as we sail it.

That we can achieve agreed upon statements of the better even though the best always eludes us is, of course, itself a statement of faith. It is the assertion that if we all deliberate together we will arrive at something that the deliberators themselves will perceive as better than the individual preferences that each deliberator brought into the deliberations and better than a greatest good of the greatest number optimization of those preferences. Behind this faith lies little more than the experience of the philosophy seminar room. In such a room a number of scholars of good will, talking together for a long time, arrive at a shared conclusion that certain resolutions of a particular human problem are more pleasing or satisfying to their combined ethical sense than are other resolutions. It remains to be seen whether seminar room results can be achieved in the wider world of strongly held preferences based on pressing economic, social and political interests. Has the post industrial world actually reached the stage of replacing the vigorous clash of preferences with the murmur of moral deliberation?

And how would we know moral deliberation if we saw it? Those espousing deliberation tend to believe that deliberation is more likely to achieve the "better," if all interested parties get to participate. So deliberative participation is hard to distinguish from pluralist participation. And how do we know whether the final agreed outcome is "better?" How do we distinguish a deliberative solution from a lowest common denominator or log rolled summation of the preferences that initially went into the deliberation? If deliberation is problematic even in "deliberative" legislative bodies, how do we know whether deliberation is occurring in administrative ones? Is our only clue one of style, that everybody talks at once rather than the taking turns at statement giving and cross-examination that characterizes adversary legalism? Or perhaps that people talk to one another rather than hiring lawyers to do their talking for them.

Deliberation has a kind of illusory, pipe dream, goody goody quality. Come let us reason together as a kind of secular equivalent of come let us pray together. We all know that the praying thing quite often ends up in preying on one another rather than praying together. The proponents of deliberation are not claiming, however, that the millennium has come and the lion and the lamb will lie down together. Rather, the assertion is that in some polities a sufficient sense of commonality and of shared public goods exists that politics can move beyond interest articulation to some tentative statements of the common good and that certain styles of negotiation and institutional arrangements can facilitate that move.

Steps Toward Deliberation

Certain steps that appear to be designed only to reduce the transaction costs of adversary legalism may, in another light, be seen as steps toward deliberation. Negotiated rule making, environmental mediation and the like may simply be devices for avoiding the adversary excesses of more formal proceedings, but they also may be seen as creating the seminar room of deliberation. Alleged "European" styles of negotiatory or consensual regulatory implementation as opposed to the American prosecutorial style[17] may be seen in the same dual light. American courts have come to recognize a "frontiers of science" exception to their normal demand for correct rules. The rule making agency is invited to demonstrate that high levels of scientific and/or technological incompleteness and uncertainty cannot presently be resolved. If it can do so, it may be permitted to openly admit its policy guesses. Then, so long as reasons are given for the guesses made, the agency may receive court approval for what it has done. It is enough for the agency to show that what it has done is better without proving (falsely) that it is best. Thus the agency and the participating interests need not parade legions of opposing scientists and technologists espousing artificially contrived, equal and opposite correct scientific "knowledge," but may more openly address uncertainties and the extra scientific reasons that lead them to various proposed resolutions of those uncertainties.[18]

Thus the discontent with adversary legalism and the search for deliberation may be two sides of the same coin. At the very least, the confirmed utilitarian pluralist seeking only to reduce transaction costs on the way to an accommodation of conflicting fixed interests may remain agnostic as to whether such devices might not sometimes produce redefinition of their interests by the participants and an end result superior to that which would have been achieved in a pure public choice game.

Globalization of Activist Judicial Review

We can certainly see some signs of the "globalization" of adversary legalism, if we mean by globalization the spread to Europe of the American style of review. Demands for transparency and participation are now rife in the European Community. Constitutional judicial review has spread to Germany, Italy and even France, the traditional home of opposition to such government of judges. The degree to which judicial supervision of administrative policy discretion has increased is in some doubt. The older civil law tradition is that an administrative court might only void a particular administrative application of a rule to the particular complainant and could not address the general validity of the rule itself. This limitation was particularly stressed where delegated legislation was involved, that is where the ministry was making legislative rules by authority delegated to it by parliamentary statute. This tradition is, however, now wavering somewhat. European complainants will now sometimes argue that the administrative application to them is unlawful because the rule being applied is unlawful. European courts sometimes accept this argument. And while as a matter of doctrine the court still only invalidates the particular application, European governments now show some tendency to revise rules that the courts have declared unlawful even though those courts have not, strictly speaking, invalidated the rule. Administrative judicial review activism seems clearest in Germany.[19] It seems most clearly to be just the wishful thinking of a small ring of academics in Great Britain.[20]

In the European Union constitutional and administrative judicial review are inextricably intermixed as are the legislative and administrative functions of the Commission. Furthermore because the national bureaucracies implement most Community law, constitutional "federalism" review and administrative review are often intermixed when courts review acts of national administration. The Court of Justice is frequently applauded or abused for the activism of its review both of the Commission and national administrations.[21] Europeans now concern themselves with the "judicialization" of politics, that is with the issue of possibly excessive judicial participation in public policy making.[22] Europeans are also concerned about the "Americanization" of law practice, that is the growth of large law firms in Europe that may be one symptom or harbinger of increased adversariness.

It is very possible that at the same time that Americans have cast an admiring eye on the nonadversarial style of European regulation making and implementation, Europeans are in the course of moving toward the American plan. National regulation is conducted in tight little islands in national capitals by bureaucrats, politicians, business executives and sometimes labor leaders, who all are part of the same elite, who grew up in the same neighborhoods, went to the same schools and travel in the same social and political circles. There is every reason for those who participate in regulation to want to keep insiders in and outsiders out, that is to limit both transparency and participation. As regulation moves to Brussels, the Paris, Rome and Madrid insiders become, at least to some degree, outsiders, a little less intimately connected to everyone who counts. The interest of national elites in transparency and participation increases.[23] Attention is paid to the reasoning giving requirement of the Community constitution. Interest is expressed in the American experience of independent regulatory commissions and the notice and comment procedures prescribed by the Administration Procedures Act and expanded by American reviewing courts. Even as Americans describe to Europeans the excesses of adversary legalism that American administrative law exhibits, Europeans are driven by increasing distrust of Eurocrats to place constraints on the Community bureaucracy and to look to administrative law and judicial review as vehicles for doing so. As Europeans start down the American path, they may hope that they can lead it to the beauties of deliberation rather than the horrors of adversary legalism.

At the moment we can certainly discern the "globalization" of distrust of technical bureaucracies, desires for transparency and participation, concern for administrative procedures governing administrative policy making, and interest in both administrative and constitutional judicial review. Globalization, of course, essentially refers to North America, Western Europe, the post-Leninist states including such Asian ones as Mongolia and Taiwan, and a scattering of former Commonwealth states, most notably Australia and New Zealand and to some minor degree India. Japan, which is such a notable participant in the globalization of markets does not, however, appear to be much involved in these particular "global" concerns. For a substantial share of the globe, but by no means all of it, there are real concerns about bringing technocratic policy discretion under some kind of outside control. So there is interest in law and courts as instruments for doing so, but without reproducing the alleged American pathologies of adversarial legalism. The open question is whether this globe can achieve deliberation, whatever that is, rather than that bundle of half-truths and high costs of which the American attempt to control technocratic discretion stands accused.

Judicial Review: Not Too Cold and Not Too Hot but Just Right

The high level of judicial activism by American courts, their announcement that they were partners and often senior partners in the business of the regulatory agencies, is certainly heavily implicated in the American pathology. Numbers of constitutional and administrative law scholars in several European countries and in the Community have applauded and often greatly exaggerated the growth of judicial review in their own jurisdictions.[24] Post-Leninist constitution builders seek to strengthen judicial review as one of the avenues to the rule of law. Human rights enthusiasts often envision a strong role for courts, as in the movement for a Bill of Rights in Great Britain, as do some environmentalists. Yet at the same time there are complaints that constitutional courts in Germany and France may have distorted the processes of parliamentary deliberation[25] and there are rumors, in the post-Maastricht mood, of impending curbs on the Court of Justice. Tentative moves to

The "Globalization" of Judicial Review 133

make the French constitutional court more available to individual complainants have dissolved. There may or may not be any progress in converting former Leninist courts into guardians of the rule of law. While some global observers see the American experience as counselling more courts, others see the U.S. as the grand example of too much.

Whether judges globally take up the task of watching technocrats is far less a matter of formal legal doctrine than of judges' individual propensities to intervene. In most of the nations of the globe we have been describing, judges have the formal legal power to invalidate the unlawful actions of administrators and the capacity to find nearly any administrative action unlawful. Whether judges choose to be active or not depends, of course, on a melange of factors, many of them entirely beyond judicial control and entirely outside the arena of legal discourse. Yet one of the major factors is clearly what judges think they should do, and that factor is in part determined by how we see law and what we say about it. If judges see judicial review as a (or the) cause of an untoward adversary legalism, they will be less active. If they can be shown that judicial review can be a path toward agency deliberation, they may well become more active. Ultimately the question is probably not more or less review but precisely what styles and doctrines of review will discourage adversary legalism and favor something like deliberation.

Very briefly my own prescription runs as follows. Judicial review as prescribed either by statute or case law should basically aim at encouraging technocrats to clearly label where their technocratic judgments leave off and nontechnical preferences begin. Review doctrines should approve and reward clearly labelled exercises of policy discretion rather than rewarding technocrats who exaggerate their expertise. While encouraging transparency and participation, review should articulate a judicial recognition that it is more important that policies be made promptly than that every avenue to perfect policy be pursued. It is not really difficult for courts to instruct lawyers that shotgun challenges to everything and everybody may be ignored by the agencies and will be ignored by courts. Finally courts should openly acknowledge that they do substantive review—that ultimately agency action that is clearly unreasonable is unlawful. Reasonableness review is hard for judges and legal commentators to talk about. How unreasonable is unreasonable enough to trigger a judicial veto? Words like "arbitrary and capricious" help very little. This is truly an area of realist jurisprudence. Deeds not words count. Courts should not veto agencies very often. They should do so on the rare occasions when they "can't help" believing the agency is dead wrong. Such review, which judges are so afraid of, is self-limiting precisely because they are so afraid of it. It is far more self-limiting than the D.C. Circuit style of review in which judicial objections to substance are camouflaged in procedural nit picking, demands for scientific perfection and insistence that the agencies respond to every pellet in every scattergun blast of issues raised by obstructive regulated parties. To put the matter only slightly differently, courts ought to say that agencies have to give *good* reasons for what they do but not every reason for what they don't do. There is some indication that the European Court of Justice is moving forward in that direction and that American courts are moving back to that position from the summit of perfection they had been insisting upon.

Setting judges to watch bureaucrats always creates the paradox of creating yet another layer of law making discretion outside the legislature. Judicial attempts to disguise that discretion by insisting that courts engage only in procedural review and in dictionary driven rather than policy driven statutory interpretation lead down one of two paths. One is judicial ineffectiveness in performing the watchdog role. The other is the disguised exercise of more judicial policy discretion than the judges would dare to exercise undisguised. A frank acknowledgement by courts that there is a point of unreason beyond which they will not allow agencies to go is more likely to achieve the useful and appropriate balance between judicial watch-dogging and judicial law-making that is sought "globally."

One facet of adversary legalism is that both agencies and courts come to lie a lot about what they are doing. Achieving a level and style of judicial review of agency action that gets both the agencies and the courts to tell the truth is far less a matter of passing new legislation, or structurally reforming institutions, or changing judicial personnel than it is of jawboning the judges. The relative rigor of review is such an intangible that it is largely a professional matter responsive to what is said in law faculties, what is pressed upon judges by litigators, and what is approved in legal commentary. The message "some review—less than in America in the 80s but more than in West Europe in the 80s" may indeed be the global message that is working itself out today.

Notes

1. See Mauro Cappelletti, *Judicial Review in the Contemporary World* (Indianapolis: Bobbs-Merrill, 1971); Alec Stone, *The Birth of Judicial Review in France* (New York: Oxford, 1992); Donald Kommers, *The Constitutional Jurisprudence of the Federal Republic of Germany* (Durham: Duke University Press, 1989).

2. Koenraad Lenaerts, *Le Juge et la Constitution aux Etats-Unis d'Amerique et daus L'Ordre Européen* (Brussels: Bruglant, 1988).

3. See Christopher Edley, *Rethinking Judicial Control of Bureaucracy* (New Haven: Yale University Press, 1990).

4. Martin Shapiro, *The Supreme Court and Administrative Agencies* (New York: Free Press, 1968).

5. Matthew McCubbins, Roger Noll and Barry Weingast, "Positive and Normative Models of Due Process," *Journal of Law, Economics and Organizations* 6:307-330 (1990).

6. Martin Shapiro, *Who Guards the Guardians: Judicial Control of Administration* (Athens, Ga.: University of Georgia Press, 1988).

7. Martin Shapiro, "Judicial Activism," in S. M. Lipset, ed., *The Third Century* (Stanford, Ca.: The Hoover Institution Press, 1979).

8. Richard Stewart, "The Reformation of American Administrative Law," *Harvard Law Review* 88:1667-1814 (1975).

9. Martin Shapiro, "The Giving Reasons Requirement in European Community Law," *University of Chicago Legal Forum* 1992:179-220.

10. See Harold Leventhal, "Environmental Decisionmaking and the Role of the Courts," *University of Pennsylvania Law Review* 122:509-563 (1974).

11. Martin Shapiro, "Globalization of Law," *Indiana Journal of Global Legal Studies* 1:37-64 (1993).

12. See Robert Cooter, *Law and Economics* (Glenview, Ill.: Scott, Foresman, 1988).

13. Shapiro, *Who Guards the Guardians*, 52-54.

14. Yehezkel Dror, *Policymaking Under Adversity* (New Brunswick: Transaction Books, 1985).

15. Shapiro, *Who Guards the Guardians*, Ch. 1.

16. See Cass Sunstein, "Factions, Self-Interest and the A.P.A.: Four Lessons Since 1946," *Virginia Law Review* 72:271-96 (1986).

17. See David Vogel, *National Styles of Regulation: Environmental Policy in Great Britain and the United States* (Ithaca: Cornell University Press, 1987).

18. Thomas McGarity, "Substantive and Procedural Discretion in Administrative Resolution of Science Policy Questions," *Georgetown Law Journal* 67:729-810 (1979).

19. See Jurgen Schwarze, *European Administrative Law* (London: Sweet and Maxwell, 1992).

20. See Susan Sterett, "Judicial Review in Britain," *Comparative Political Studies* 26:421-442 (1994).

21. Cf. Hjalte Rasmussen, *On Law and Policy in the European Court of Justice* (Dordrecht: Nijhoff, 1986) with Lenaerts, *Le Juge et la Constitution;* and Joseph Weiler, "A Quiet Revolution, the European Court of Justice and Its Interlocutors," *Comparative Political Studies* 26:510-534 (1994).

22. See "Judialization of Politics," a special issue of the *International Review of Political Science* 26:99-201 (1994).

23. See Sonia Mazey and Jeremy Richardson, eds., *Lobbying in the European Community* (Oxford: Oxford University Press, 1993).

24. See Shapiro, "The Giving Reasons."

25. See Cappelletti, *Judicial Review*; Karen Alter and Sophie Meunier-Aitsahalia, "Judicial Politics in the European Community," *Comparative Political Studies* 26:535-561 (1994).

6

Americanization of Law:
Reception or Convergence?

Wolfgang Wiegand

... he could see the island of Manhattan off to the left. The towers were jammed together so tightly, he could feel the mass and stupendous weight. Just think of the millions, from all over the globe, who yearned to be on that island, in those towers, in those narrow streets! There it was, the Rome, the Paris, the London of the twentieth century, the city of ambition, the dense magnetic rock, the irresistible destination of all those who insist on being *where things are happening* ... (Tom Wolfe, *The Bonfire of the Vanities*)

I. Introduction

When I first published my study about the "Reception of American Law,"[1] I tried to describe a development which up to that time had not been analyzed or recognized in the literature.[2] Although there were remarks here and there about the (bad) influence of American law and American "legal imperialism," there was no real study of the reasons for this "imperialism," or its consequences.[3] I got interested in the topic when I taught a course on the history of private law, beginning with the re-discovery of the Roman law in the eleventh century. This led to the so-called "reception of the Roman law" throughout Europe, the dominant and still most important development in European legal history, which has recently gotten even more important after the break-down of the communist regimes in Eastern Europe and the Soviet Union—an aspect I will return to. This Roman basis bias survived, despite important philosophical and theoretical innovations in European legal theory and practice. Such a background made it at least surprising to find a broad and deep change in law and legal culture in Europe in the middle of the 20th century. Was this change just a personal impression, or could it be verified? I focused on Switzerland because it is a small country where it is relatively easy to combine personal experience, empirical studies and analysis of court decisions and jurisprudential literature. In the end, I concluded that a reception of American law has indeed taken place, which could and should be compared to the reception of Roman law in Europe at the dawn of the period of modern European legal thought.

This thesis—that there is a parallel between the reception of Roman law in the Middle Ages in Europe and the reception of American law in today's Europe—seemed obvious and helpful to some, inadequate and misleading to others. Hans Schlosser, in the 1993 edition of his popular book, "Neuere Privatrechtsgeschichte" (that is, his history of modern private law)[4], adopted the thesis. In any event, the concept of "reception" was important but not crucial; it was merely an aid in explaining what was actually going on. The process of reception of American law is indeed connected to significant and important changes in substantive law, legal procedures and legal thinking in Europe.[5] The process has continued and gotten stronger since my article appeared in 1986-7. This essay points out some aspects of the process.

II. New Aspects of the Reception of American Law

A. The Universities

American styles and methods of university education have become more influential. Although the traditional style of law teaching on the Continent remains, there are some important innovations which owe much to American models.

First, the examination system has been altered. Normally, in German speaking areas of Europe, students used to attend lectures, and then prepare for final examinations on all the material they had learned. It is a major change to grant "credits" for particular courses, and to give exams for those specific courses.

Especially with regard to legal education, there is much discussion on whether this system is helpful or not. Nonetheless, it has been becoming more common. The European Community has introduced the so-called ERASMUS-program, which offers students the opportunity to study in all EC-countries. The idea behind this system is to make examinations interchangeable. Universities participating in the program tend to introduce the new mode of credits and examinations. Since this program is of high prestige, all leading faculties will soon, at least partly, introduce the new system.

A second important innovation is the introduction of post graduate studies in European community law as well as in American law. Many European faculties offer programs taken by an increasing number of students who are not able or willing to study in the United States. Especially in the Netherlands, Belgium, Italy and now also in Germany programs are offered which are in style as well as in structure copies of American post-graduate education which leads to an LL.M. or M.C.L.

There are several reasons for this development. First, the number of professors who have studied in the United States is growing. These teachers bring their experience back home, and try to reform traditional legal education, sometimes without realizing that they are importing American models.

The importance of postgraduate education is growing, since both industry and law firms prefer young lawyers who have American legal education in addition to their regular training- a point I will return to. European Universities that wish to compete with American universities therefore have to offer comparable opportunities.

In this manner, European Universities are becoming more and more "Americanized," in a double sense: first, they adopt the style and structure of American legal teaching and, second, they become more competitive—an obvious aspect of education in the United States but quite unknown on the Continent in Europe.

B. Law Firms

1. Traditionally, law offices in the German speaking area had three, two or even only one practicing lawyer. Over the last twenty years there has been a trend toward larger law firms; and a major change took place from about 1990 on. There have been waves of mergers of law firms; large firms now have offices in all major German cities and other European cities, sometimes also with branches in New York and Tokyo. In Switzerland there have been mergers of several large Zürich- and Geneva-based law firms which at the same time have opened bureaus in Eastern Europe and in Brussels.

2. Firm structure is also becoming more similar to the US style of structure, with senior and junior partners, associates and young lawyers as assistants. Many of these young lawyers have—and are sometimes required to have—an additional American education, leading to a LL.M. or comparable degree.

3. It goes without saying that the style of legal argument, and modes of handling litigation, are increasingly influenced by American models; this is evident as well in the drafting of contracts. In the seventies, a merger of two Swiss firms with more than 1 billion dollars turn-over per year was effected through a contract of less than ten pages. Nowadays I am sure the contract would run to 100 pages or more.

The continuing influence of the American legal system and legal education causes changes in traditional European structures. These changes in university teaching and examination are not confined to legal education. As I explained earlier,[6] these changes are part of a broader development. America is dominant in science and culture. The leading role of American universities in nearly all fields is a well-known fact that needs no further explanation or documentation. It is therefore quite natural that students from all over the world come to these universities and that universities in other countries pick up elements of the American system or even copy it. This occurred first in the natural sciences, then spread to other branches of learning.

Education in *economics*, very notably, is totally dominated by American models. The books and articles students read are written in English. They also often write their papers and doctoral theses in English. More and more universities give degrees with American names (e.g. the M.B.A). They do so to meet a demand from industry and law firms.

The need for these degrees, and the interest of students in American education, leads some American Universities to organize courses in Europe, where students can get an LL.M. or M.B.A. So, for example, the Rochester Graduate School of Business Administration offers in cooperation with the University of Berne a postgraduate program in Switzerland. In short, the "Americanization" of legal education is part of a wider phenomenon.

III. Procedural Law

A. Civil Procedure

The rules of civil procedure on the Continent were developed during the Middle Ages by Italian and French jurists. Of special importance was the canon law, which formed the basis of the main structures and the theory of procedure. American ideas or techniques have not influenced "normal" civil procedure,[7] but there are important American influences in some special areas:

Arbitration. International arbitration is becoming more and more a kind of industry. The main players are lawyers of international law firms, judges and sometimes professors. Under most arbitration regulations, the arbitrators are free to follow whatever procedural rules they wish. I have noted, in discussions with people involved in this kind of arbitration, that they more and more adopt American models. This is especially true for pretrial discovery.

Bankruptcy. In the German speaking area, rules about bankruptcy are mainly conceived of as aspects of the law of procedure. During the last decades, these laws have been reformed or even completely revamped in many European countries. In 1994, the German legislature adopted, after nearly twenty years of work and discussion, an entirely new code of bankruptcy.[8] The so-called "Reform des Insolvenzrechts" was strongly influenced by American ideas and conceptions. This is especially true of the totally new concept of reorganization ("Reorganisation" or "Sanierungs-verfahren"), which follows the concept of Chapter 11 of the US bankruptcy code of 1978.[9] The new law also establishes the new principle of "Restschuldbefreiung" (forgiveness of dept), also taken from American models. Reorganization and "Restschuldbefreiung" are more than reforms. They give up the traditional principles of German bankruptcy law and introduce new principles developed in the United States. In this rather technical area of law, the United

Americanization of Law 141

States, as a highly industrialized nation, first developed modern concepts to solve problems caused by changing economic and social conditions.[10]

B. *Criminal Procedure*

Besides changes in substantive penal law[11] there have been major changes in criminal procedure. An excellent example is Germany where new laws relating to witnesses were introduced into German "Strafprozessordnung" (i.e. criminal procedure law). These new laws were a sharp break with the tradition of criminal procedure in the German speaking area.[12] The association of German jurists ("der deutsche Juristentag"), the most important body of German lawyers, with strong influence on legislation, has also discussed and approved allowing plea bargaining in German criminal procedure.[13]

C. *Constitutional Courts*

The law of basic constitutional rights has changed, under American influence, during recent decades all over Europe. Hand in hand with that development, the power of constitutional courts has grown to an extent nobody could have imagined in, say, 1950. This is especially true for Germany where the Bundesver-fass-ungsgericht (Federal Constitutional Court) in many aspects resembles the Supreme Court of the United States. The functions of the Bundesverfassungsgericht—its decision-making as well as its importance and influence—are without precedent in European legal history. But they closely correspond to the practice and role of the United States Supreme Court. That is also true of many details of the work of the court. For example dissenting opinions and especially the publishing of dissenting opinions were introduced under the influence of the American model into German constitutional courts. This practice was totally unknown before.

D. *Summary*

Thus, the influence of American law can be shown in civil procedural laws, in the work of constitutional courts, and in innovation in criminal procedure. The reception of parts of American bankruptcy law is of great significance. The take-over of American bankruptcy rules is not the result simply of studying law comparatively; rather, the United States, here as in many others fields, was the first to confront certain problems of industrial and post-industrial society. American innovation and leadership is perhaps the most important reason for the permanent and ongoing reception of American legal models.

In the field of constitutional law, an additional reason is the dominant position of constitutional law in American legal history as well as in the legal system generally. In the European counties, especially in the German-speaking area, this new concept was accepted gradually and leads to a new conception of and role for the constitutional courts.

IV. Substantive Law

Although changes in legal education, or the implanting of American models in procedural law, are remarkable and important, the influence of American law and legal conceptions on substantive law is even more significant—perhaps the most important development in legal culture in Europe and globally since the Second World War.

American expressions and phrases, American models and principles—these cause deep changes in legal structure and in the dogmatics of civil law. I will give some examples from fields I teach, or in which I act as a consultant. In Switzerland, by long tradition professors are asked by lawyers, banks and other industries for legal opinions on questions which are either too complicated for the average lawyer or which are new. I take my first example, which is both curious and typical, from that realm.

A. The So-called Letter of Intent

In 1992 a downtown lawyer in Bern sought a legal opinion. She explained that a client had presented her a document which caused some difficulties. When I read the document I could understand the difficulties the lawyer had with it. The title was 'letter of intent.' The following German text had nothing to do with any kind of declaration about the formation of a contract or something comparable to that. Instead it turned out to be a kind of letter of awareness, in the so-called "soft" version.[14]

The document was formulated to secure bank credit for one firm in a Swiss group of companies doing business in the construction industry. It was formulated and presented to the firm by representatives of the bank.

The first remarkable point is that a contract between two Swiss parties, whose text is German, carries an English name. This underlines one aspect of the reception of American law. It looks modern, international and professional to use English phrases or topics in business and legal texts. That this phenomenon is not restricted to the business or legal worlds is well-known and needs no further explanation.[15]

More astonishing is the fact that the banker who used the formula "letter of intent" obviously did not know what it actually meant. Had this heading been written at the beginning of an ordinary German text of a contract of guarantee, it would be easy to say that this was a mistake made by someone who simply wanted to be fashionable. This would be misleading however, because, as I mentioned before, the German text does not follow a traditional contract model, or that of any kind of traditional credit security instrument. It is nothing less than an exact translation of clauses well known to a "letter of awareness" in the American sense. These were introduced into the German-speaking area during the seventies and eighties and are now part of German and Swiss commercial law. They are called

Americanization of Law 143

"Patronatserklärung," and, as in American usage, have both a soft and a hard version. For our topic two aspects are of importance:

The wording of the Patronatserklärung is a translation nearly word by word, of American clauses. Moreover, the whole concept is an import from America; and so too of the function. European lawyers learned the clauses from their American counterparts, in contracting with American companies. They soon realized that European groups of companies would and could need this special form of security for partners of group members. In the meantime, the "Patronatserklärung" became part of university courses on commercial law, and is discussed in books of authority on commercial law as well as used in business life. The bank representative used the right formula of the Patronatserklärung—probably taken from an in-house form book of the bank—but used it incorrectly. This simple example shows American *terms* have been received which are independent of the Americanization of the law; but the general trend of Americanization is nonetheless quite real, and this example shows the strength of the trend.

B. Commercial Law[16]

It is no coincidence that the example just given stems from what in Europe is traditionally called commercial law, which includes corporate, banking and capital market law. This is the field where Americanization in terminology and in substance is strong and accelerating.

As I mentioned earlier, the field of economics is entirely dominated by American literature and the American language. Even in German and Swiss newspapers, phrases like "corporate identity" or "corporate culture" as well as "corporate financing" are not translated but are simply used as they are. The terms are well-known and so are the concepts linked to these terms. In corporation law, too terms and concepts of American Corporation law influence traditional European business law. Sometimes American models are introduced to cope with problems that were unrecognized earlier in European law—e.g. the corporate opportunity doctrine[17] or the business judgment rule. Examples could be multiplied. The general development of European corporation law owes a great deal to American legal theory in this field.

This is especially clear for the rules the European Community developed for harmonization of European corporation law.[18] Some of those EC-directives directly import American models into European law. The EC-Accounting Directives are one example.[19] The same trend is even more pronounced in Switzerland. The new Swiss corporation law of 1991[20] is fairly traditional; but many Swiss companies on a voluntary basis have adopted so-called "International Accounting Standards,"[21] which are basically American law.

Thus both the EC and Switzerland have embraced the concepts of transparence—one of the main principles of American corporation law. In so doing, they reversed the legal acceptance of the traditional European attitude of companies, that is, to hide as much as possible.[22]

But this development is just a piece of a mosaic. The whole picture is that capital market law (including the corresponding part of criminal law) has been restructured totally under strong influence or by direct reception of American rules.

C. Capital Market and Security Law

Perhaps the most significant example of this development is the new Swiss Stock Exchange Law ("Börsengesetz"). The government introduced it in February 1993; it passed both Chambers in June 1994, needing only some small adjustments between the two Chambers as of late 1994.[23] This law includes detailed rules on stock ownership notification and take-over regulations, as well as a special criminal provision on stock price manipulation. It is evident from the text that American models were at work here. American market theory and American legal doctrine underlie all of the law's provisions. The government's commentary, on publication of the draft, spoke for example about the "efficient functioning of the Swiss financial system" and "the confidence of market participants in a clean and undistorted capital market offering equal opportunities." Boeckli remarks that "this sounds like a newspaper clipping" from an American business newspaper, though it is in fact "the language of the Swiss White Book."[24]

There is another branch of the law of capital markets where the terminology and the form of business transactions have been completely Americanized. The economic as well as the legal definitions of financial futures or derivatives stem from American capital market theory, and the legal doctrines based on these theories. More examples could be given; but it is already clear that American legal concepts and terminology dominates the law of capital markets.

D. Antitrust Law

That the antitrust law of the EC as well as that of Germany has been strongly influenced by American theory and practice is common knowledge.[25] Especially significant is the development in Switzerland. There cartels were considered quite natural and were tolerated or even esteemed. Nevertheless a new cartel law of 3 September 1993 implants the American principles of antitrust law as well as American theory and practice directly into Swiss law. The same is true for the prooposed control over mergers; and the duty to notify concerning "presumably unlawful cartels."[26]

E. Insider Trading and Money Laundering

Switzerland was the first country in Europe to introduce a criminal provision on insider trading, which was explicitly called a "Lex Americana"[27]: many European countries are preparing or have already enacted insider trading rules. Switzerland also promulgated a money laundering provision on August 1, 1991, and is preparing additional provisions against illegal financial transactions related to international terrorism and crime.[28] All of legislation and the rules themselves betray strong American influence.

Thus commercial law shows strong evidence of direct and significant reception of American law. The reasons for this development are very clear. There are two major factors:

The first is that economics has developed a body of theory and doctrine on capital markets and related areas. But economics as a field is completely dominated by American theory and models. These theories and models, of American origin, were taken up and spread widely in European circles. They also opened the door to the introduction of legal institutions based on these economic insights.

Second, many questions related to capital market or to new financial instruments have—as mentioned above—first arisen in the United States. So, for example, takeovers as well as new financial instruments have been phenomena of economic life in the United States. Legal practice, legislatures, and legal scholars have all been forced to find rules and concepts to deal with these phenomena. This brings us back to my central thesis: after the Second World War nearly all major new concepts of law, and new developments in legal theory and practice, had at least their starting point in the United States.

V. Change of Conception

A. Liability

The tendency to extend forms of liability, discussed in my earlier article,[29] has been continued and even intensified. Liability of lenders was totally unknown some years ago anywhere in Europe. Nowadays there are several doctoral theses about lender's liability and the tendency to adopt it.[30] There is also a strong trend to extend liability for providers of services, which is manifest in the proposed EC Directive for Services Rendered.[31]

Finally, the responsibility of company officers, though discussed, was not a major legal issue until recently. Now in Switzerland as well as in Germany, there are more and more suits; and the chances that creditors or shareholders will win their cases seems to be improving every year.[32]

B. Change of Civil Law Doctrine

The fundamental structures of the civil law are based on Roman law traditions. The influences and receptions described here and elsewhere in my work may change aspects and bring about new rules in fields of commercial law or in areas where no rules existed; the traditional core structures of the law are apparently untouched by these developments. But even in the core areas one can detect the growing influence of American legal concepts. A prominent example is the United

Nations Convention on Contracts for the International Sale of Goods (CISG). This convention may, in the next century, dominate international trade in goods. It has been signed by all important trading nations of the world. It is interesting to note that this law follows American tradition in matters that concern performance and failure to perform. Americanized rules about breach of contract or anticipatory breach will replace Roman-based rules about failure to fulfil and the like. It goes without saying that rules of international sale contracts will influence national laws of sales. Thus, a German commission to reform that part of the German civil code which concerns non-performance has proposed new rules, much influenced by CISG, or more accurately by American law.[33]

C. A New Style

Whereas the CISG has partly taken over some rules of American law, in other fields, there is an astonishing amount of reception of the *style* of American legal culture. All the directives of the EC follow the American pattern of legislation: they begin with definitions and explanations which determine the range and application of the law. When the members of the EC fulfil their obligation to create national rules within the framework of EC directives, they also follow that style, starting with definitions of subjects and terms. This technique, well-known to American lawyers, has no basis in European legal history. The canons of interpretation in Europe have been developed with an eye to the traditional style of European laws and their application. There may then be some difficulties in applying and interpreting EC law, and the national laws which follow EC directives, since European lawyers feel unable to use their customary tools of interpretation and analysis.[34]

The same phenomenon appears with regards to contracts: All over Europe, lawyers impressed by their American education or influenced by patterns used by their American counterparts, have adopted the American style of drafting contracts. These begin, too, with definitions of terms. European lawyers thus may also find it hard to adjust to modes of interpretation of such contracts. European contract interpretation rules are derived from and are similar to the rules for interpreting statutes. They are adequate to the traditional European style of contracting. Their application to contracts styled the American way may be rather difficult.

European legal scholarship thus faces a problem. To interpret these new laws or contracts we may have to use American forms of interpretation; otherwise one should perhaps return to the traditional European style of legislation and contracting. Since this latter seems unlikely, the situation leads necessarily to a further degree of reception. In fact, the reception of American law proceeds step by step; it is not restricted to regulations and legal models but also takes place at a higher level, the level of legal theory and legal thought.

D. General Aspects

In my prior article, I argued that reception of general models and concepts from American laws had taken place. I mentioned the "law and economics" movement and, more generally, the interdisciplinary approach of American legal reasoning and doctrine. This process continues in many areas of legal life.

Important is the ongoing intrusion of constitutional law into other fields of legal theory and practice. This is still for European lawyers a frightening or at least surprising experience, exemplified particularly by the judgments of the German Bundesverfassungsgericht. This court, in many decisions, has directly intervened in matters of private law,[35]—a process once unthinkable in Germany.

The American conception of constitutional law tends to break down the traditional walls between public and private law and replaces them with a pragmatic approach, concerned with problem-solving, and indifferent to whether the rules to be applied are traditionally labelled public or private. This tendency is seen in banking law, health law and in many other fields as well.

Finally, as a natural consequence of all aspects discussed before, the importance of codified law itself has been step by step reduced; and the importance of court decisions has increased. Many European countries, despite their "gapless" codes, are more and more oriented toward case law. Case law grows in importance, perhaps because legislators are not able to react to social and economic developments as quickly as courts. Courts confront the problems of the modern society in the first instance; that is why they play a leading role in dealing with those problems. Perhaps here, as in many of the other examples, the so-called reception of American law is nothing more than a common reaction to the needs of modern society which may have little or nothing to do with Americanization.

VI. Conclusion and Consequences

It would be easy to say that industrialized nations share certain problems; hence the harmonization of legal rules and techniques is simply, and naturally, part of a process of convergence.

It is certainly true that many legal problems are consequences of industrialization, and of the structure of modern society and of modern states. There is no doubt for example that risk-spreading, and the urge to find compensation for accidental losses, is a worldwide phenomenon and is independent of the legal influence of the United States.[36] Nevertheless this does not explain why so many legal solutions and legal arguments used in solving new problems come from American legal patterns and models. Yet reasons for this aspect of development are not hard to find.

The United States, as the most industrialized nation, dealt with many of these problems earlier than other countries. Legal scholarship and the judiciary developed solutions; and the solutions, because of the high standards of universities and the legal profession, were themselves at a high level. These are again results of the leading role of the nation. To summarize: I would say that the reception of American legal thought (as well as of procedural institutions and legal patterns) is a natural phenomenon. It is not the result of simple convergence brought about by the identity of problems faced by industrialized countries. It is a true *reception*, in a sense well-known from history: the leading power, the most developed society, acts as a model; other societies adopt this model, including the legal culture of the dominant nation.[37]

This explanation of a process going on in Europe and many other parts of the developed world is not of purely academic interest. There are indeed many practical consequences.

Since this is reception and not simply convergence, nations are free to follow American models or not. That means, concretely, that, if a problem has to be solved, they can decide which solution they want. This includes the option to choose a model other than American. This is important with respect to such fields as property law or the law of torts where, in my view, the traditional European system is much better than the American.

In other fields it is evident that we have no traditional models; we are thus nearly forced to accept American patterns. This is especially true in very young fields—some dealing with such things as the capital market. But it is also true of others very far from the commercial world. Thus laws against discrimination of all sorts—race, gender, handicapped, or sexual minorities—tend to be copies of American patterns. Here convergence is clear, because problems of discrimination exist everywhere in the world. But on the other hand, the society which first developed legal instruments to fight discrimination in an efficient form is the United States.

Finally: The societies of the former communist states are on their way back to the rule of law. In many fields, they return to their 19th century situation, dominated by German law and ultimately based on the Roman legal tradition. In other fields, this will not be the case. What happens in Eastern European forms a kind of natural experiment on the modernization of law. It will perhaps give us a broader and surer basis for discussions of convergence and reception.

Notes

1.   Wolfgang Wiegand, "Reception of American Law in Europe,"*American Journal of Comparative Law* 39:229 ff., (1991). A (longer) German version was published in 1988: "Die Rezeption amerikanischen Rechts," in *Die schweizerische Rechtsordnung in ihren internationalen Bezügen, Festgabe zum Schweizerischen Juristentag* 1988 (the manuscript was conceived and written in 1986/87). Some of the main topics and arguments are repeated

Americanization of Law 149

here in the Introduction.

2. Marc Galanter anticipates some aspects in his article "The Modernization of Law," in *Modernization*, ed. Myron Weiner (1966).

3. For Germany see Rolf Stürner, "Die Rezeption U.S.-amerikanischen Rechts in der Bundesrepublik Deutschland," in *Festschrift Rebmann* (München: C.H. Beck, 1989), 839 ff.

4. Hans Schlosser, *Neuere Privatrechtsgeschichte*, 7th edition (Heidelberg: C.F. Müller, 1993), 212 f.

5. The remarks in this article are confined to the legal situation in Europe and especially to the German-speaking area.

6. Wiegand, supra n. 1, "Reception of American Law."

7. On the contrary: some American scholars, such as John Langbein, have suggested reforming American civil procedure through use of German models; Walter K. Olson *The Litigation Explosion: What Happened When America Unleashed the Lawsuit* (1991) suggests replacing the "American rule" with the traditional European rule on partition of costs in civil procedure.

8. New bankruptcy code of July 8, 1994, which will come into force on January 1, 1999.

9. This legal institution was partly developed in the twenties and thirties by German emigrants, so that we can speak now of a "re-reception."

10. On the connection between new business concepts and the corresponding new legal concepts, see Wiegand (supra n. 1) 236 ff. It was Germany on the other hand that developed the first system of social security—as a response or reflex to the social situation at the end of the 19th century in central Europe.

11. Cf. Wiegand (supra n. 1) 239, with reference to Art. 161 Swiss Penal Code of December 17, 1987, in force from July 1, 1988 (insider trading). For further development both in criminal procedure law and in criminal substantive law, see below at n. 27 and 28.

12. Cf. Uwe Bocker, *Der Kronzeuge: Genese und Funktion der Kronzeugenregelung in der politischen Auseinandersetzung mit dem Terrorismus in der Bundesrepublik Deutschland* (Pfaffenweiler: Centaurus, 1991.)

13. See Bernd Schünemann, "Absprachen im Strafverfahren? Grundlagen, Gegenstände und Grenzen, Gutachten B für den 58." *Deutschen Juristentag* (München: C.H. Beck, 1990), and id., "Die informellen Absprachen als Überlebenskrise des deutschen Strafverfahrens," in *Festschrift für Jürgen Baumann*, ed. Arzt, Fezer, Weber, Schlüchter, Rössner, (Bielefeld: E. und W. Gieseking, 1992), 361 ff.

14. See e.g. on the letter of intent Marcus Lutter, *Zur rechtlichen Bedeutung von Absichtserklärungen* (Köln/Berlin: C. Heymann, 1982); Peter Siebourg, Der *"Letter of intent"*: Ein Beitrag zum US-Amerikanischen und deutschen Recht mit vergleichenden Anmerkungen (diss., Bonn, 1979); and on the letter of support or awareness Michalski, "Die Patronatserklärung," *Wertpapier Mitteilungen* (WM) 1994, 1229 ff. for Germany; Anton K. Schnyder, "Haftungsgrundlage für Konzernobergesellschaften?" *Schweizerische Juristen-Zeitung* (SJZ) 1990, 57 ff. for Switzerland. The terminology is partly also misleading in the Swiss juridical literature, e.g. in Guhl/Merz/Koller, *Das Schweizerische Obligationenrecht*, (8th ed., Zürich: Schulthess, 1991) 168; and Guach/Schluep, "Schweizerisches Obligationenrecht," *Allgemeiner Teil*, Bd. II, Rz 3896 (5th ed., Zürich: Schulthess, 1991).

15. Cf. Wiegand (supra n. 1) 231 ff. American phrases and words have taken hold in all aspects of life; however, the penetration of Americanisms into everyday German or French faces stiff opposition. France adopted a bill about the protection of the French

150 *Wolfgang Wiegand*

language on June 30, 1994. By this law, the French language becomes obligatory for spoken and printed advertising as well as for all radio and TV transmissions. The same is true for official communications and for operating instructions. English terms are to be banished from the French language. Sanctions are fines and revocations of subventions. The French Constitutional Council moderated the French Language Law on July 30, 1994. It ruled that the law could be declared obligatory only in the domain of the state itself, and not for private and legal persons who do not act by order of the state. See for that *Neue Zürcher Zeitung* (NZZ), August 2, 1994, 4 (Nr. 177); NZZ, July 2-3, 1994, 3 (Nr. 152); NZZ, May 10, 1994, 7 (Nr. 108); NZZ, May 6, 1994, 2 (Nr. 105).

16. See for the following Peter Böckli, *Swiss Business Law: Osmosis of Anglo-Saxon Concepts* (1993) (an as-yet unpublished paper, for which I am grateful.). Böckli's main conclusion is that Switzerland is heading generally more and more toward the use of Anglo-American concepts (p. 12).

17. Cf. Wiegand (supra n. 1) 238.

18. See the documentation by Marcus Lutter, *Europäisches Gesellschaftsrecht* (2nd ed., Berlin/New York:W. de Gruyter, 1984).

19. Cf. in particular the 4th EC Council Directive on Company Law concerning annual accounts of companies of July 25, 1978, L 222/11 and the 7th Directive about the consolidated annual accounts of June 13, 1983, L 193/1.

20. Law of October 4, 1991, put into force on July 1, 1992.

21. IAS, *International Accounting Standards* (revised edition, London, 1993).

22. Cf. Böckli (supra n. 16) 10.

23. Federal Law on Stock Exchanges and Securities Trading (Stock Exchange Law), based on the (in part considerably) amended draft of the Federal Government which was published with a commentary (Government White Book) on 24 February 1993 in the *Federal Gazette* (FG) 1993 I 1369 ff. For further information about the newest development in Swiss Capital Market Law see the following references: Böckli (supra n. 16); Urs Brügger, "Schweizerisches Börsenrecht im Wandel, in *Aktuelle Rechtsprobleme des Finanz- und Börsenplatzes Schweiz* (Bern: Stämpfli, 1994), 48 ff.; Peter Nobel, "Reform of the Swiss Securities Markets, The proposed Federal Law on Stock Exchanges and Securities Trading," *Swiss Review of Business Law*, 1993, 209 ff.; Rolf H. Weber, *Neuere Entwicklungen des Kapitalmarktrechts*, Aktuelle Juristische Praxis (AJP), 1993, 275 ff. For Germany see the new law of June 17, 1994, on markets (Zweites Finanzmarktför-derungsgestz), which contains much new law about securities trading.

24. Böckli (supra n. 16) 5 f.

25. Germany's Antitrust Law (Gesetz gegen Wettbewerbsbeschränkungen, GWB) goes back to the middle fifties and came into effect on January 1, 1958, the same day Art. 85 ff. of the EEC Treaty became effective. Hence Germany had an interest in getting trade regulation rule on the European level parallel to that in its own country. Germany's law stems basically from the decartelization law of the occupying powers after World War II. See Wernhard Möschel, "Deutsches und Europäisches Recht der Wettbewerbsbeschrän-kungen—ein Vergleich," in JA 1986 7 ff. and id., *Recht der Wettbewerbsbeschränkungen* (1983).

26. Cf. Böckli (supra n. 16) 10 ff.

27. Cf. Official Minutes "Nationalrat" 1987 1370 ff. and Böckli (supra n. 16) 4 f.; Wiegand (supra n. 1) 239; further see Peter Böckli, "Schweizer Insiderrecht und Banken, Einfluss der EG-Richtlinie von 1989", AJP 1993 769 ff.; Peter Forstmoser, *Das neue Schweizer Insider-Recht* (Zürich: Bank Vontobel, 1988); Christoph Peter, "Erfahrungen mit

Americanization of Law 151

dem Insidertatbestand, *Aktuelle Rechtsprobleme des Finanz- und Börsenplatzes Schweiz* (Bern, Stämpfli, 1993), 105 ff.; Niklaus Schmid, "Insiderdelikte und Geldwäscherei—neuere und künftige Aspekte aus der Sicht der Banken," in *Berner Tage für die Juristische Praxis'* ed. Wolfgang Wiegand (Bern: Stämpfli, 1993), 189 ff. with further references.

28. The Swiss Government proposed to the Parliament two packages of legal rules. The first package contained the money laundering provision and a rule about wrongful financial transactions, articles 305bis and 305ter Swiss Penal Code. Therefore the Swiss Bank Regulatory Authority put into force a directive concerning money laundering. The second package of measures against organized crime includes a provision defining criminal organizations (Art. 260ter of the draft bill, published in FG 1993 III 295, 331), and a new regulation about seizure of property (Art. 59 of the draft bill). See Peter Müller, "Organisiertes Verbrechen—Gegenstrategien des Gesetzgebers, AJP, 1993, 1180 ff.; Gunther Arzt, "Organisierte Kriminalität—Bemerkungen zum Massnahmepaket des Bundesrates vom 30. Juni 1993," AJP 1993, 1187 ff.; Daniel Zuberbühler, "Die Geldwäschereibekämpfung," *Aktuelle Rechtsprobleme des Finanz- und Börsenplatzes Schweiz* ed. Nobel, (Bern: Stämpfli, 1993), 126 ff.

Developments in this field are proceeding very fast; see the Bill for a new provision in the Swiss Penal Code punishing "stock price manipulations" (cf. Böckli (supra n. 16) 5 ff. and FG 1993 I 60, 1369); Government White Book of 12 January 1994 concerning creation of central office for fighting organized crime (FG 1994 I 1145); preliminary draft of 12 January 1994 of an administrative law against money laundering in the financial sector; exchange of letters of 3 November 1993 between the U.S. and Switzerland concerning legal assistance connected with the offer, purchase and sale of securities and derivative financial products (enacted on 3 November 1993).

29. Cf. Wiegand (supra n. 1) 241 ff.

30. Cf. e.g. Andreas Länzlinger, *Die Haftung des Kreditgebers, Beurteilung Möglicher Haftungstatbestände nach schweizerschem und nach amerikanischem Recht* (diss. Zürich, 1991); *ibid* (Zürich: Schulthess, 1992).

31. Official Journal of the European Communities (OJ) C 12/8 of 18 January 1991.

32. See Wolfgang Wiegand, "Die Verantwortlichkeit des Verwaltungsrats," *Grundfragen des neuen Aktienrechts (Festschrift Rolf Bär)* ed. von Büren, Hausheer, and Wiegand (Bern: Stämpfli, 1993), 1 ff.

33. See Eugen Bucher, "Überblick über die Neuerungen des Wiener Kaufrechts; dessen Verhältnis zur Kaufrechtstradition und zum nationalen Recht," *Berner Tage für die juristische Praxis,* ed. Bucher, (Bern: Stämpfli, 1991), 13 ff. On German reform of the law of obligations see *Abschlussbericht der Kommission zur Überarbeitung des Schuldrechts* (Bundesminister der Justiz), Bonn, 1992, 29 ff, 192 ff.; Ulrich Huber, "Leistungsstörungen (Empfiehlt sich die Einführung eines Leistungsstörungsrechts nach dem Vorbild des Einheitlichen Kaufgesetzes? Welche Änderungen im Gesetzestext und welche praktischen Auswirkungen im Schuldrecht würden sich dabei ergeben?" *Gutachten und Vorschläge zur Überarbeitung des Schuldrechts,* Band I (Bundesminister der Justiz, Bonn, 1981, 647 ff.

34. See Marcus Lutter, "Die Auslegung angeglichenen Rechts," *Juristenzeitung* (JZ) 1992 593 ff. and Wolfgang Wiegand, "Die zentralen Elemente des Konsumkreditgesetzes," *Berner Bankrechtstag* (BBT Band 1), *Das neue Konsumkreditgesetz* ed.Wolfgang (Bern: Stämpfli, 1994), 37 ff.

35. See Friedrich Krauss, *Der Umfang der Prüfung von Zivilurteilen durch das Bundesverfassungsgericht* (Köln/Berlin: C. Heymann, 1987); and for example Erwin Deutsch, "Neues Verfassungszivilrecht: Rechtswidriger Abtreibungsvertrag gültig—Unter-

haltspflicht aber kein Schaden," *Neue Juristische Wochenschrift* (NJW) 1993, 2361 ff.

36. See the remarks in Wiegand (supra n. 1) 242 f.

37. Cf. e.g. for Japan, Hideo Nakamura, "Der Einfluss des amerikanischen Rechts auf den japanischen Zivilprozess," *Gedächtnisschrift für Peter Arens* ed. Leipold, Lüke, Yoshino (München: C.H. Beck, 1993), 309 ff.

7

Courts and the Construction of Racial and Ethnic Identity: Public Law Litigation in the Denver Schools

Rachel F. Moran

In this paper, I review the public law litigation model, which was designed to accommodate complex, multipolar conflicts in a judicial setting. Desegregation cases were considered an avatar of this type of lawsuit. I also examine the most prominent criticisms of this model, which focus on the institutional limitations of the courts and the threats to judicial legitimacy that public law litigation poses. By conducting an empirical study of a long-running case involving desegregation and bilingual education in the Denver public schools, I provide new evidence on the mixed impact of this type of proceeding. I also make some predictions about the future of public law litigation in educational policymaking based on the growing multipolarity of school governance.

I. Introduction: Public Law Litigation, Desegregation, and the Denver Schools

In 1976, Professor Abram Chayes wrote a seminal piece that set forth what he termed a model of "public law litigation."[1] He contrasted this model with the received tradition of civil adjudication. Under the traditional approach, Chayes contended, a lawsuit is bipolar and backward-looking. Two parties with unitary and diametrically opposed interests initiate and control the lawsuit, which is a self-contained and discrete episode. The judge plays a relatively passive role, allowing the parties to direct the fact-finding process. As a neutral arbiter of the law, the judge's key role is to fashion relief that is carefully tailored to remedy the substantive violation of the plaintiff's rights.[2]

By comparison, public law litigation is much more sprawling and amorphous with parties representing multipolar interests. The lawsuit is not merely retrospective in orientation; instead, factfinding can be far more predictive and legislative. The judge plays an active role in shaping the litigation; the remedy is no longer neatly tailored to fit the violation but is ad hoc, flexible, and designed to address not private rights but the operation of public policy. As a consequence, the lawsuit tends to require ongoing judicial supervision, and the decree is often negotiated among the parties to facilitate its enforcement.[3] In illustrating this model, Chayes declared that school desegregation cases were among the avatars of public law litigation.[4]

In a later article, Chayes bemoaned the decline of public law litigation due to unsympathetic, conservative judges.[5] Although Chayes did not focus on desegregation cases in particular in evaluating the obstacles to implementing his model, other authors have repeatedly noted the tenuous state of desegregation litigation.[6] In this paper, I take a close look at one well-known, long-running desegregation case in the Denver public schools, *Keyes v. School District No. 1.*[7]

This study will permit a more nuanced evaluation of the utility of public law litigation in the pursuit of educational equity than any general lament on the state of desegregation can. Drawing on interview material as well as on court records, school district documents, and media reports, I will review the legal development of the case, the perceptions of the lawsuit in different sectors of the Denver community, and the insights the case provides into the future of institutional reform lawsuits like this one.

Keyes is in many ways the avatar of public law litigation that Chayes described. The suit attracted a number of intervenors who sought to multiply the issues addressed by the court. The case has gone on for over two decades; ultimately, the remedial decree encompassed a wide array of operations throughout the district despite the fact that initial claims of violation focused on segregated conditions in certain core schools. The trial court has relied heavily on experts to formulate a decree and has repeatedly sought to enlist the parties' cooperation in fashioning appropriate remedies. In keeping with the generally mixed reviews for public law litigation, various parties to the case have expressed increasing doubts about the propriety of long-term judicial intervention in the Denver public school system.

A closer examination of *Keyes* reveals that public law litigation faces several key obstacles in desegregation cases. First, as has been widely reported by commentators like David Horowitz,[8] the judiciary is not designed to accommodate a multipolar, quasi-legislative factfinding process and to implement wide-ranging, long-term institutional remedies. These procedural and structural limitations lead parties to question the legitimacy and efficiency of judicial intervention.

A second problem, which has not been noted in the general literature, however, stems from the fact that while the remedy is ongoing and flexible, the finding of an original violation is largely fixed. The fixity of the constitutional wrong can leave the court with justifications for intervention that seem outdated. Even if the remedy is not tightly tailored to the violation under public law litigation, the sense that the original finding of harm is obsolete casts additional doubt on the legitimacy of judicial intervention.

Despite these obstacles, however, the data collected here indicate that public law litigation can make a useful contribution to reconstructing intergroup conflict and advancing the ideological debate about educational equity. If a lawsuit serves this purpose, alternative avenues of political reform may become feasible and attractive ways to deal with competing claims about educational equity. However, the opportunity to bring public law litigation remains an important safety valve should these channels of political discourse break down.

II. A Quick Sketch of National Reform Initiatives
and the Denver Public Schools

I chose to study the *Keyes* case for several reasons. My primary research interest had been bilingual education, and I was beginning to explore the interaction of this reform agenda with desegregation. Indeed, the potential conflict between African-American and Latino claims regarding educational equity reflected a rising level of multipolarity in school policymaking. The timing of the *Keyes* case was ideal for my purposes. The lawsuit began in 1969, at about the time that bilingual education advocates were mobilizing to demand nationwide reform.[9] By 1974, when Latinos intervened in the case to demand a bilingual education remedy, federal support for bilingual education was reaching its apex.[10] The case persisted after 1978 when federal support for bilingual education began its decline.[11] Throughout this period, and especially after the mid-1970's, policymakers and scholars questioned whether desegregation decrees could promote equal educational opportunity.[12] *Keyes* permitted me to examine how these changes in national policy affected the evolution of desegregation and bilingual education in a particular school district.

Not only did *Keyes* span a critical period of flux in national education policy, but it also took place in a Western school district that experienced demographic shifts similar to those reshaping race relations nationwide. These population changes further enhanced the perception of school policymaking as a multipolar process. When the lawsuit was filed in 1969, Denver was a tri-ethnic district composed of whites, African Americans, and Latinos. Shortly before implementation of a desegregation decree in 1974, the majority of the district's student body was white with approximately one-fourth of the student body consisting of Latinos and slightly less than one-fifth of African Americans.[13]

Once a desegregation order was implemented, white flight began to occur; at the same time, the district experienced an influx of Latino and Asian-American students. As a consequence, the Denver school district became predominantly non-white with Latinos representing an increasingly large plurality of the student body. By the fall of 1991, for example, Latinos made up about 40% of Denver's student body, while whites made up one-third and African Americans, slightly more than one-fifth of the student population.[14] The complex composition of the Denver student body made *Keyes* an excellent vehicle for examining the reconstruction of racial and ethnic relations in the schools as a result both of the lawsuit and larger social and demographic forces.

As Chayes' work on public law litigation makes clear, the Denver schools were not unique in facing the challenges of a transformed student body while sometimes chafing at legal strictures. Denver did, however, represent the special image of the West as an open, fluid environment, one that might be particularly receptive to the reforms motivating public law litigation. Before *Keyes* was filed, the school district prided itself on its progressive educational initiatives. In fact, though, until the 1960's, the Denver school board operated in a closed way. The members deferred heavily to the superintendent and consulted with him in private conferences. School board elections were small contests that attracted little interest.[15] Coupled with general demands for citizen participation during the 1960's and 1970's, the *Keyes* case opened the educational decisionmaking process to public scrutiny. After the 1960's, school board elections became competitive, and meetings were open to the public.[16] Grappling with the demands of a newly vocal minority community, this "school government in the sunshine" became a cipher for people's anxieties about the increasingly complex role of race and ethnicity in educational policymaking.

The promise of the new West as a bastion of progressive race relations and an avatar of public law litigation dimmed amid the *Keyes* controversy. Although the United States Commission on Civil Rights hailed Denver as a model for implementing a desegregation decree,[17] Professor Lino Graglia at the University of Texas Law School labeled the same effort a "disaster by decree."[18] Through it all, Denver school officials considered themselves forward-looking educators who were widely misunderstood and deeply unsettled by the racial and ethnic politics engulfing the public schools. Fairly interpreted by lawyers and lay people alike, *Keyes* has been neither an unqualified success nor an unmitigated disaster. Denver's struggle, though unique in some respects, provides universal lessons for Americans doubtful about the utility of public law litigation in transforming racial and ethnic relations.

II. A Brief History of the *Keyes* Litigation

A case never starts on the day it is filed. A lawsuit is always the product of events that have gone before, a highly stylized and formal reminder of previous conflict. *Keyes* is no exception in this regard. The lawsuit reflected demographic changes that had been occurring for decades, changes that local officials eventually were unable to contain through conventional methods of decisionmaking.

After World War II, there was a rapid influx of African Americans into the Denver area. Many had served in the military and, after being stationed in Denver, determined to make it their permanent home.[19] This African-American population

Courts and the Construction of Racial and Ethnic Identity

was well-educated, relatively affluent, and upwardly mobile. The new arrivals crowded into the northeast sector of Denver due to housing segregation.[20] Soon the schools that served this area were overcrowded; ambitious African-American parents expressed a growing dissatisfaction with the school board's allocation of resources to their neighborhoods.

The Latino population, by contrast, had grown steadily for many years except for a brief period during the Depression.[21] Some Latinos were long-term residents of Denver; others were recent arrivals, only some of whom planned to stay permanently. The Latino population was on average less well-educated and less affluent than either African Americans or whites in the city. Part of the Latino population was concentrated in northwest Denver, but the population in general was more geographically dispersed than African Americans.[22] That is, affluent, well-educated Latinos were less likely than African Americans to be barred from moving into white neighborhoods by segregative housing practices.

African Americans, believing that their middle-class aspirations were blocked by segregative practices, began to agitate for reform. First, African-American leaders along with other minority community representatives expressed concern about overcrowding, high drop-out rates, and low achievement in segregated schools.[23] Minority community leaders demanded that the board take steps to rectify unequal educational opportunity stemming from racially identifiable neighborhood schools. In response to these complaints, the school board created two blue-ribbon panels to examine conditions in the schools and make appropriate recommendations. In their reports, these panels laid the foundation for a voluntary open enrollment plan and resolutions to integrate elementary and secondary schools in certain predominantly African-American and white sections of Denver.[24]

The voluntary open enrollment plan permitted parents to enroll their children in schools outside their neighborhood if spaces were available and students at the new school were predominantly of a different race.[25] This plan sparked little protest, but when the school board adopted resolutions to integrate some predominantly African-American and predominantly white schools through busing, the measures triggered a huge public outcry. The *Denver Post* described the heavily attended meeting at which the board adopted the resolutions:

> Some [in the audience] reacted with cold fury, threatening lawsuits, recall of board members, and reprisals at the polls in the May school board election. Others seemed near tears as they pleaded with the board not to do this fearful thing. Still others welcomed the chance to make a contribution to the welfare of their city.[26]

After a vitriolic school board election, anti-busing candidates were elected by a 2-1 margin.[27] With their electoral mandate, these new board members quickly rescinded the integration resolutions.[28] Shortly thereafter and to no one's surprise, the National Association for the Advancement of Colored People (NAACP)'s Legal Defense Fund filed the *Keyes* case on behalf of a class of African-American, Latino, and white students and their parents.[29]

158   *Rachel F. Moran*

Keyes can be broken down into three stages. The first addressed whether the school district had committed a constitutional violation; the second, how to remedy that violation; and the third, when that remedy should come to an end. Here, I will describe each stage of the lawsuit, noting the distinctive roles played by African Americans, Latinos, and whites in constructing this public law litigation. Asian Americans have played a very limited part in the case; where relevant, their participation also will be mentioned.

Stage One: The Demonstration of a Constitutional Wrong (1969-1974): During the first stage of *Keyes* from 1969 to 1974, the plaintiffs concentrated on showing that the Denver school board had violated the equal protection clause of the Constitution by engaging in segregative practices. Originally, the NAACP considered using *Keyes* as a test case to establish that patterns of segregated schooling in and of themselves violate the Constitution, regardless of whether they result from intentional discrimination. Later, however, the attorneys abandoned this strategy in favor of demonstrating through comprehensive statistical evidence that the board had intentionally promoted segregation in the schools.[30]

The plaintiffs' evidence revealed that attendance zones, school construction, and teacher assignments were heavily influenced by shifts in the racial composition of neighborhoods. Attendance zones moved block by block as African Americans entered a neighborhood. Schools were built at the center of predominantly white or predominantly African American neighborhoods, rather than at the periphery in potentially integrated, transitional areas. African-American teachers were assigned to predominantly African- American schools, while white teachers were assigned to predominantly white schools. The plaintiffs therefore contended that the board had manipulated the neighborhood school policy to perpetuate segregation.[31] Perhaps believing that it could not be held liable based on purely circumstantial evidence, the board never fashioned an effective rebuttal to the plaintiffs' showing.[32] After hearing the evidence, Judge William Doyle, a long-time Denverite, remarked that "this [case] has been a revelation to me."[33] He ordered desegregation of the predominantly African-American and white schools that were the subject of the bulk of the statistical evidence.

Predominantly Latino schools were largely untouched by the initial decision.[34] The plaintiff class nominally included Latino students and their parents, but the Latino community played a minimal role in the early development of the lawsuit. There was little evidence about segregative practices affecting predominantly Latino schools in northwest Denver. The paucity of Latino teachers was not extensively addressed, either, because the trial court initially focused on teachers' school assignments, overall experience, and turnover rates rather than teacher recruitment.[35]

The omission of predominantly Latino schools was no accident. Despite the complex, multipolar interests in the district, the lawsuit at first assumed a bipolar structure under the direction of the NAACP and African-American leaders in Denver by focusing on the segregation of whites from non-whites with a heavy emphasis on predominantly African-American schools. Yet, African Americans

Courts and the Construction of Racial and Ethnic Identity

were poorly situated to raise Latino claims because African Americans and Latinos also were segregated from each other. In part because African Americans and Latinos lived in separate parts of Denver, there were few strong links between the two groups. As Dr. Richard Koeppe, a former superintendent of the Denver Public Schools and now a professor at the University of Colorado at Denver, explained: "[T]he Hispanic community lives over here and does their thing, and the Black community lives over here . . . , and they really did not dialogue with each other very much. . . . "[36]

This inattention to Latino interests was significant because the Latino community had quite a different perspective on desegregation than the African-American community. In the school board election preceding the lawsuit, Latino neighborhoods supported anti-busing candidates.[37] Latino leaders uniformly expressed doubts about the utility of desegregation as a remedy for educational inequity. Bernard Valdez, a former school board member, explained:

> I felt all along that integration was not going to improve education, because I just couldn't see how it would . . . I thought it might improve the human relations aspect, . . . when children get to know each other and things of that nature. But my mind never changed. I always maintained that the busing and the mixing of the kids didn't do anything for the educational achievement of children.[38]

In disbelief that the federal court could find intentional discrimination based on what school board members considered to be purely circumstantial evidence, the board appealed Judge Doyle's ruling ordering busing in certain core city schools. To the board's dismay, the United States Supreme Court found that Judge Doyle's integration remedy might be too limited because it confined relief to selected schools and did not contemplate district-wide remedies. In an opinion by Justice William Brennan, the Court concluded that a finding of intentional discrimination in one portion of the district gave rise to a presumption that similar wrongdoing had taken place in other parts of the district. Moreover, intentional segregative acts in one segment of the district were apt to affect student assignments in other parts of the school system.[39] The Court strongly suggested that district-wide relief was appropriate, and on remand, Judge Doyle held that such a remedy was necessary.[40]

Stage Two: The Formulation of District-Wide Relief (1974- 1984): The expansion of the integration remedy to cover the entire school district led to the second stage of the case, a period from 1974 to 1984 in which a broader range of parties sought to influence the fashioning of relief. Once the remedy became district-wide, the multipolarity of interests emerged in the lawsuit. In 1974, a number of parties intervened in the *Keyes* litigation; several were members of neighborhood associations hoping to exempt their schools from busing on the ground that they already were naturally integrated.[41] Others were members of the Citizens Association for Neighborhood Schools (CANS), a group of parents from the primarily white, working-class area of southeast Denver who registered strong opposition to busing as an unconstitutional and unwarranted remedy.[42] These intervenors were involved only briefly in the case and dropped out after a comprehensive desegregation decree was entered, perhaps because they concluded that their participation added little to the defenses and objections raised by the school board.

Although most of the intervenors were short-term players, one was not. Represented by the Mexican-American Legal Defense and Education Fund (MALDEF), the Congress of Hispanic Educators and a class of Latino children and parents intervened in 1974; these intervenors hoped to convince the district court that certain predominantly Latino schools in northwest Denver should be exempted from the desegregation decree to preserve bilingual education programs.[43] Despite early legal disappointments, these intervenors have continued to participate in the lawsuit, probably because their long-term interests were not adequately represented either by the original plaintiffs or by the school board.

Judge Doyle was generous in permitting a wide array of parties to intervene in the case; however, these intervenors arguably had little impact on the ultimate scope of relief. The multipolarity of the lawsuit at the remedial phase could not wholly counteract the bipolar structuring of the original finding of a violation. After all, the federal judiciary had a constitutional violation to remedy; the vestiges of past segregative practices had to be eliminated root and branch. Ultimately, the district court adopted a comprehensive plan for desegregating the Denver schools; the Tenth Circuit Court of Appeals systematically rejected Judge Doyle's efforts to soften the impact of the decree by using part-time integration or by excluding certain schools.[44] For instance, Judge Doyle's decision to preserve five predominantly Latino schools as sites for model bilingual education programs was overturned on appeal; the Tenth Circuit explained succinctly that "[b]ilingual education . . . is not a substitute for desegregation."[45]

For years after this setback, the Latino intervenors' demands for bilingual education reforms languished; only in 1984 did the school board enter into a consent agreement to provide more extensive bilingual education services.[46] Latino intervenors spearheaded these negotiations; Asian Americans played a peripheral role in the process.[47] Circumstantial evidence suggests that the board entered into the agreement in anticipation of the next stage of the case, the push to have the school district declared unitary and terminate court supervision. The board hoped that the agreement would help to establish a record of good faith compliance with legal requirements to provide equal educational opportunity to racial and ethnic minority students.[48]

Stage Three: The Quest for Unitariness (1984-1995): In the third stage of *Keyes* from 1984 to1995, the school board made repeated attempts to convince the district court that the Denver public school system had complied with desegregation orders, eliminated the effects of past discrimination, and should have its full autonomy restored.[49] The board has redoubled its efforts after the United States Supreme Court entered in 1991 and 1992 two decisions favorable to other districts that sought unitary status in 1991 and 1992.[50]

Courts and the Construction of Racial and Ethnic Identity 161

The board made these arguments to Judge Richard P. Matsch, who replaced Judge Doyle after the latter was appointed to the Tenth Circuit Court of Appeals. Judge Matsch denied the board's 1984 motion to declare the district unitary and instead directed to the board to experiment with flexible student assignments that rely on natural, residential integration in some neighborhood schools.[51] In particular, the judge authorized changes in school assignments, even if the result was somewhat lower levels of racial balance so long as the district did not revert to a dual system.[52] Meanwhile, community leaders negotiated with the board to reach a mutually acceptable resolution of the case, and the Mayor's Office expressed its support for declaring the school district unitary.[53] In 1992, the school board filed another motion to be declared unitary; Judge Matsch granted this motion three years later but retained jurisdiction over the portion of the case relating to language discrimination and bilingual education.[54]

III. Perceptions of the *Keyes* Case as Legal Process and Educational Policy

My interviews with attorneys, litigants, school officials, and community leaders who participated in *Keyes* indicated that they evaluated the case's impact on several different levels. First, they assessed the legitimacy of the legal process, drawing on some of the concerns about public law litigation described earlier. Next, they measured the case's impact in educational terms by weighing its effect on the academic achievement of minority students. Finally, the persons I interviewed understood *Keyes* as a response to the breakdown of school politics in the area of race and ethnicity and evaluated its consequences accordingly. Here, I describe each of these levels of response, linking them where appropriate to the public law litigation model.

Perceptions of the Legal Process. Attorneys took a very different view of public law litigation in *Keyes* than did their lay clients. Lawyers were much readier to accept the legitimacy of judicial intervention than their lay counterparts. Regardless of whom they represented, the attorneys tended to emphasize the rule of law and the judge's role as a constitutionalist. Typically, they portrayed the judges as erudite persons of integrity who had to remain unswayed by community passions. Attorneys uniformly expressed great respect for jurists who paid a heavy price in community notoriety and isolation to respect the rule of law.

Charles Brega, who represented a neighborhood association, remembered Judge Doyle as having "kind of a constitutional bent. I think he was an intellectual . . . person; I mean this was probably an intellectual exercise to him and that was more intriguing than it would be for some other judges who want to get to the next case and get on about it."[55]

A. Edgar Benton, an attorney and former school board member, described Judge Doyle as "fiercely devoted to the Constitution."[56] To illustrate this point, he recalled the following anecdote:

162 *Rachel F. Moran*

> I remember one colloquy between the court and school district counsel when the lawyer for the district said: 'Your honor is aware that in 1969 we had an election in Denver for the school board and the community by a substantial vote rejected this whole thing [busing].' Judge Doyle . . . was looking down and when this lawyer finished, Doyle leaned forward out over the bench and in a thunderous voice, he said: 'The Constitution of the United States is not to be determined by a vote of the people. Surely you don't disagree with that.'[57]

Mr. Benton also said of Judge Matsch that he knew of "no judge elsewhere who has a more fervent and determined conviction to uphold the Constitution of the United States."[58]

By contrast, lay people were much more inclined to view the judge as a political power broker. On the one hand, African-American leaders who supported integration generally praised the judiciary but at times were exasperated with the legal system's potential for delay and foot-dragging. These leaders sometimes thought that the judges could and should have gone further to promote equal educational opportunity but struck political compromises to avoid confrontation. They questioned the efficacy of public law litigation as an avenue of reform because of the constraints on judicial intervention.

Rachel Noel, the first African-American school board member in Denver and a principal architect of the resolutions to integrate the Denver schools, remarked that "I always wanted to talk to [Judge Doyle]. I wanted to tell him how much I admired his strength, and I thought he was very . . . courageous presiding over the case. . . . "[59] But she added that:

> I think we were all glad to see the decision in our favor. We may have thought it might have been stronger. I thought that in a sense we were vindicated in bringing the suit. But you see, after the decision, then it was just chipped away, chipped away, chipped away in non-action and . . . rhetoric. . . . And that to me is a sad reflection on this district.[60]

School officials, on the other hand, doubted the propriety of public law litigation, viewing it as an unfounded expansion of the judicial role. They depicted the jurists as authoritarian figures who abused their power. Board members who participated in the first stage of the case characterized Judge Doyle as biased in favor of the plaintiffs and duped by the plaintiffs' experts. Frank Southworth, who was elected on an anti-busing platform and was instrumental in rescinding the integration resolutions in 1969, said that:

> I can tell you my own opinion [is] that Bill Doyle already had his mind made up and there wasn't anything we could have said that would have changed his mind. He wanted to run the school district.[61]

Another former school board member who served in the 1970's, William Berge, echoed these views:

Courts and the Construction of Racial and Ethnic Identity   163

Neither Judge Doyle nor Dick Matsch understood the Denver Public Schools. It's impossible for a federal judge to sit in the courtroom and to listen to what I'd call conjured testimony and make a realistic decision. The judge would have to go out in the community; he would have to devote his entire time the way the school board members did, to become familiar with the members of the community and to become familiar with the problems that existed in each area of the community and then to respect the wishes of the people involved as to the solution of those problems.[62]

Interestingly, the perception that judicial intervention was inappropriate shifted over time. Based on critiques of public law litigation, one might predict that the more prolonged the decree, the more suspect the court's initial decision to get involved would become. In fact, however, board members who were involved in the later years of the case were more prone to acknowledge that Judge Doyle had grounds for finding intentional discrimination and consequently was compelled to intervene. William Schroeder, a school board member during the 1980's, stated that "I think the *Keyes* decision was right and proper because as you reviewed the things that occurred before *Keyes*, there is no doubt and no question that the school district had vitally hurt the education of children and had actually limited the education of black children, in my mind."[63] However, these board members often felt that judicial oversight had gone on long enough and that Judge Matsch had become overinvested in his managerial role.[64] This shift in board members' positions may reflect a grudging acceptance of the federal district court's role over time, or it may derive from a strategic effort to enhance the district's chances of being declared unitary.

The intervenors' views paralleled those of the principal litigants. That is, intervenors who supported integration tended to see the judge as a benign, albeit not wholly effective figure. Intervenors who opposed integration saw the judge as autocratic and biased. Unlike the plaintiffs and defendants, however, the intervenors tended to feel that they had been bypassed by the judicial process. These perceptions may reflect the strength of bipolarity in the adjudicative process; even when multipolar interests are represented in the courtroom, some perspectives are muted because of the court's tendency to understand the litigation in terms of unitary and diametrically opposed interests. Some intervenors responded by redirecting their energies to the political process, while others persisted in seeking judicial recognition of their claims perhaps because they were not well-mobilized politically.

The white, working-class intervenors expressed deep skepticism about the judicial process. They viewed the judge as an elitist unreceptive to their populist arguments. These intervenors questioned the judge's preference for equality over liberty and generally expressed doubt that the Constitution could embody such deeply anti-majoritarian principles. Thomas Quentin Benson, the attorney who represented CANS, described one of its leaders, Nolan Winsett, in terms that call to mind populist heroes:

Here is a good example of America; it really is. Nolan Winsett is a regular guy realtor. When he really felt strongly about something, he rose up and became a leader. People may question his tactics or brilliance or whatever, but he became a leader, filling a niche that needed to be filled. And after all is said and done, he went back to the level of seeking houses. . . . It's a common, recurring theme in America because our system allows ordinary people to do extraordinary things. And you'll find it not just here but in so many other ways in which, given particular circumstances, you'll find the Boris Yeltsins of the world standing on tanks and rallying troops to do things that nobody ever thought they could do before.[65]

Disappointed by the judicial process, white intervenors did grass-roots organizing to elect anti-busing candidates to the board and to pass a state constitutional initiative banning busing. Despite their electoral successes, desegregation proceeded under the court order, and the intervenors felt stymied by the court's seeming monopoly on school policy regarding pupil assignments. As Mr. Winsett put it:

We knew going in that we could not fight the federal court. Or, at least many of us knew that and were not even attempting to fight the federal court. A federal judge has the power of God on earth. And you don't get in their way unless you want to get stepped on.[66]

Mr. Benson echoed this frustration by telling the following story:

You remember the story of a judge who goes to heaven. He stands in this long line waiting to get in. He sees this other judge, law book in his hand with his black robes, charge right by him, wave at St. Peter and go right in. He says to St. Peter, 'I've been a judge. I've been waiting for all this time. You let this other judge go right in.' [St. Peter replies,] 'That wasn't a judge. That was God. He likes to pretend he's a judge.'[67]

Following the decision, the judge asked all parties to submit names for an advisory panel composed of community representatives to assist in monitoring and implementing the decree. As Mr. Benson explains, CANS submitted five names including that of Mr. Winsett. However, none of the CANS nominees was selected by Judge Doyle. Mr. Benson concluded that: "[Judge Doyle] froze us out. The judge made his own decision that he didn't want anything to do with us and arbitrarily and capriciously denied access to . . . the common folk."[68]

Despite the white intervenors' limited judicial success, they soon found avenues to flee the desegregation decree. A key legislative change prevented Denver from annexing adjacent school districts without the latter's consent, thereby leaving open the opportunity for white flight. Mr. Winsett described this strategy in colorful terms:

Courts and the Construction of Racial and Ethnic Identity

> [A]s it turns out, all we did was to stage an action with the federal court ruling right over us, allowing the populace sufficient time to be orderly, quietly evacuated. And did they evacuate! They hit the county lines so fast, north, south, east and west, that it absolutely blew the minds of developers.[69]

White flight ultimately undermined the possibilities for meaningful desegregation, but it did not vindicate the intervenors' position that busing was an unconstitutional usurpation of their freedom as citizens. For the white, working-class intervenors, then, the constitutionalist became the enemy of the citizen.

Latino intervenors also felt bypassed by the judicial process but for different reasons. First, Latinos felt that many of their concerns about language, culture, and class did not fit neatly into a civil rights reform model based exclusively on race. As Robert Peña, a former official of the Congress of Hispanic Educators, explained: "We're much more diffused in our appearance. Although we are segregated . . . to some extent . . . , we don't carry the blackness, you know, which makes us distinct. We're spread out in our features. . . . "[70]

Latinos believed that African Americans dominated the *Keyes* case in part because their claims derived from well-established precedents based on the African-American experience with de jure segregation. This bipolar paradigm derived from relations between African Americans and whites did not usefully address many facets of the Latino experience. Katherine Archuleta, a community leader in Denver, noted that: "Initially, certainly [*Keyes*] was perceived to be a black/white issue. . . . I don't think that there is a widespread understanding of why there was a joining of the case by Hispanics."[71]

Second, despite being granted the opportunity to intervene, Latinos found themselves with few resources to compete with African Americans for judicial acknowledgement of their distinctive claims. MALDEF, unlike the NAACP, was a fledgling organization,[72] and there was heavy turnover among the young, local attorneys from small firms who represented the Congress of Hispanic Educators and the class of Latino students and parents. By contrast, the NAACP drew on a pool of experienced staff attorneys and obtained a local lawyer, who has represented the plaintiffs throughout the case and drawn on the resources of his large Denver law firm.

Mr. Peña described the difficulties most vividly:

> Everything . . . has been done piecemeal . . . ; it's very fragmented. . . . You know, MALDEF did what they could and then when they say, 'We'll get somebody local; we'll get somebody here,' it was very frustrating. . . . [I]f you check the history of the *Keyes* case, the [original plaintiff class represented by the NAACP] always had top-notch lawyers. . . . [Local counsel for the NAACP] has been on it from day one. . . . [W]e'd have a Chicano lawyer. Well, he'd be here for three months and all of a sudden he's gone and here we'd come with a new guy. We'd have to break him in, give him all the information, and then—bam!—he'd be gone.[73]

Like white, working-class intervenors, Latinos also resorted to grass-roots organizing. The most prominent organizer was Rodolfo (Corky) Gonzales, who led the Crusade for Justice (or "la Cruzada") in Denver. A charismatic ex-boxer, Gonzales used colorful protest tactics to draw attention to Latinos' problems; he was quickly labeled a dangerous radical. In fact, some Denver residents reportedly believed that the way to solve Latinos' educational difficulties was to "get rid of Corky Gonzalez."[74]

Gonzales mobilized elements of the Latino community in a highly visible way, but it is not clear that much resulted in the way of concrete reforms. Looking back on Gonzales' activism during the 1960's and 1970's, James Voorhees, a Denver attorney and former school board member, recalled:

> The Hispanic community was very passive. I don't know what they are [like] now, but in those days they didn't vote. They talked a lot, and Corky Gonzales, who was an ex-professional boxer, nice guy, . . . headed something called the Brown Beret. . . . The Hispanics talked a lot but they never did much. They didn't vote, for sure.[75]

Today, Latinos continue to feel frustrated by their limited success in mobilizing constituencies to elect school board candidates and lobby for educational reforms. This political undermobilization may explain in part why Latinos have continued to participate actively in *Keyes*; their lack of electoral victories may make judicial relief an even more compelling need than would otherwise be the case.

Given their disappointments in *Keyes*, however, Latinos have by no means abandoned their quest for a strong political presence in Denver school politics. Rather than resort to street demonstrations and rallies as Gonzales did in the 1970's, Latino leaders in Denver are emphasizing electoral changes such as redistricting to improve their representation on the school board.[76] Thus, as their numbers grow, Latinos are seeking to capitalize on constitutional principles to empower themselves as citizens.

Perceptions of Educational Impact and Continuing Political Relevance. Critics of public law litigation often assert that courts must rely heavily on experts to implement reform initiatives. In their view, courts can become mired in a battle of the experts that jeopardizes sound policymaking. While these dangers are undoubtedly real ones in the short term, the *Keyes* case demonstrates that over the somewhat lengthy lifespan of a decree, a case can provide a forum for airing findings regarding the schools openly and consistently. Through the series of reports and hearings that are generated, some degree of consensus about the efficacy of reforms can emerge. With respect to the educational impact of *Keyes*, there was remarkable consensus among those interviewed. The interviews covered two aspects of the case: (1) academic achievement among minority students; and (2) race relations among all students.

Courts and the Construction of Racial and Ethnic Identity   167

As to academic achievement among minority students, everyone agreed that the desegregation order had not led to drastic advances in minority student achievement. Some felt that minority students' achievement had improved somewhat,[77] while most believed that the case had little, if any, impact on their academic performance.[78] Different explanations for this shortfall were offered. Some blamed the school board's ambivalence, arguing that its foot-dragging and resistance had undermined any chance for desegregation to work effectively.[79] Others blamed white flight, which made meaningful desegregation impossible and reduced popular support for the Denver public schools.[80]

Whatever the proffered explanation, most seemed to agree that these impediments could not be removed by modifications in the present court order; this perception prompted an interest in having the district declared unitary so that officials could experiment with alternative reforms in a neighborhood school system. As Omar Blair, an African American and former school board member, testified before Judge Matsch during hearings on whether the district should be declared unitary:

> I think that generally speaking we have been under the Court order long enough. . . .
>
> I think . . . the turmoil and trauma . . . caused the school district to lose a lot of its students. I think that's counterproductive. I think we are almost to the point of no return now. . . . [81]

As to the impact on race relations, the interviewees again expressed a surprisingly consistent view that the case had transformed these relations in generally beneficial ways. Even those who criticized the legal process indicated that *Keyes* had helped to raise the racial consciousness of Denverites. Lawyers and lay participants alike reported that whites are more tolerant and accepting of minorities after the lawsuit. Whites and minorities also are more apt to have positive relationships with one another today as compared to two decades ago.[82]

Interviewees often contended that this decline in prejudice meant that the persistence of racially and ethnically identifiable neighborhoods was a product of legitimate personal preferences, not racism. Consequently, these persons were comfortable with terminating judicial oversight in *Keyes*, even if racially and ethnically identifiable schools resulted. As Assistant District Attorney Stan Sharoff explained the Mayor's position regarding unitariness:

> [E]ven in situations where the price of the housing stock is not a factor, the Mayor chooses to live in a black area of Denver. He doesn't want to live in southeast Denver where the majority of people are Anglo. . . . [The Mayor and other prominent black officials] can afford to live in other areas, but [they] like living in the black community. And this is true with Hispanic people, too, according to the people I've talked to. So, we don't expect a random distribution [of racial and ethnic groups across neighborhoods]. We expect people to live in areas where

they want to live. . . . [Concentration of Hispanics in west Denver is] consistent with what the Mayor believes are people's voluntary choices, that it isn't the forces of discrimination that are dictating where Hispanics live.[83]

Thus, with respect to both educational achievement and interracial relations, most believed that *Keyes* had little left to contribute to the welfare of the Denver public schools. Only certain African-American leaders who spearheaded the case and the plaintiffs' local counsel expressed the view that perpetuating the decree was essential to ensure equal educational opportunity. These participants were deeply invested in the role of the judge as a watchdog over the political process. Many of those involved in the case seemed ready to experiment with flexible school policymaking unencumbered by judicial monitoring. Several expressed the view that if discrimination reappeared in the schools, minority students and their parents could return to federal court to seek appropriate relief, either under a final injunction in *Keyes* or by filing a new lawsuit.[84] Thus, public law litigation did continue to serve as a potential safety valve for the political process in the minds of a number of participants.

IV. The Future of Public Law Litigation in Desegregation Cases: Some General Lessons from the *Keyes* Case

As mentioned at the outset of this essay, the success of public law litigation in general and desegregation cases in particular has been mixed. The *Keyes* case is no exception, as my empirical account reveals. In addition to providing a retrospective assessment, this study provides some insights into the future of public law litigation in Denver and elsewhere.

First, the multipolarity contemplated by Chayes' public law litigation model is a source of its appeal as a reform mechanism and perhaps the root of its undoing as a judicial exercise. In *Keyes*, the analysis of racial and ethnic relations in *Keyes* was framed in bipolar terms by contrasting the school assignments of whites and non-whites; the court equated African Americans and Latinos as non-white minorities in measuring racial balance in pupil assignments. In fact, as the case evolved and district-wide remedies were imposed, the multipolar nature of racial and ethnic relations in Denver emerged. By affording a carefully cabined role to Latino intervenors, the court was able to accommodate some of these competing interests.

Today, however, the level of multipolarity in school politics is rising. This array of interests manifests itself in internal conflict within racial and ethnic groups as well as conflict among these groups. Most significant in this regard has been the rising internal disagreement within the African-American community in Denver. Because African Americans spearheaded the litigation, these divisions imperil the legitimacy of class representation in *Keyes*. Even if the court does not formally recognize this factionalization by revisiting the issue of representativeness, the disagreements will be aired through other channels and cast doubt on the continuing viability of the lawsuit.

Before and during the early years of *Keyes*, the pro-integration segment of the African-American community dominated legal and political discourse. Those who preferred community control of racially and ethnically identifiable schools were marginalized, often being labeled as extremists in pursuit of "black identity, black solidarity, and black power."[85] During the later years of the case, especially recently, those African-American leaders questioning the benefits of integration have become more prominent than before.[86]

An intergenerational divide looms between African Americans who want to preserve the integrationist ethic of *Keyes* and those who want the case to draw to an end. Older African Americans who experienced the sting of legally mandated segregation are reluctant to adopt any position that appears to acquiesce in a return to racially and ethnically identifiable schools.[87] Younger African Americans who often bore the brunt of court-ordered busing are less interested than their elders in preserving a seemingly hollow victory that elevates numerical balancing over educational quality.[88]

One of the great political strengths of the African-American community has been its remarkable cohesion. Moreover, this internal solidarity has enabled African Americans to present a seemingly unitary front in demanding that school boards desegregate public schools, thus conforming to more traditional images of litigants with monolithic and diametrically opposed interests. The emerging generational divide in the African-American community threatens to weaken its leadership in political circles and judicial proceedings. The precise impact of this division will depend on the extent to which younger African-American leaders feel some deference to older members of their community, who were trailblazers for civil rights; the impact also will depend on the extent to which older members feel pride in younger African Americans' newly won positions of power and authority. At present, an intergenerational relationship of mutual respect appears to have muted the development of harsh, open conflicts in Denver. Whether this uneasy truce will last remains an unanswered question.[89]

In addition to intergenerational divisions, African Americans in Denver also face class-based disagreements. One by-product of residential segregation was an extremely effective network of African-American organizations, including most prominently the church system, which united members across class lines.[90] In Denver, churches in the African-American community played a vital role in mobilizing the population for reform. Ironically, desegregation has undercut the vitality of these organizations in several ways. Housing reforms have permitted middle-class members of the African-American community to move to integrated suburbs if they wish. These people often provided significant leadership in urban neighborhoods, and their departure undermines the pool of able spokespeople and organizers. The departure of the African-American middle class not only undermines urban organizations but also could accentuate class differences that now divide the African-American population.[91]

At the same time that African Americans are confronting new internal divisions based on age and class, they find themselves the captives of demographic changes that threaten to dilute their political clout even further. African Americans find their unique leadership role jeopardized by the ever increasing multipolarity of racial and ethnic politics in the schools. The Latino and Asian-American populations are growing more rapidly than the African-American population.[92] The Latino population in particular threatens to outstrip the African-American population in sheer numbers; in some areas like Denver, Latinos already outnumber African Americans by a considerable margin.[93] Moreover, Latinos and Asian Americans are themselves internally divided groups. Because Latinos in Denver constitute a larger and more vocal group than Asian Americans, most of the discussion will focus on the former, although the latter will be mentioned when appropriate. Race and ethnicity have been somewhat artificial organizing principles for Latinos. Latinos have different racial origins and come from a range of countries. Asian Americans, too, have diverse ethnic origins that hinder their unification.[94] These internal racial and ethnic differences often have been obstacles to overcome, not natural bases for mutual identification and support. A traditional civil rights model, as developed by African-American litigants, in which race is the dominant dimension of self- definition has not worked well for Latinos, nor is it apt to work well for Asian Americans.[95]

Class-based issues have long been of concern to inner-city Latinos. Affluent Latinos typically have been able to integrate by moving to predominantly white suburbs, thus diluting their participation in reform efforts. For less economically secure members of the Latino community, however, educational reform has been seen as a key to escaping menial work. These images of upward mobility are especially powerful for Latinos who are recent immigrants and members of the working poor.[96]

Rising multipolarity among and within racial and ethnic groups strains the limits of a public law litigation model and makes legislative and administrative solutions seem more suitable than judicial intervention. The universalist principle of colorblindness permitted African Americans to pursue judicial remedies under an anti-discrimination principle. Today, as cities become ever more racially and ethnically diverse, many advocates are questioning a norm of colorblindness. Instead, they demand that institutions like the schools adopt pluralistic norms, such as multiculturalism.

The shift to a pluralistic vision entails real costs for African Americans. A pluralistic norm provides no obvious reason for privileging African Americans more than other racial and ethnic groups.[97] Yet, African Americans have played a leading role in the definition of the civil rights agenda in the United States. To preserve their preeminent position in the definition of race relations, African Americans, especially those living in urban poverty, must continue to emphasize the historical uniqueness of their experience and the imperatives of corrective justice. To the extent that this conceptualization of civil rights is accepted, public law litigation will remain a proper enforcement mechanism.

The emphasis on the special status of African Americans in racial and ethnic relations may alienate other groups, such as Latinos and Asian Americans. These groups could respond with their own histories of harm, but the resulting competition for remedial assistance itself will be divisive and potentially strain the judiciary's ability to reach mediated solutions in public law litigation. No other racial or ethnic group (except perhaps native Americans) is apt to displace the strongly etched and compelling case for corrective intervention that African Americans have made. Latinos and Asian Americans therefore will strive to change the framework of analysis to emphasize current and future needs in a pluralistic society, rather than past transgressions.[98] To the degree that this conceptualization is endorsed, public law litigation will decline and be replaced by legislative and administrative responses. This divergence of reform strategies may undermine racial and ethnic minority groups' ability to build effective coalitions for educational change.

The immigrant experience of Latinos and their concern with language and culture may provide the foundation for some natural alliances with Asian Americans, many of whom share the same immigrant experience.[99] As in *Keyes*, these groups may find common ground when pursuing equal access to education for those who are linguistically and culturally different. If these groups can build a shared agenda, the coalition is likely to seek enlarged political influence. Latinos in Denver, for instance, have pursued redistricting reforms to enhance their chances of electing school board representatives.[100] Asian Americans, because their population is much smaller, may benefit from alliances with a Latino community that is politically empowered.

The reconceptualization of racial and ethnic politics in pluralistic terms leads to complex, political compromises rather than judicial interventions as illustrated by Latinos' frustration with the remedies available in the *Keyes* case. For Latinos, bilingual education has captured only a small portion of their reform agenda. Bilingual education focuses on a subset of Latinos who use Spanish as their primary language; these Latinos tend to be members of immigrant families. Most Latinos in Denver and elsewhere do not fit this description; yet as a group, they too suffer from unequal access to education.

In 1974, when Latinos first intervened in *Keyes*, Dr. Jose Cardenas, an education expert, testified on their behalf. He emphasized a comprehensive approach to education that would examine not only issues of language but also culture and class. Dr. Cardenas wanted to ensure that the curriculum, extracurricular activities, and staff were compatible with students' needs; he urged that students' nutritional, health, and other material needs be incorporated into school services.[101] In fact, Dr. Cardenas advocated a reconstruction of the case that moved beyond race and ethnicity to account for a wider set of differences in a pluralistic student body.

This testimony reflected Latinos' greater preoccupation with class-based concerns as well as with race, ethnicity, language, and culture. When MALDEF was in its infancy, one of its first educational initiatives was school finance reform

172   *Rachel F. Moran*

that would reduce class-based differences in the delivery of educational services.[102] These efforts have been largely unsuccessful because class, unlike race, is not a suspect category that triggers strict judicial scrutiny of state action. Latino concerns about class, like those about language and culture, do not fit neatly into a civil rights paradigm that elevates race and ethnicity to a position of singular importance. Robert Peña described this dilemma most strikingly:

> It was so frustrating, I can't tell you. I remember crying literally with [the Latino intervenors' attorney] Peter Roos and arguing with him about 'let's go for the big banana and quit screwing around with bilingual and the little stuff, and let's go after the . . . ' and he said, 'Bob, we have no legal recourse on those things.'[103]

Latino efforts to build a reform agenda around a wider array of differences are hindered not only by prevailing legal paradigms but also by internal group differences. Like African Americans, Latinos have not come fully to grips with the implications of divisions among themselves and their likely impact on organizational efforts. Unfortunately, these shortcomings are apt to hamper effective participation in legislative and administrative processes, thus resuscitating the need for public law litigation without eliminating the conceptual limitations of available court-ordered relief.

Throughout my interviews, African Americans and Latinos uniformly expressed strong support for affirmative action; all agreed that the requirement that the Denver school district hire more African-American and Latino teachers had been a pivotally important aspect of the case. Robert Peña explained that in *Keyes*, "we never made connections with the Blacks at all, ever, except when we did the affirmative action. . . . "[104] African Americans and Latinos focused on continuing affirmative action efforts to ensure that African Americans and Latinos assumed positions of leadership in the school hierarchy.[105] Partly in response to these concerns, the school board recently appointed the first African-American superintendent in its history.[106] Board members went to great lengths to assure me that the superintendent had been selected because of her individual merit,[107] but it also was plain from some of the interviews that African Americans and Latinos are vying for coveted administrative positions in the school system.[108]

At the same time, whites are questioning programs that create a blanket privilege for some racial and ethnic groups in a multicultural society. In Denver, several white persons whom I interviewed expressed serious reservations about affirmative action programs. This was true even among whites who had been sympathetic to integration. In their view, integration and affirmative action were temporary remedies that eventually had to end. Just as they felt that integration had served its purpose, many believed that the justifications for affirmative action had become attenuated. They believed that at some point, individuals had to compete based on their merits, apart from their racial or ethnic identities. These individuals distinguished a respect for racial and ethnic difference from a preference in employment and higher education for particular racial and ethnic groups.[109]

If, as I believe, these attitudes toward affirmative action are representative of more general views among African Americans, Latinos, and whites, these differences of opinion assume the sort of bipolar construction that makes these claims eminently suitable for litigation. The conflict appears to involve unitary, diametrically opposed interests of whites and non-whites. Because numerical guidelines for teacher hiring can be set, manageable, long-term judicial remedies seem available.

Even in this realm, however, multipolarity may create pressures on public law litigation. Already, gender, age, and disability have been added to the list of traits receiving special protection in education and employment.[110] With the proliferation of protected traits comes increasingly unwieldy public law litigation. The courts confront a heightened need for mediated settlements regarding affirmative action plans, especially where the number of potential job openings is small; at the same time, the chances for such agreements may decrease as groups seeking to be included under the plans or opposing the plans engage in political debate outside the courts.

The specter of multipolarity has not arisen in *Keyes* because the affirmative action component of the case is tied to the underlying violation of students' rights to attend an integrated school system. Thus, the fundamentally bipolar structuring in that regard arguably has preserved the appearance that affirmative action is a bipolar dispute. If the affirmative action issues were ever unlinked from the desegregation context, multipolar conflicts might develop. In the meantime, affirmative action issues as defined in the *Keyes* case could provide a springboard for building effective coalitions between African Americans and Latinos, even though their interests diverge in other areas.

V. Conclusion

Keyes has to some extent become an anachronism. Larger demographic and philosophical changes have engulfed the lawsuit. With the combination of white flight and a burgeoning number of racial and ethnic groups in urban areas, the quest for a colorblind world through desegregation seems chimerical. Demands for a pluralist system that nurtures racial and ethnic difference have become increasingly commonplace. African Americans, Latinos, and whites have different stakes in the reconstruction of American race relations; their varying perspectives will affect the coalitions that are built and the reform strategies of the future. In all likelihood, cases like *Keyes* will be replaced with multipolar conflicts played out most dramatically in the political arena, rather than the courts.

Nevertheless, the legacy of *Keyes* is not a death knell for public law litigation. Rather, the *Keyes* case suggests that such litigation provides an important safety valve when legislative and administrative processes break down. Should such a failure occur in a pluralistic system of school governance, the courts undoubtedly could be called upon to recast a polarized dialogue about race and ethnicity in legal terms despite all the obstacles confronting public law litigation. An avatar, after all, takes many shapes, but the basic entity continues.

Notes

1. Abram Chayes, "The Role of the Judge in Public Law Litigation," *Harvard Law Review* 89:1281, 1284 (1976).

2. Chayes, "The Role of the Judge," 1282-83.

3. Chayes, "The Role of the Judge," 1302.

4. Chayes, "The Role of the Judge," 1284.

5. Abram Chayes, "Foreword—Public Law Litigation and the Burger Court," *Harvard Law Review* 96:1, 56-60 (1982).

6. See Drew S. Days, "Turning Back the Clock: The Reagan Administration and Civil Rights," *Harvard Civil Rights-Civil Liberties Law Review* 19:309, 319-30 (1984); Joel L. Selig, "The Reagan Justice Department and Civil Rights: What Went Wrong," *University of Illinois Law Review* 1985:785, 795-817.

7. 313 F. Supp. 90 (D. Colo. 1970), *modified,* 445 F.2d 990 (10th Cir. 1971), *modified and remanded,* 413 U.S. 189, *on remand,* 368 F. Supp. 207 (1973), *order entered,* 380 F. Supp. 673 (1974), *modified,* 521 F.2d 465 (1975), *cert. denied,* 423 U.S. 1066 (1976), *on remand,* 576 F. Supp. 1503 (1983), *motion to terminate jurisdiction denied,* 609 F. Supp. 1491 (1985), *order modified,* 653 F. Supp. 1536, *interim decree issued,* 670 F. Supp. 1513 (1987), *aff'd,* 895 F.2d 659 (1990), *cert. denied,* 111 S. Ct. 951 (1991).

8. David Horowitz, "Decreeing Organizational Change: Judicial Supervision of Public Institutions," *Duke Law Journal* 1983:1265, 1303-07. See generally David Horowitz, *The Courts and Social Policy* (Washington: Brookings Institution, 1977) (using case studies to illustrate the limits of judicial intervention).

9. Rachel F. Moran, "The Politics of Discretion: Federal Intervention in Bilingual Education," *California Law Review* 76:1249, 1259-65 (1988).

10. Moran, "The Politics of Discretion," 1268-83.

11. Moran, "The Politics of Discretion," 1284-1314.

12. See, e.g., David J. Armor, "The Evidence on Busing," *Public Interest* 28:90, 99-105 (1972).

13. 380 F. Supp. at 674 (in fall 1973, whites made up 54.1% of the elementary school population, 56.7% of the junior high population, and 63.8% of the senior high population; Latinos made up 27% of the elementary school population, 24% of the junior high population, and 17.8% of the senior high population; and African-American students made up 17.6% of the elementary school population, 18.5% of the junior high population, and 17.3% of the senior high school population.)

14. Mark Stevens, "Hispanics Propose An End to Busing," *Denver Post*, Nov. 26, 1991, 1A.

15. Mary Jean Taylor, "Leadership Responses to Desegregation in the Denver Public Schools: A Historical Study, 1959-1977," 45-52 (June 1990) (unpublished Ph.D. dissertation, University of Denver).

16. Taylor, "Leadership Responses," 52-64, 84-85.

17. Taylor, "Leadership Responses," 270.

Courts and the Construction of Racial and Ethnic Identity   *175*

18. Lino Graglia, *Disaster by Decree: The Supreme Court Decisions on Race and the Schools* (Ithaca, NY: Cornell University Press, 1976).

19. Carl Abbott et al., *Colorado: A History of the Centennial State*, 300, 302 (rev. ed. Boulder, Co: Colorado Associated University Press, 1982); Stephen J. Leonard and Thomas J. Noel, *Denver: Mining Camp to Metropolis*, 368, 375-76 (Niwot, CO: University Press of Colorado, 1990).

20. Abbott et al., *Colorado*, 299, 302; Leonard and Noel, *Denver*, 374-76.

21. Abbott et al., *Colorado*, 298-302; Leonard and Noel, *Denver*, 389-90; Jessica Pearson and Jeffrey Pearson, "The Denver Case: Keyes v. School District No. 1," in Howard I. Kalodner and James J. Fishman, eds., *Limits of Justice: The Courts' Role in School Desegregation*, 167, 169 (Cambridge, MA: Ballinger Publishing Co., 1978).

22. Abbott et al., *Colorado*, 302-03; Leonard and Noel, *Denver*, 392, 394; Franklin J James et al., *Discrimination, Segregation & Minority Housing Conditions in Sunbelt Cities: A Study of Denver, Houston & Phoenix*, 49-50 (Denver, Co: Center for Private Sector Cooperation, 1983); Pearson and Pearson, "The Denver Case," 169.

23. "Report and Recommendations to the Board of Education, School District Number One, Denver, Colorado by a Special Study Committee on Equality of Educational Opportunity in the Denver Public Schools," 2 (Mar. 1, 1964).

24. "Report and Recommendations," 1; Advisory Council on Equality of Educational Opportunity in the Denver Public Schools, "Final Report and Recommendations to the Board of Education, School District Number One, Denver, Colorado," 15-16 (Feb. 1967).

25. Walt Lindenmann, "Board Approves Changes in School Attendance Boundaries," *Denver Post*, May 7, 1964, 30; Charles Carter, "Open Enrollment Policy—School Tranfers Analyzed," *Denver Post*, Mar. 19, 1967, 3.

26. "School Board Takes Historic Step," *Denver Post*, Feb. 2, 1969, G3.

27. Charles Carter, "Perrill, Southworth Win; City Pay Raises Okayed," *Denver Post*, May 21, 1969, 1.

28. Charles Carter, "Forced Busing Plan Killed: 'Voluntary' Program OK'd—New Board Votes 4-3 For Changes," *Denver Post*, June 10, 1969, 1, 10.

29. Interview with Gordon Greiner (Sept. 17, 1991); Leonard and Noel, *Denver*, 337-78.

30. Complaint for Permanent Injunction and Declaratory Judgment (June 19, 1969) at 24-25, *Keyes* (No. C-1499); Plaintiffs' Preliminary Memorandum of Law (July 15, 1969) at 14-15, 21-27, *Keyes* (No. C-1499).

31. 313 F. Supp. 60, 69-73, 79-80, 83 (D. Colo. 1970); see also Taylor, "Leadership Responses," 148-49.

32. Interview with Stephen Knight (Oct. 21, 1991).

33. Trial Transcript (July 23, 1969), at 765, *Keyes* (No. C-1499).

34. 313 F. Supp. at 83-84, 97-100 (decree primarily affected predominantly African-American schools in northeast Denver).

35. Compare 313 F. Supp. at 79-80 (teacher experience and turnover) with 380 F. Supp. at 680 (teacher recruitment).

36. Interview with Dr. Richard Koeppe (Oct. 7, 1991). See also James J. Fishman and Lawrence Strauss, "Endless Journey: Integration and the Provision of Equal Educational Opportunity in Denver's Public Schools: A Study of *Keyes v. School District No. 1, Howard Law Journal* 32:627, 634 (1989) (describing lack of cooperation between African-American and Latino communities in Denver).

37. Carter, "Perrill, Southworth," 1.

38. Interview with Bernard Valdez (Oct. 1, 1991).

39. 413 U.S. at 189, 198-213.

40. 368 F. Supp. at 208-10.

41. See, e.g., "Motion to Intervene by Montbello Citizens' Committee, Inc." (Dec. 17, 1973), *Keyes* (No, C-1499); "Memorandum in Support of Applicant's Intervention" (Dec. 17, 1973), *Keyes* (C- 1499); "Motion to Intervene by Moore School Community Association and the Moore School Lay Advisory Committee" (Feb. 8, 1974), *Keyes* (C-1499).

42. "Motion to Intervene by Citizens' Association for Neighborhood Schools" (Feb. 20, 1974), at 1-3, *Keyes* (No. C-1499); Interview with Thomas Quentin Benson (Sept. 16, 1991); Interview with Frank Southworth (Oct. 17, 1991); Interview with Nolan Winsett (Oct. 1, 1991).

43. "Motion to Intervene as Parties Plaintiffs" (Jan. 8, 1974) at 3, *Keyes* (No. C-1499); "Complaint in Intervention" (Jan. 8, 1974) at 6- 7, *Keyes* (No. C-1499).

44. 521 F.2d 465, 477-80 (10th Cir. 1975).

45. Id. at 480.

46. Denver Public Schools, "Report to the Board of Education: A Program for Limited English Proficient Students" (June 1984); see also Taylor, "Leadership Responses," 262-64 (describing the board's reluctance to adopt bilingual education programs through informal negotiations in the 1970's).

47. 576 F. Supp. 1503, 1516-18 (1983); Interview with Ba Vovan (Oct. 9, 1991).

48. Fishman and Strauss, "Endless Journey," note 36, at 702-03.

49. 895 F.2d at 661-63.

50. *Dowell v. Board of Education*, 111 S. Ct. 630 (1991); *Freeman v. Pitts*, 112 S.Ct. 1430 (1992).

51. 609 F. Supp. 1491 (D. Colo. 1985), order modified, 653 F. Supp. 1536, interim decree issued, 670 F. Supp. 1513, aff'd, 895 F.2d 659 (1990), cert. denied, 111 S. Ct. 951 (1991).

52. 670 F. Supp. at 1515-16.

53. "Webb Moves to Halt Court Role," *Denver Post*, July 14, 1991, 11A; "Webb: End Mandatory DPS Busing," *Denver Post*, Mar. 29, 1991, 1B; Interview with Stan Sharoff, Denver Assistant District Attorney (Oct. 10, 1991); "City and County of Denver's Motion to Intervene and Notice of Motion" (Mar. 18, 1992) at 2-4, *Keyes* (No. C-1499); Mark Stevens, "Hispanics Propose An End to Busing," *Denver Post*, Nov. 26, 1991, at 1A; Mark Stevens, "Leaders Push for Settlement to End Busing: Blacks Join Hispanics in Plan," *Denver Post*, Nov. 27, 1991, 1B, 5B. Judge Matsch denied the City and County of Denver's Motion to intervene in *Keys* in an order dated October 12, 1993.

54. "Motion of Denver School District to Terminate Jurisdiction" (Jan. 31, 1992) at 5, *Keyes* (No. C-1499); 1995 v.s. Dist., LEXIS, 14143 (No. C-1499 [69-M-1499], Sept. 12, 1995).

55. Interview with Charles Brega (Sept. 21, 1991).

56. Interview with A. Edgar Benton (Oct. 2, 1991).

57. Id.

58. Id.

59. Interview with Rachel Noel (Oct. 8, 1991).

60. Id.

61. Interview with Frank Southworth (Oct. 17, 1991).

62. Interview with William Berge (Oct. 23, 1991).

63. Interview with William Schroeder (July 13, 1992).

Courts and the Construction of Racial and Ethnic Identity

64. Interview with William Schroeder (July 13, 1992); Interview with Frank Southworth (Oct. 17, 1991).

65. Interview with Thomas Quentin Benson (Sept. 16, 1991).

66. Interview with Nolan Winsett (Oct. 1, 1991).

67. Interview with Thomas Quentin Benson (Sept. 16, 1991).

68. Interview with Thomas Quentin Benson (Sept. 16, 1991).

69. Interview with Nolan Winsett (Oct. 1, 1991).

70. Interview with Robert Pena (Oct. 24, 1991).

71. Interview with Katherine Archuleta (July 21, 1992).

72. Karen O'Connor & Lee Epstein, "A Legal Voice for the Chicano Community: The Activities of the Mexican American Legal Defense and Educational Fund, 1968-82," *Social Science Quarterly* 65:245, 249-50 (1984).

73. Interview with Robert Pena (Oct. 24, 1991).

74. Alan Cunningham, "Hispanos Push for Unity to Effect School Change," *Rocky Mountain News*, Mar. 24, 1969, 8.

75. Interview with James Voorhees (Oct.7, 1991).

76. Mark Stevens and Eric Anderson, "DPS Election Bill Now Law: Districts to Fill Five Board Seats," *Denver Post*, June 5, 1992, 8B.

77. Interview with Gordon Greiner (Sept. 17, 1991); Interview with Superintendent Evie P. Dennis (Oct. 14, 1991).

78. Interview with Katherine Archuleta (July 21, 1992); Interview with A. Edgar Benton (Oct. 2, 1991); Interview with William Berge (October 23, 1991); Interview with Charles Brega (Sept. 21, 1991); Interview with Stephen Knight (Oct. 21, 1991).

79. Interview with Rachel Noel (Oct. 8, 1991); Interview with James Voorhees (Oct. 7, 1991).

80. Interview with Thomas Quentin Benson (Sept. 16, 1991); Interview with James Voorhees (Oct. 7, 1991).

81. Trial Transcript (Apr. 19, 1984) at 799-800, *Keyes* (No. C- 1499). See also Interview with Omar Blair (Oct. 23, 1991).

82. Interview with A. Edgar Benton (Oct. 2, 1991); Interview with Charles Brega (Sept. 21, 1991); Interview with Gordon Greiner (Sept. 17, 1991); Interview with Dr. Richard Koeppe (Oct. 7, 1991).

83. Interview with Stan Sharoff (Oct. 10, 1991).

84. Interview with Katherine Archuleta (July 21, 1992).

85. Martin Moran, "Community School Control Urged," *Rocky Mountain News*, Oct. 17, 1969, 70. See also "Blacks Seek Control of Cole Area Schools," *Denver Post*, Aug. 20, 1969, 40.

86. Interview with Bernard Valdez (Oct. 1, 1991) ("Not one of the [black] leaders came out against the busing idea. Some change is going on now, but in those days . . . they felt that [integration] was the answer to their problems").

87. Interview with Rachel Noel (Oct. 8, 1991).

88. Interview with Edward J. Garner (July 27, 1992) ("I would think that in the African-American community, [the split over the benefits of integration] would be intergenerational").

89. See Carl Upchurch, "I Still Have a Dream," New York Times, Aug. 27, 1993, A15.

90. Harold Cruse, *Plural but Equal: Blacks and Minorities in America's Plural Society*, 230-31 (New York: William Morrow, paperback ed. 1987).

91. Cruse, *Plural but Equal*, 389-91; Cornel West, *Race Matters*, 36-37 (1993); see also Nicholas Lemann, "The Origins of the Underclass," *Atlantic Monthly*, June 1986, 51-53.

92. Tony Bizjak, "383 Million Americans by 2050?," *Sacramento Bee*, Dec. 4, 1992, A1; Ramon G. McLeod, "U.S. Population in 2050 Will Be Half Minorities," *San Francisco Chronicle*, Dec. 4, 1992, A1.

93. U.S. Department of Commerce, Economics and Statistics Administration, Bureau of the Census, *1990 Census of Population, General Population Characteristics, Colorado* 22 (June 1992) (of a total of 467,610 residents in the city of Denver, 60,046 were African American, 107,382 were Latino, 11,005 were Asian American, and 5,381 were native American).

94. See Ronald Takaki, *A Different Mirror: A History of Multicultural America* 415 (Boston, MA: Little, Brown and Company, 1993) (citing differences in education and socioeconomic status among Asian-American groups); Bill Ong Hing, "Beyond the Rhetoric of Assimilation and Cultural Pluralism: Addressing the Tension of Separatism and Conflict in an Immigration-Driven Multiracial Society," *California Law Review* 81:863, 923- 25 (1993) (collecting sociological studies identifying the distinctive acculturation experiences of Korean Americans, Japanese Americans, and Southeast Asian refugees.)

95. Douglas S. Massey, "Latino Poverty Research: An Agenda for the 1990s," *Items* 47:7, 8-9 (March 1993).

96. See Harriett Romo, "The Mexican Origin Population's Differing Perceptions of Their Children's Schooling," *Social Science Quarterly* 65:635 (1984).

97. See Cruse, *Plural but Equal*, 278, 282 (pessimistically assessing the pitfalls of a pluralist ethic for African Americans).

98. See, e.g., Carnegie Corporation, *Hispanics in an Aging Society* (New York: Carnegie Corporation of New York,1986) (documenting role that young Latinos will play in financing retirement benefits for a predominantly white and aging population); Jonathan Gaw, "Report Says Latino Education in Decline," *Los Angeles Times*, Sept. 22, 1990, B1 (describing National Council of La Raza report highlighting the problems of undereducating a youthful and rapidly growing population of Latinos who eventually will shoulder a disproportionate burden of supporting social welfare programs, such as social security and Medicare); "Retirement Security May Be Illusion," *Chicago Tribune*, Dec. 3, 1989, 1 (same).

99. Ronald A. Taylor, "The Multicultural Melting Pot: Decades Later, Still A Racial Battleground," *Washington Times*, Jan. 19, 1992, K6 (describing preliminary efforts to build coalitions between Asian-American and Latino communities around problems of immigration); Bob Liff, "New Realities May Count In City Politics; Census Shows New Ethnic Diversity," *Newsday*, Feb. 24, 1991, 23 (noting rapid growth of Latino and Asian-American populations in New York and their ongoing need to build coalitions to succeed in city politics).

100. See Stevens and Anderson, "DPS Election," and accompanying text.

101. Trial Transcript (Feb. 25, 1974) at 991-1050, *Keyes* (No. C- 1499).

102. O'Connor and Epstein, "A Legal Voice," 250, 253.

103. Interview with Robert Pena (Oct. 24, 1991).

104. Interview with Robert Pena (Oct. 24, 1991).

105. Interview with Al Aguayo (Oct. 22, 1991).

Courts and the Construction of Racial and Ethnic Identity

106. Superintendent Evie P. Dennis took office in the 1990-91 school year. Members, Board of Education, 1913 - Current (n.d.) (available from Public Information & Services, Denver Public Schools).

107. Interview with Edward J. Garner (July 27, 1992); Interview with Dorothy Gotlieb (July 13, 1992).

108. Interview with Dorothy Gotlieb (July 13, 1992).

109. See, e.g., Interview with Charles Brega (Sept. 21, 1991).

110. See, e.g., Title IX of the 1972 Education Amendments, 20 U.S.C. § 1681 (gender); Age Discrimination in Employment Act, 29 U.S.C. §§ 621-634 (age); Individuals with Disabilities Education Act, 20 U.S. §§ 1400-1485 (disability); Rehabilitation Act, 29 U.S.C. §§ 701-797b (same).

About the Contributors

Lawrence M. Friedman is Marion Rice Kirkwood Professor of Law at Stanford University Law School. He is author or editor of many books on American legal history, and on the relationship between law and society, including *Contract Law in America* (1965); *American Law and the Constitutional Order: Historical Perspectives* (co-editor, Harry N. Scheiber, 1978); *A History of American Law* (2nd ed., 1985); *Total Justice* (1985); *The Republic of Choice* (1990); and *Crime and Punishment in American History* (1993). Prof. Friedman is past-President of the Law and Society Association and of the American Society for Legal History. He is a fellow of the American Academy of Arts and Sciences.

Marc Galanter is Evjue-Bascom Professor of Law and South Asian Studies at the University of Wisconsin-Madison and is Director of Wisconsin's Institute for Legal Studies. Drawing on a background as a comparativist, he has been engaged for many years in the empirical study of the legal system of the United States. He has written extensively on patterns of disputing and litigation and on the organization of the legal profession. His book *Tournament of Lawyers* (with Thomas Palay, 1991) attempts to explain the growth and transformation of large law firms. He was editor of the *Law and Society Review* and has served as President of the Law and Society Association.

Robert A. Kagan began teaching political science at Berkeley in 1974, and in 1988 became a member of the law faculty at Boalt Hall, where he also serves as Director of the Center for the Study of Law and Society. He has been a visiting scholar at Oxford University, Ohio State University, the Netherlands Institute for Advanced Study, the Russell Sage Foundation, and the Center for Advanced Study in the Behavioral Sciences.

Recent publications include "Banning Smoking: Compliance Without Coercion" (with Jerome Skolnick) and "The Politics of Smoking Regulation: The United States, Canada, and France" (with David Vogel) in *Smoking Policy: Law, Policy, and Politics*, Robert Rabin and Stephen Sugarman, eds. He has also written a number of articles on labor law, labor relations, and environmental law.

Rachel F. Moran was educated at Stanford University and the Yale Law School. Professor Moran clerked for Chief Judge Wilfred Feinberg of the U.S. Court of Appeals for the 2nd Circuit and then worked for the San Francisco firm of Heller, Ehrman, White & McAuliffe. She joined the Boalt Hall faculty in 1983.

Professor Moran has written numerous articles on bilingual education policy and is currently working on a case involving desegregation and bilingual education in the Denver school system. Recent publications include "The Future of

182   *About the Contributors*

Multicultural Education in the United States" (1995) and "Of Democracy, Devaluation, and Bilingual Education" (1993). She was a visiting professor at UCLA in 1988 and at Stanford in 1989. Professor Moran serves as chair of the Chicano/Latino Policy Project at the U.C. Berkeley Institute for the Study of Social Change.

Harry N. Scheiber did postdoctoral work in law while a fellow at the Center for Advanced Study in the Behavioral Sciences. He taught at Dartmouth from 1960-71, and then became a professor of American History at the University of California at San Diego. He joined the Boalt Hall faculty in 1980.

Professor Scheiber has held Guggenheim, Rockefeller, American Council of Learned Societies, National Endowment for the Humanities, and Social Science Research Council fellowships. He was a Distinguished Fulbright Lecturer in Australia, and he has been president of the Agricultural History Society, the Council for Research in Economic History, and the ACLU of New Hampshire. His principal books include: *American Law and the Constitutional Order; American Economic History; Ohio Canal Era—A Case Study of Government and the Economy; The Wilson Administration and Civil Liberties; The Old Northwest—Studies in Regional History; Perspectives on Federalism; and Federalism and the Judicial Mind.*

Martin Shapiro received his Ph.D. in Political Science from Harvard University and has taught there and at Stanford and at three campuses of the University of California. Currently he teaches at Boalt Hall School of Law, U.C. Berkeley. He has held visiting appointments at the Yale Law School, at Amherst, and in France, Italy, Mexico and Australia. He publishes in the fields of constitutional, administrative, comparative and European Union law.

Among his books are *Courts: A Comparative and Political Analysis* (1981), *The Politics of Constitutional Law* (with Douglas Hobbs, 1974), and *Who Guards the Guardians? Judicial Control of Administration* (1988).

Wolfgang Wiegand studied Law and Economics at the Freie Universität, Berlin (1961-62) and at the Ludwig Maximilian Universität, Munich (1962-66). He finished law school in 1966 and worked as a Wissenschaftlicher Assistant with Professor Sten Gagner, one of Europe's leading scholars in legal history (1966-76). During that period Professor Wiegand was also practicing law in Munich. His dissertation (plus petitio/1972) focussed on civil procedure in the Middle Ages. This was followed by a major book on the reception of Roman law in central Europe, which was accepted as a Habilitationsschrift by the Law Faculty in 1976.

After teaching at the University of Göttingen (1976-77) Professor Wiegand was appointed Professor at the University of Bern. He has also been a visiting professor at the University of Geneva, and a visiting scholar at the University of California at Berkeley (1991-92). He was Dean of his Faculty, 1981-82.

In Switzerland Professor Wiegand has worked on Swiss civil law and banking law as well as on medical law problems. Recent publications include books and articles about the information of the patient in the doctor-patient relationship (1993 and 1994). He is also the editor or author of several books on banking law, and commentary on property law in the German Civil Code.

About the Book

The American legal system is under heavy attack for the impact it is supposed to have on American culture and society generally. A common complaint of the anti-lawyer movement is that under the influence of lawyers we have become a "litigious society," in the process undermining traditional American values such as self-reliance and responsibility.

In this volume a group of distinguished scholars in law and the social sciences explores these questions. Neither an apology for lawyers nor a critique, *Legal Culture and the Legal Profession* examines the successes and the problems of the U.S. legal system, its impact on the broader culture, and the spread of American legal culture abroad.

Lawrence M. Friedman is Marion Rice Kirkwood Professor of Law at Stanford University. **Harry N. Scheiber** is the Stefan Riesenfeld Professor of Law and History, Boalt Hall School of Law, in the University of California at Berkeley.